Alexander's Successors and the Creation of Hellenistic Kingship

Also available from Bloomsbury

Alexander the Great: Themes and Issues by Edward M. Anson
Philip II, the Father of Alexander the Great: Themes and Issues
by Edward M. Anson
Ptolemy I Soter: Themes and Issues by Edward M. Anson

Alexander's Successors and the Creation of Hellenistic Kingship

John Holton

BLOOMSBURY ACADEMIC
LONDON • NEW YORK • OXFORD • NEW DELHI • SYDNEY

BLOOMSBURY ACADEMIC
Bloomsbury Publishing Plc, 50 Bedford Square, London, WC1B 3DP, UK
Bloomsbury Publishing Inc, 1385 Broadway, New York, NY 10018, USA
Bloomsbury Publishing Ireland, 29 Earlsfort Terrace, Dublin 2, D02 AY28, Ireland

BLOOMSBURY, BLOOMSBURY ACADEMIC and the Diana logo are trademarks of
Bloomsbury Publishing Plc

First published in Great Britain 2025

Copyright © John Holton, 2025

John Holton has expressed his right under the Copyright, Designs and Patents Act, 1988,
to be identified as Author of this work.

For legal purposes the Acknowledgements on p. x constitute an extension of this
copyright page.

Cover image: Bronze statue of a Hellenistic prince, Palazzo Massimo alle
Terme, Rome, Italy
MasterBliss/Alamy Stock Photo

All rights reserved. No part of this publication may be: i) reproduced or transmitted in any
form, electronic or mechanical, including photocopying, recording or by means of any
information storage or retrieval system without prior permission in writing from the
publishers; or ii) used or reproduced in any way for the training, development or operation
of artificial intelligence (AI) technologies, including generative AI technologies. The rights
holders expressly reserve this publication from the text and data mining exception
as per Article 4(3) of the Digital Single Market Directive (EU) 2019/790.

Bloomsbury Publishing Plc does not have any control over, or responsibility
for, any third-party websites referred to or in this book. All internet addresses
given in this book were correct at the time of going to press. The author and
publisher regret any inconvenience caused if addresses have changed or sites
have ceased to exist, but can accept no responsibility for any such changes.

A catalogue record for this book is available from the British Library.

A catalog record for this book is available from the Library of Congress.

ISBN:	HB:	978-1-3503-9902-0
	PB:	978-1-3503-9901-3
	ePDF:	978-1-3503-9903-7
	eBook:	978-1-3503-9904-4

Typeset by RefineCatch Limited, Bungay, Suffolk
Printed and bound in Great Britain

For product safety related questions contact productsafety@bloomsbury.com.

To find out more about our authors and books visit www.bloomsbury.com
and sign up for our newsletters.

Contents

Preface	vi
List of Illustrations	viii
Acknowledgements	x
List of Abbreviations	x
Chronology	xi
1 Approaching the World of Early Hellenistic Kingship, 323–276 BC	1
2 The Performance of Status in the Early Hellenistic World: Craterus at Delphi	35
3 Heroic Paradigms of Rulership and the Politics of *imitatio*	71
4 Diadem and *basileia*: A Zelotypic Model	99
5 Spear-won Land in Hellenistic Imperial Discourse	127
Conclusions	147
Notes	153
Bibliography	187
Index	213

Preface

There has been no shortage of excellent scholarly works on Hellenistic kingship, but the majority of these are devoted to specific personalities, dynasties or institutional aspects. There remains a need for a generalist approach to the category or typology of Hellenistic kingship as an international phenomenon; and although recent inroads have been made, a comparative approach is still underdeveloped. In particular, a properly comparative study of the Hellenistic kingdoms in their first generation is needed: the period of the *diadochoi*, Alexander's Successors, from the death of Alexander in 323 BC to the accession of Antigonus Gonatas in 276. I do not pretend that this book is a complete study of early Hellenistic kingship, but I hope at least that it begins to fill the gap. A companion study, *Royal Traditions and the Consolidation of Power by Alexander's Successors*, also examines this period, though from a different perspective.

The introductory Chapter 1 establishes the key methodological underpinnings of the book and its context in scholarly trends and approaches in the connected fields. Beyond this, it elaborates on key scholarly questions surrounding royal ideology, what the genealogies of Hellenistic kingship are, and how a model of competition helps us to frame its ideological development.

Chapter 2 is a detailed case study of royal ideology development from the very early years after Alexander's death (323–320 BC). It focuses on Craterus' spectacular monument at Delphi, commissioned in perhaps 322/321 BC and commemorating a lion hunt alongside Alexander the Great, and scrutinizes in particular the poetic inscription attached to the monument. It combines literary and historical analysis to establish that Craterus made use of archaizing modes of status enhancement as well as royal imagery that was typically associated with the Argead monarchy, all in order to lay claim to superiority of status and royal suitability in the earliest years after Alexander's death. This study is heuristic in that many of the specific registers evoked in this monument are also early prefigurations of, and perhaps influences on, what would become some typical features of royal ideology in the early Hellenistic world.

Building on some of the frameworks trailed in Chapters 1 and 2, Chapter 3 explores the use of heroic paradigms of rulership and the politics around *imitatio*, namely the complex imitation of heroic models embedded in broader society and culture. Opening with a vignette of Ptolemy's heroic single combat, the chapter then segues into models for *imitatio* and then develops three extended case studies: Ptolemy's use of the *aegis* symbol and Alexander's body in the establishment of his regime in Egypt; Lysimachus' use of lion symbolism to create his own authority in Thrace; and Pyrrhus' adaptable use of Achilles and Heracles as royal models. Through these studies, the chapter demonstrates that engagement with heroic templates was not limited to Alexander but was widely used by his Successors, too, in framing their personal authority after his death.

Chapter 4 examines the act of creation for the Hellenistic kingships, namely the series of accessions between 306 and 304 BC that sees five new kingdoms created on the basis of two things: wearing a diadem, a headband of cloth analogous to a crown; and taking the royal title. It then develops a study of the political underpinnings of the ritualized (self-)coronations to frame the significance of these accessions. Finally, it demonstrates how the invented images and stories of Alexander after his death created a specific association with the diadem symbol, which was not widely (or perhaps at all) used in his own lifetime to signify his royal status and office. The chapter overall provides analysis of the defining moment in which Hellenistic kingship came into existence and how the use of symbolism and staging underpinned the creation of this new reality.

Chapter 5 explores one of the primary recurrent ideologies widely regarded to have underpinned Hellenistic royal power, namely the specific claim to dominate territory as 'spear-won land' (*doriktētos chōra*). The chapter opens with two historically significant moments at which claims to *doriktētos chōra* are made: in 196 BC, when the Seleucid king Antiochus III claims to Roman envoys that his ancestor had conquered Thrace so now it was his, and in 334 BC, when Alexander landed his Persian campaign in Asian soil by casting a spear into the land. Both moments create a claim by selective use of ideology and the historic or mythic models it conjures up. As the next sections of the chapter demonstrate, there was a myth-historical tradition of 'spear-won land' that underpinned Alexander's usage, and the *diadochoi* themselves used it symbolize participation in Alexander's conquests and, later, to frame the consequences of defeating Antigonus at Ipsus in 301.

Illustrations

Figures

1. Silver tetradrachm of Alexander, 336–323. Staatliche Museen zu Berlin, Münzkabinett 18254121 / Dr Karsten Dahmen. [CC PDM 1.0]   16
2. Exedra of Craterus' votive offering, Delphi. Wikimedia Commons / Dennis Jarvis. [CC BY-SA 2.0]   39
3. Bronze coin of Amyntas III, 392–370. Yale University Art Gallery 2004.6.1475. [CC0 1.0]   58
4. Silver stater of Tarsus, 333–324. Staatliche Museen zu Berlin, Münzkabinett 18259497 / Dr Karsten Dahmen. [CC PDM 1.0]   61
5. Gold stater of Alexander the Great, 334–323. Staatliche Museen zu Berlin, Münzkabinett 18250205 / Lutz-Jürgen Lübke (Lübke und Wiedemann). [CC PDM 1.0]   62
6. Silver tetradrachm of Ptolemy, c. 316/315. Staatliche Museen zu Berlin, Münzkabinett 18203058 / Dirk Sonnenwald. [CC PDM 1.0]   79
7. Bronze statuette of Alexander with silver inlay, 1st–3rd centuries AD. The Walters Art Museum, Baltimore 54.1075. [CC0 1.0 Universal]   82
8. Gold stater of Ptolemy, c. 290. Staatliche Museen zu Berlin, Münzkabinett 18200178 / Lutz-Jürgen Lübke. [CC PDM 1.0]   84
9. Silver tetradrachm of Lysimachus, c. 301–297. Staatliche Museen zu Berlin, Münzkabinett 18249715 / Lutz-Jürgen Lübke. [CC PDM 1.0]   87
10. Lion-head from the Belevi Mausoleum, c. 285. Selçuk, Museum of Ephesus / Jona Lendering. [CC0 1.0]   89
11. Silver didrachm of Pyrrhus, c. 280. Staatliche Museen zu Berlin, Münzkabinett 18203180 / Dirk Sonnenwald. [CC BY-SA 4.0]   93
12. Bronze hemiobol of Ptolemy, c. 312. Staatliche Museen zu Berlin, Münzkabinett 18214374 / Reinhard Saczewski. [CC PDM 1.0]   121
13. Gold double-daric of Seleucus, c. 300–298. Staatliche Museen zu Berlin, Münzkabinett 18200205 / Lutz-Jürgen Lübke (Lübke und Wiedemann). [CC PDM 1.0]   122

14 Silver tetradrachm of Lysimachus, *c.* 297–282/281. Staatliche
    Museen zu Berlin, Münzkabinett / Lutz-Jürgen Lübke (Lübke und
    Wiedemann). [CC PDM 1.0]   122
15 Silver tetradrachm of Demetrius, *c.* 290/289. Staatliche Museen
    zu Berlin, Münzkabinett 18203027 / Dirk Sonnenwald.
    [CC BY-SA 4.0]   123
16 Silver tetradrachm of Antiochus I, *c.* 276–274. Staatliche Museen
    zu Berlin, Münzkabinett 18228232 / Reinhard Saczewski.
    [CC PDM 1.0]   123
17 Silver tetradrachm of Antiochus I, 278–261. Staatliche Museen
    zu Berlin, Münzkabinett 18203079 / Dirk Sonnenwald. [CC PDM 1.0]   124
18 Gold octodrachm of Ptolemy II Philadelphus, *c.* 260–240. Staatliche
    Museen zu Berlin, Münzkabinett 18203062 / Dirk Sonnenwald.
    [CC PDM 1.0]   125
19 Fresco from the villa of P. Fannius Synistor, Boscoreale, *c.* 40–30 BC.
    Wikimedia Commons / ArchaiOptix. [CC BY-SA 4.0]   134

Map

1 Greece, the Aegean and the eastern Mediterranean. © John Holton   xiv

Acknowledgements

I am very grateful to a number of superb teachers and colleagues for their support and scholarly engagement over the years, including Lloyd Llewellyn-Jones, Daniel Ogden, Keith Rutter, Douglas Cairns, Calum Maciver, Gavin Kelly, Stephanie Winder, Ben Gray, Mirko Canevaro, Ulrike Roth, Federico Santangelo, Joseph Skinner, Marijn Visscher, Kyle Erickson, Boris Chrubasik, Emma Nicholson, Simon Glenn, Shane Wallace and Alexander Meeus. I am especially grateful to Maria Pretzler, who first taught me Hellenistic history and was a boundless source of inspiration as an undergraduate; Andrew Erskine, who as my doctoral supervisor taught me an enormous amount, and went above and beyond many times; and Annie Tindley, for her ongoing support.

The team at Bloomsbury has been brilliant: quick, supportive and highly professional. They are a model for what a modern academic press should be. A huge thanks to Lily Mac Mahon and Zoe Osman in particular for their enthusiasm and their patience. The referees they engaged have likewise been extremely helpful, constructive and (crucially) very timely in their feedback.

The biggest thanks are owed to my wonderful wife Stephanie and our joyful son Hector, who have provided the best support and encouragement at every step of the way. To them this book is dedicated.

Abbreviations

The majority of the abbreviations used in this book follow standard conventions of the field, which can be found most easily in *The Oxford Classical Dictionary* (4th edition). The following usages, relating to corpora of important numismatic evidence, are worth specifying explicitly.

ANS	American Numismatic Society, New York, 1858–
	Link to collection: https://numismatics.org/
PCO	Ptolemaic Coins Online, 2019–, American Numismatic Society
	Link to collection: https://numismatics.org/pco/
SCO	Seleucid Coins Online, 2018–, American Numismatic Society
	Link to collection: https://numismatics.org/sco/

Chronology

Alexander and the Successors, 336–276 BC

336	Accession of Alexander the Great
336/335	Alexander confirmed as *hegemon* of League of Corinth
335	Destruction of Thebes
335/334	Production of Athena/Nike gold coinage begins
334	Alexander crosses the Hellespont
	Battle of the Granicus
334–333	Takeover of Asia Minor
333	Battle of Issus
333/332	Production of Heracles/Zeus silver coinage begins
332	Sieges of Tyre and Gaza
332/331	Takeover of Egypt; visit to Siwah
331	Foundation of Alexandria in Egypt
	Battle of Gaugamela
	Takeover of Babylon
331/330	Takeover of Persian heartlands: Persepolis, Pasargadae, Susa
330	Murder of Darius; acclamation of Bessus
329	Arrest and execution of Bessus
329–327	Bactrian and Sogdian campaigns
327	Marriage of Alexander and Rhoxane
327–325	Indian campaigns
326	Battle of the Hydaspes
	Mutiny at the Hyphasis
	Voyage down the Indus
325	March across Gedrosia
	Periplus of Nearchus
325/324	Winter in Carmania: administration of justice
324	Return to Babylonia
	Mutiny at Opis; Craterus begins repatriation of veterans
	Receipt of Greek embassies
	Exiles' Decree

323	Preparations for Arabian campaign
	Death of Alexander
	Babylon Settlement: accession of Philip III and Alexander IV; regency of Perdiccas begins; distribution of satrapies
	Revolt of Greek settlers
323–322	Revolt of Athens and Aetolia: Lamian War
	Death of Leonnatus
	Return of Craterus to Greece
322	Ptolemy's annexation of Cyrene
322/321	Plans for Craterus monument at Delphi (?)
321	Flight of Antigonus to Europe
	Ptolemy's seizure of Alexander's body
	Antipater and Craterus invade Asia Minor
	Death of Craterus
320	Perdiccas' invasion of Egypt
	Assassination of Perdiccas
	Offer of regency to Ptolemy (declined); interim regency of Peithon and Arrhidaeus begins
	Settlement at Triparadeisus (Syria): regency of Antipater begins; Antigonus made royal *strategos* in Asia; distribution of satrapies; outlawing of Eumenes and Perdiccan faction
319	Death of Antipater
	Regency of Polyperchon begins (contested by Cassander)
319/318	Polyperchon invests Eumenes as royal *strategos* in Asia
317	Assassination of Philip III and Eurydice by Olympias
	Cassander captures Athens: oligarchic regime of Demetrius of Phalerum begins
316	Battle of Gabiene: execution of Eumenes
312	Battle of Gaza
312–311	Seleucus retakes Babylonia
311	Peace between the Successors (Antigonus, Lysimachus, Cassander, Ptolemy)
310/309	Assassination of Alexander IV and Rhoxane by Cassander
309/308	Seleucus defeats Antigonus and solidifies control in Babylonia
308–305	Eastern *anabasis* of Seleucus
307	Demetrius Poliorcetes liberates Athens: end of oligarchy, divine honours for Antigonus and Demetrius

306	Battle of Salamis (Cyprus)
	Antigonus declares himself king; installs Demetrius as joint king
	Antigonus and Demetrius invade Egypt, defeated by Ptolemy
	Ptolemy declares himself king
305	Seleucus declares himself king
304	Lysimachus declares himself king
	Cassander declares himself king
302	Antigonus and Demetrius re-found Hellenic League at Corinth
301	Battle of Ipsus
	Death of Antigonus
	Division of Antigonus' Asian domains between Seleucus, Lysimachus, Cassander
297	Death of Cassander
296/295	Demetrius takes over Macedon and Athens
294	Seleucus installs Antiochus I as joint king
291/290	Demetrius in Athens: ithyphallic hymn performed
288	Lysimachus and Pyrrhus take over Macedon
285	Ptolemy installs Ptolemy II Philadelphus as joint king
282	Death of Ptolemy; first Ptolemaieia festival in Alexandria
	Death of Demetrius
281	Battle of Corupedium; death of Lysimachus
	Seleucus crosses the Hellespont to Thrace
	Seleucus assassinated by Ptolemy Ceraunus
281–279	Reign of Ptolemy Ceraunus in Thrace and Macedon
279	Death of Ptolemy Ceraunus
279–276	Succession of short-lived kings in Macedon
278	Second Ptolemaieia festival in Alexandria
277/276	Antigonus Gonatas defeats Celts at Lysimachia
	Antigonid power base in Macedon installed

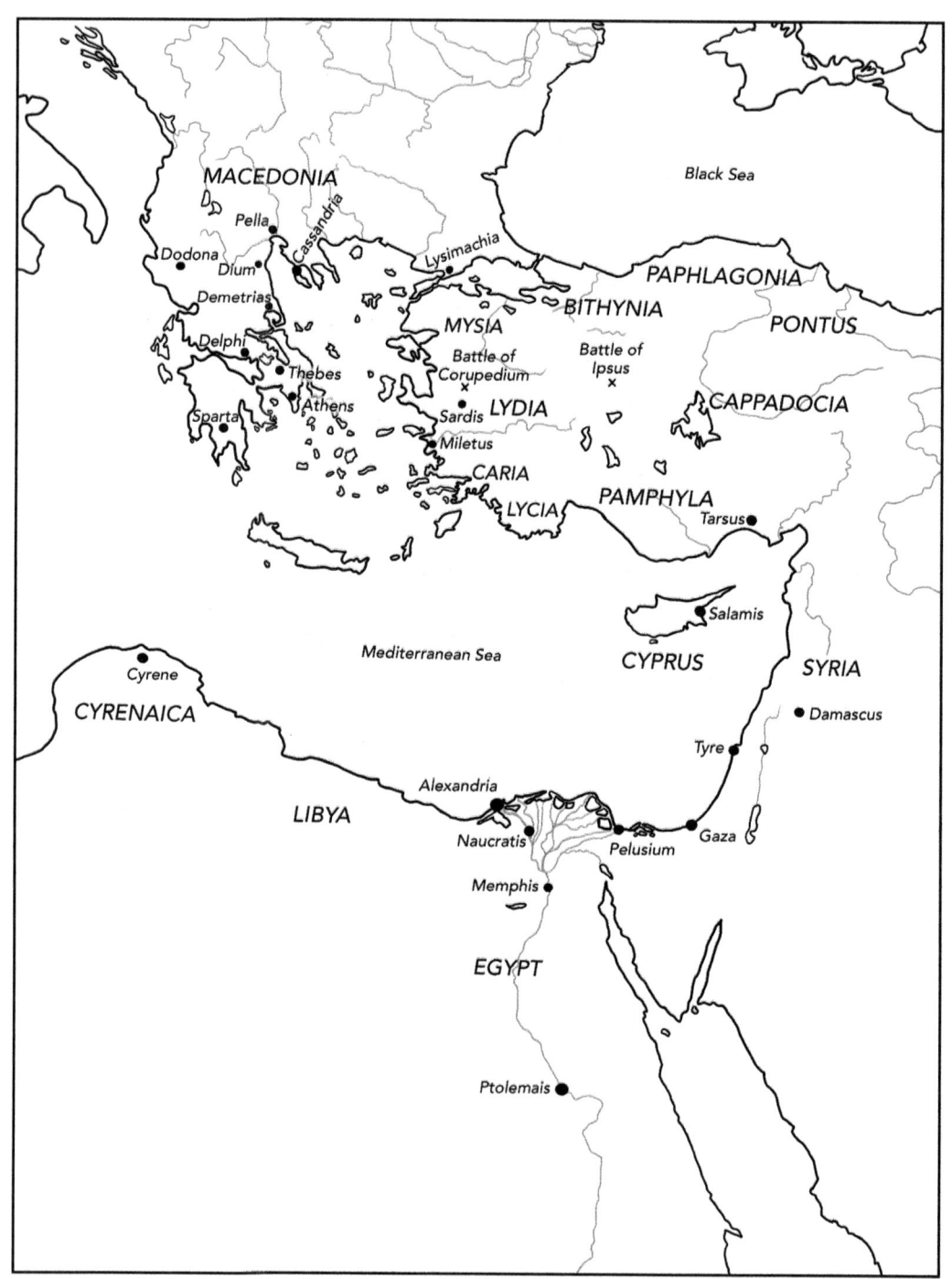

Map 1 Greece, the Aegean and the eastern Mediterranean. © John Holton.

1

Approaching the World of Early Hellenistic Kingship, 323–276 BC

In 306 BC, seventeen years after the death of Alexander the Great, Demetrius Poliorcetes ('Besieger of Cities') decisively defeated Ptolemy and his brother Menelaus in a naval engagement at Cyprian Salamis.[1] Demetrius, son of Antigonus Monophthalmus ('One-Eyed'), was culminating a wider campaign against the cities of Cyprus, which had been controlled by Ptolemy for at least a decade. The victory was a resounding one in strategic terms: Demetrius not just forced Ptolemy's withdrawal and took control of the entire island, so disrupting Ptolemy's strategy for maintaining the security of his power base in Egypt,[2] he also suborned the remaining Ptolemaic garrisons, significantly diminishing Ptolemy's overall military capability while enriching his own.[3] The functional position of Antigonus as the most powerful of the *diadochoi* – Alexander's 'Successors', who had been waging military and political war against each other since the conqueror's death – was affirmed to all onlookers at the expense of one of his great rivals. His subsequent manipulation of the victory's magnitude took full advantage of its symbolic potential; as Diodorus records:

> Antigonus, on learning of the victory that had occurred, and buoyant at the height of his superiority, put a diadem around his head and thereafter took the title of king (διάδημα περιέθετο καὶ τὸ λοιπὸν ἐχρημάτιζε βασιλεύς), consenting that Demetrius, also, should hold the same title and honour.
>
> Diodorus Siculus XX 53.2

Antigonus thus capitalized on the significance of the victory by asserting into existence a new kingship. This was the first new kingship, or *basileia*, since the appointment of Philip III Arrhidaeus and Alexander IV in the immediate aftermath of Alexander's death in June 323.[4] These heirs of Alexander had not held power but had been dominated by a series of regents and protectors, and when they were assassinated in 317 and 310/309, respectively, they were not replaced with new kings.[5] The years leading immediately up to Salamis in 306 were thus notionally an interregnum, though in reality the Macedonian empire had long since ruptured into unofficial power bases controlled autonomously, and without imperial oversight, by Alexander's former generals and companions. Even so, the fiction of a unified empire had remained, even to the point of recording the dead Alexander IV as the reigning king in official documents from some parts of the empire down the new kings' accessions.[6]

Strikingly, Antigonus' new *basileia* was not explicitly construed as a succession to Alexander, his heirs, or the wider Argead dynasty to which they had belonged.[7] Rather, this was a formalization of how much power and position he (and his son) had independently accrued in the years since Alexander's demise. In being the first to break convention and formally claim royal status for himself, Antigonus' self-coronation was also an act of systematization, at attempt to impose order on the unstable, informally delineated world of the interregnum; it was also an unrestricted, unqualified claim to the whole of that world, not just to the particular niches that he had carved out within it. As Diodorus goes on to tell us, this did not go uncontested:

> And Ptolemy, not dispirited by the defeat, in equal measure took the diadem himself, and towards everyone styled himself as king. In rough equivalence with these, the remaining dynasts emulously proclaimed themselves as kings (οἱ λοιποὶ δυνάσται ζηλοτυπήσαντες ἀνηγόρευον ἑαυτοὺς βασιλεῖς): Seleucus, who had recently added the Upper Satrapies to his acquisitions, and also Lysimachus and Cassander, who were carefully maintaining the allotments they had been granted originally.
>
> Diodorus Siculus XX 53.3–4

Thus, within the space of at most two years, Antigonus' rival dynasts – not just Ptolemy, but also Seleucus, Lysimachus and Cassander – formalized their positions in a like manner with their own accessions, projecting their own claims to system-wide dominance in an attempt to delimit but also replicate the universalistic implications of Antigonus' claim to kingship. So came into existence the first Hellenistic royal dynasties.

In Diodorus' characterization, this was a competitive series of self-declarations of royalty, motivated by ζηλοτυπία ('emulous rivalry'). We cannot uncritically accept the imputation of emotional motive, though it does offer an interesting explanatory model.[8] Even so, the historical fact of the accessionary series happening over a short space of time, like a sequence of dominoes, taken with the fact that they evidently shared the same means of framing, speaks for itself: the accessions were a series of competitive reactions, triggered first by Antigonus' ascension and then continued in motion. Once Antigonus had broken new political ground with his independent accession, the other major dynastic players began to follow his precedent, while also following the wider emerging trend. In this way, although it was trend-bucking in terms of constituting a new development, Antigonus' accession was also trend-setting, and it became paradigmatic. Equally, it is as much owing to the remaining dynasts' competitiveness, their attempt to emulate but simultaneously to divest Antigonus' actions of distinction, that *basileia* and the specific means of claiming it seen here gained its subsequent dominance in the post-Alexander world. Its influence stretches still further forward in time, even after the dissolution of the Hellenistic kingdoms themselves.[9] Antigonus' creation of a new kingship was thus also a game-changing moment, in the immediate climate of the diadochan struggles but in a much longer term, too.

To read Diodorus' above account of the 'Year of the Kings' in isolation is to minimize the acquisition and solidification of political power and authority that had preceded the accessions, over the long years of struggle between 323 and 306. Much more can be unpacked out of the lead-up to this complex scenario, the scenario itself, and its legacy.[10] Nevertheless, his brief account aptly captures wider issues that were centrally important in the development and formalization of the new kingships over a longer period. We see a snapshot of how complex strategies evolve for developing and signifying ideology, performing status, and competing with rival means of staging royal power. These are foundational strategies that are found widely across the international world of early Hellenistic kingship and have recurrent dynamics across even geographically disparate contexts. Examining these further throughout the early, formative years of Hellenistic kingship, the period 323–276, is the objective of this book.

The subsequent chapters focus on different ideological strategies and performances that unify the first Hellenistic kingships, and they are developed through comparative case studies and contextualization in the historical dynamics of the broader period. Before this, it is important to frame the book's unifying approach to early Hellenistic kingship, and then outline a clear position on some crucial questions. What is meant by royal ideology and performance, and how significant are they for illuminating the institution of kingship? What were the genealogies behind the development of Hellenistic kingship? Why is competition a meaningful model for understanding it?

1. Unifying early Hellenistic kingship

It is difficult to overestimate the importance, but also the immensity, of the topic of kingship in a historical study of the Hellenistic period. If there is one factor that meaningfully sustains our periodization of the Hellenistic era (323–30), it is the institution of kingship.[11] Kingship can be considered a defining feature of the Hellenistic world in terms both temporal (Alexander to Cleopatra) and geographic (Macedon to Bactria). But how can we provide a unified study of this vast institution? A typical answer might be that we cannot. In the 1996 volume *Aspects of Hellenistic Kingship*, it was agreed by the editors in their programmatic introduction, and by Gruen in his contribution, that 'no single model accounts for Hellenistic kingship' and that 'no single formula existed for a Hellenistic king'.[12] These conclusions have been often repeated.[13] Essentially, they emphasize the need to pay close attention to how the Hellenistic kingdoms legitimated their regimes over various regions via local discourses of power and culture. In this line of thought, since the regions governed by each monarchy, and the ethno-cultural groups that populated them, were inherently different, no two kingdoms can or should be considered substantially alike.

Although it rightly points towards the importance of specific local contexts, the 'no single model' contention runs into problems of method and has shortcomings as an interpretative model. Especially in its first generation of 323–276, Hellenistic kingship is a naturally unifiable phenomenon according to at least three key characteristics. First, the first Hellenistic dynasties shared an evolutionary history in the backdrop of the fragmentation of the Macedonian empire after Alexander's death in 323. Secondly, the major players that emerged as kings from that fragmentation – Antigonus and Demetrius, Ptolemy, Seleucus, Lysimachus and Cassander – came from comparable cultural and political backgrounds, the majority belonging to the families of Macedonian elite who had campaigned with Alexander. Thirdly, the first Hellenistic kingdoms developed not just similar institutional features – both broadly and specifically, as one might expect of new states developing coterminously within a single historical context, faced with similar challenges of state-building – but also highly similar modes of ideologically representing royal power and status. Simply put, the early Hellenistic kingships developed in broadly the same time and circumstances, had developers from shared backgrounds, and evolved comparable royal structures and ideologies. This gives a solid basis for a unified study of the institution in its foundational period.

The world of the Hellenistic kingdoms can also be unified through the perspective of multipolarity, as an international system of peer-powers dominated, from 276, by three competing dynasties: the Antigonids in Macedon, the Seleucids in Asia, and the Ptolemies in Egypt – later to be joined by the Attalids of Asia Minor, among others.[14] For the kingdoms of this period, there was no 'balance of power', but rather a political environment characterized by continual conflict among great powers which shared interests and recognized each other's sovereignties, while nonetheless competing for pre-eminence on the world stage.[15] This is a helpful model for the years after 276, but in itself offers no explanation for the preceding years: we need to account for the origins of this multipolarity. Indeed, in larger terms, the period 323–276 was the transitional and formative phase for the Hellenistic era, with a unitary imperial state – the Macedonian empire, nominally ruled on behalf of Alexander's heirs Philip III and Alexander IV – being replaced by a multiplicity of new, independent imperial enterprises; at the same time, a single empire with a universalist ideology was replaced by several with universalist ideologies.[16] A shared trajectory towards independent *basileia* unifies this period and the major actors in it, and this created the basis for the entire institutional existence of Hellenistic kingship, down to the collapse of the Ptolemaic state and its annexation by Octavian in 30.

Ideology, its performance, and its competitive negotiation and take-up are significant historical dynamics in reconstructing the development of early Hellenistic kingship. How kings – or the dynasts with regal aspirations – developed their self-images in this period is of vital importance to understanding how they came to embed their power and status, especially since no single diadoch could claim legitimacy in the traditional terms of genetic inheritance;[17] nor could he, as a usurper, straightforwardly draw on and fit into available, pre-existing paradigms of monarchic rule.[18] Although one major method by which the *diadochoi* sought to secure and legitimize their route to kingship was through local negotiation – of the ideology and practice of rulership – equally important was the orchestration of a royal image on an international level. Their programmes of image-making were inherently interactive: the *diadochoi* did not just articulate their own internally developed imagery of kingship but also responded to – and often strategically co-opted – a series of rival attempts to do the same. At least on an international level, the ideological discourse of kingship in the early Hellenistic period was thus a continually evolving one, characterized by mutuality and reciprocity. Because of this, we find not just typologically comparable representations of royal power and status, but also extremely close parallels in the specifics of these, for instance in numismatic iconography.

Examining the wider world of the early Hellenistic kingships, therefore, enables a unified yet still qualitatively significant study of Hellenistic kingship as a whole in its formative generation; the examination of major commonalities can function as a heuristic device for exploring the evolution of the institution of Hellenistic kingship.[19] Moreover, it is through an inclusive study of the dynamics of ideology, performance and competition that we can achieve a deeper understanding of how early Hellenistic kingship was developed and sustained – a question which has significant bearing on understanding the long life of Hellenistic kingship as a whole, not to mention its post-Hellenistic influence.

2. Framing an international view

Despite the popularity of the Hellenistic kingdoms as a subject of scholarly study, there remains no single unified study of Hellenistic kingship in its first generation of 323–276, though it has been long-awaited.[20] There are serious obstacles to be surmounted to develop such a synthetic view. Although there are exceptions,[21] one important tendency already mentioned is to suggest that Hellenistic kingship cannot be meaningfully considered a single construct: aphoristically, 'no single model accounts for Hellenistic kingship', or 'no single formula existed for a Hellenistic king'.[22] This kind of view has its origins in attempts to correct Hellenocentric priorities that were entrenched in earlier scholarship, and it is complementary with the regionalist, biographical or dynastic approaches that dominate studies of Hellenistic history generally. It has been a necessary recalibration of scholarly priorities, and a productive shift in conceptual horizons. In its own way, however, the axiomatic 'no single model' stance over-simplifies as much as the one-sided views it seeks to modify. In promoting perspectival plurality it downplays the common (often Graeco-Macedonian) aspects that were shared in Hellenistic kingship's genetic make-up, as discernible from its institutional and behavioural practice and, particularly, royal ideology. Since this contention is deep-rooted, some historiographical reflection is necessary.

Droysen's original conceptualization of the Hellenistic period, in his monumental *Geschichte des Hellenismus* (1836–43), took as its defining feature inter-cultural 'Verschmelzung' (fusion), via the 'Hellenization' of non-Greek peoples.[23] The nature and extent of Greek and non-Greek interactions have since been central issues in scholarship, and Hellenistic history at broad brushstrokes remains concerned, accordingly, with questions of periodization and definition.[24] Droysen's vision of *Hellenismus* dominated for a long time, and although pockets of Droysenian teleology linger still,[25] it lost most of its force in the wake of the post-colonialist position that developed after the twentieth-century World Wars.[26] According to this revisionist model, the Hellenistic kingdoms were structured along lines of separation, rather than fusion, for the Graeco-Macedonian 'dominant ethno-class' and its native subject populations. These were fault lines, for although the ethno-cultural groups remained separate, they frequently conflicted and erupted into violence.[27] Often given the moniker of 'two solitudes' or 'cultural apartheid',[28] this model enjoyed its own period of dominance but has been scrutinized and re-evaluated in turn in more recent scholarship.[29]

More recently, Ma advocated that scholars embrace paradoxicality, rather than rely on paradigmatic uniformity, in both our evidence base and our analytical mindset.[30] It certainly seems true that the binary options for conceptualizing cultural interaction in the Hellenistic world, namely the alternation between the diametrically opposed interpretations of fusion and separation, are increasingly untenable and expose some crucial problems of method.[31] Nevertheless, fusion and separation remain the dominant paradigms in scholarship, however critically positioned. This pendulum swing on the issue of cultural interaction has also characterized the progression of studies of the Hellenistic kingdoms, since one of their defining features was Graeco-Macedonian domination of non-Greek peoples and cultures, which has been characterized as the development of a Graeco-Macedonian 'dominant ethno-class'.[32] Although it is not the aim of this current study to generate a new paradigm for understanding cultural relationships in the Hellenistic kingdoms *in toto*, it is important to outline recent trends to see where the main issues lie.

* * *

The post-colonialist response to Droysenian 'fusion' influenced scholars of Hellenistic monarchy to emphasize non-Greek subject peoples dominated by a Graeco-Macedonian colonial elite. This has led to greater focus on the nature of that domination and how, through acculturation and accommodation, the kings negotiated ruling over their unfamiliar and potentially hostile subjects.[33] This has been a necessary act of rebalancing perspectives, and it has been historiographically productive. However, it has led to over-compensation in places. Particularly, the Hellenistic kingdoms' Graeco-Macedonian background, and its varied traditions of monarchy, have been a minor key in recent scholarship.[34]

Since a shared political and cultural background of the major actors is one of the unifying features underpinning the original development of the Hellenistic kingdoms, whereas it is their respective native populations and their rulers' specialized modes of local acculturation that are differentiating, a fragmented understanding of Hellenistic kingship has necessarily followed. Particularly for the period 323–276, this fragmented view has been affirmed by the preponderance of studies which adopt singular regional, biographical or dynastic focuses.[35] Such emphasis on the local and on the particular also inhibits a general conceptualization of Hellenistic kingship, since only rarely does it have recourse to cross-dynastic comparatives.[36] Formulae such as 'no single model accounts for Hellenistic kingship', then, can be said to represent the logical trajectory of recent decades of scholarly engagement with the topic of Hellenistic kingship.

None of this is to suggest that scholars have been unaware of, or have not engaged with, these very problems and complexities. Some scholarship, particularly with regard to Ptolemaic Egypt – and more recently, by imitation of approach, Seleucid Babylonia[37] – attempts to assess both the Greek and the non-Greek constituent populations of a Hellenistic kingdom (or a particular region thereof) in a single conspectus. Peremans argued for a 'monarchie bicéphale' for Ptolemaic Egypt, which argued that the situation of the Ptolemaic king astride two opposing subject cultures necessitated the development of discrete Egyptian and Hellenic faces of kingship.[38] This is a modified reiteration of the post-colonialist position, even in its recent evolution as a more harmonized construct wherein one merged face of kingship incorporated dual cultural registers.[39] This latter formulation is influenced by Stephens's 'seeing double' approach to Hellenistic Egyptian poetry, which holds that a systematic inter-permeation of Egyptian and Hellenic cultural codes took place in the artistic environments of Ptolemaic Egypt, resulting in literary works which exhibit both Greek and Egyptian resonance and interest.[40]

This conceptualization of a world of overlapping cultural codes and systems is a refinement of the basic premise of the post-colonialist contention, and potentially ramifies for framing more nuanced ideas of how Hellenistic kings ruled over heterogeneous bodies of subjects. One could easily contemplate, for instance, that the assimilation of double or even multiple cultural codes into a unitary expression of royal power and identity might have been strategically effective for a ruler.[41] However, this model also entails limitations for its potential application. It encourages a more sophisticated approach to cultural interaction and the interpenetration of royal power on a particular regional level, but it inhibits meaningful cross-dynastic comparanda and complex institutional generalizations. Despite 'seeing double', or speaking of a 'two-headed monarchy', we are still in the post-colonialist realm of 'no single model' and 'no single formula',[42] and this limits our ability to develop a holistic picture.

* * *

The international perspective adopted in this book – looking at the interactive evolution of Hellenistic kingship in the wider world of Alexander's former empire, focusing on ideology, performance and competition – is intended to present a productive way of unifying and further understanding the historically significant institution of Hellenistic kingship. This international perspective is not simply an imposed scholarly convenience, however: it reflects, and aims to expose, the internationality that inhered in the evolving monarchic discourse in the early Hellenistic period. Even though the regal-aspirant *diadochoi* were undeniably regional actors, attempting to negotiate and embed royal power and status (before and after the fact of actual accession) in the diverse localized environments they controlled, they were also international actors, competing for and performing their power and status, and seeking to obtain recognition thereof, on a much broader supra-regional stage. Moreover, none of the aspirant kings devised his ideology and self-representation in a vacuum, isolated and insulated from the corresponding activities of his rivals. Without denying the value of a regional perspective, our perspective should also be an international one because the *diadochoi* themselves, in their own context, were also international actors.

As this book argues, the performance of early Hellenistic kingship on an international level substantially incorporated Graeco-Macedonian elements (see section 4, below). This does not deny or diminish the significance of non-Graeco-Macedonian influences in the early kingdoms' ideological programmes. Rather, it is important to recognize that we cannot transpose the expediency that motivated local acculturation to the formulation of royal imagery at an international level, an arena in which different strategic concerns applied. Among these, there were different intended audiences for royal performances, not least the Graeco-Macedonian soldiers and settlers that would support military, political and economic state objectives. The *diadochoi* were competitors in particular for the support of Greek *poleis*, new and old, and the individuals, resources and networks they could supply.[43] Another consideration is that ideological projections were offensively directed against inter-state rivals (see section 5, below). In short, there were important reasons as to why an international face of early Hellenistic kingship developed, just as much as the series of local faces that we can reconstruct.

Conceptualizing the *diadochoi* as international actors is also an important point for understanding how they used reputational power – ideology and its performance – to create and embed their royal positions. Validation of projected positions through international recognition, by as many operators on that level as possible, was an important precondition of success in terms of creating long-term, stable structures of rulership and mutually recognized sovereignties, and it resulted in the multipolar world discussed above. The *diadochoi* did not just need to legitimate their self-constructed positions for an internal audience: they also needed to concretize and impress these positions in the eyes of an international world of potential subjects, allies and competitors. It is also reasonable to postulate that continued stress across an international system was a means by which the newly developed ideologies were negotiated, achieving acceptance or not, permanence or not.

An international level of representational activity also tallies with the fact that there the ambitions of the *diadochoi* were not regionally circumscribed. They were opportunistic and outward-looking, not introspective, in their geopolitical ambitions and in the ideologies that were developed to structure and express those ambitions.[44] In addition to securing and retaining rule in lands they had acquired, whether from settlement or conquest, the *diadochoi* continually sought new acquisitions to their existent domains and alliance systems; by extension, there were no internally devised limitations on the reach and impact of diadochan self-projection. The inherent triumphalism of the diadochan ideological discourse conceptually promoted, however counterfactually, the wide internationalism of their power and status. But perhaps most importantly, an international view enables us to perceive the ways in which competition (see section 5, below) between the emergent dynasties was a persistent and highly significant force in shaping kingly ideology and the evolution of the royal institution more broadly.

Finally, it could be objected that a discussion of the institution of kingship in the early Hellenistic world does not need to be defined by the cultural discourses that the kings encountered and manipulated. Why not speak about the symbolic language of kingship per se, rather than royal imagery with a particular cultural turn? There are virtues to such an approach, as many of the issues involved – how royal display and ceremonial sustains the wider monarchic institution, for instance – are perennial questions that pertain to monarchic societies across vastly different periods and geographies.[45] At the same time, it is important not to lose the opportunity to analyse the meaning of royal ideology and performance in their contemporary contexts.

3. Royal ideology and performance

Quigley suggests that the purpose of all ritual, a cultural construct fundamentally involving 'installation', 'is either to transform a person from one status to another or to maintain him in that status'.⁴⁶ This is clearly true in royal contexts, such as in coronation or accession rituals – that is, differential situations of status can be affected by rituals of kingship. But they can also be impacted by the articulation and performance of ideology, especially if they are designed to showcase how a leader is embodying ideals, values and traditions of kingship.⁴⁷ In this, I would agree with Fowler and Hekster's definition of royal ideology:

> [T]he entire scheme or structure of public images, utterances, and manifestations by which a monarchical regime depicts itself and justifies its right to rule. It is the display and also … on occasion the creator of power.⁴⁸

To be more specific, royal ideology is a coordinated programme of royal representation across various modes and media, potentially taking the form of speech, text, dress, regalia, symbol, image and action. These may claim to represent and communicate royal power and status, yet they also can act to construct, solidify, maintain and augment them through their capacity to shape perceptions and resonate with ingrained expectations and knowledge of royal traditions.⁴⁹ Thus, ideology and its performance can tap into reality and also help transform it, sometimes both simultaneously, for a world of subjects within a realm but also the world beyond it. In the context of the unstable post-Alexander years, and particularly the series of regencies and then interregnum leading to usurpatory regime-formation, developing robust schemes of royal ideology and modes for performing them was of paramount concern for the *diadochoi* in their competition for superiority and lasting power.⁵⁰

Taking cue from Weber, much has been written about the 'charismatic' authority underpinning the institution of kingship, and this has been applied to the Hellenistic kingships no less than to other monarchic rulers in world history.⁵¹ It is a particularly appropriate model here given the instability of the post-Alexander world, the exemplarity of the first Hellenistic kings in establishing a long-lived institution, the centrality of military victory in their programmes of activity, and their self-styled heroic standing, close relationship to divinity, and capacity to attract followers.⁵² At the same time, 'charisma' is not all-explanatory,⁵³ and there is significant distinctiveness in the Hellenistic kingships that requires framing them in the specialized contexts to which they belong. Further, any 'charisma' that might have been attached to the kingly offices of the *diadochoi*, on which any descendants could later capitalize, was first and foremost a product of the their own ideological foundations, so the natures of those foundations are worth scrutinizing, too.⁵⁴

Studies on kingship, often called the predominant form of governance in human history, with a global ubiquity across time and space before the modern age,[55] have widely discussed how kingship is constructed, what role it plays in society, and what its social, political and above all religious underpinnings are. This is extremely helpful in a whole range of respects, yet it also constitutes substantial conceptual baggage for any new study of kingship. This, combined with the unprecedented situation represented in the early Hellenistic period, of the emergence of five new great power kingships out of the ashes of a single empire, means fresh reflection and synthesis is worthwhile for achieving the substantive aim of this book: investigating the significance of royal ideology and its performance in the development of early Hellenistic kingship.

3.1. Contexts and functions

Royal imagery and ideology in basic terms are concerned with pomp and display, and are designed to inspire awe, reverence and respect for the monarchic figure at the centre of the representational spectacle. In this line of thought, it is an attempt to give tangible, perceptible form to the abstract concept of the monarch's superiority of power and status.[56] In other words, it is designed to articulate the 'majesty' of the monarch,[57] his (or her) unique eminence, and to reify the socio-political boundaries separating the ruler from the ruled.[58] Along these lines we can easily conceive of the value of royal ideology and performance to the monarchic state, and the ways in which symbolic constructions of royalty could be put into the service of power.[59] One might think it especially useful, in that vein, for an ailing or insecure regime, which has recourse to more imaginative strategies for maintaining an illusion of unassailable dominance, or for a comparatively powerless monarch, who lacks real political power but whose office nonetheless constitutes a symbolic, highly visual component of his state's corporate identity (so-called 'theatrical' monarchies).[60]

This same potency makes royal ideology and performance useful, and much more necessary, for emergent royal regimes and new royal states. For rulers aspiring to declare themselves and be acknowledged as fully fledged monarchs – by whatever strategy of legitimation open outside of legal recourse – there is a greater need to create, embed and fulfil a robust monarchic image. Further, this necessity needs to be attended to well before the fact of formal accession – hence, on the road to royal power, creating an ideological narrative towards it – as well as continually reinforced afterwards. A monarch cannot simply count on having the direct support of his or her subjects, so royal ideology and performance importantly serves as a persuasive and communicative tool; it also helps to develop ruler–subject consensus, before as well as after the actual acquisition of a formal title structuring his power and control.⁶¹ However, just as it does not preclude more subtle and indirect attempts at shaping perceptions, ideological negotiation of this kind does not preclude direct coercion.⁶²

There is a tension observable in many royal societies across world history, namely the divergence between how royal ideology is devised and performed and how royal power is exercised, structured, and situated. Although the image and practice of any kingship are fundamentally interconnected and mutually informative – image can dictate practice, and practice can in turn generate image – they are often in disagreement, and often intentionally so.⁶³ Examining the nature and form of such disagreement can expose some of the intentionality behind it, and thus also elucidate some of the core functions of royal ideology and performance in a given context and its contingent purposes.⁶⁴ Some of these intentions might be to paper over the cracks appearing in the edifice of power, or to facilitate an aspirational trajectory to higher status, or to justify a transgressive action, or to magnify a policy beyond its natural field of significance – that is, ideology and imagery have the potential to support material changes in political realities, all in service of a (would-be) regime. Equally, the specific models and concepts involved in the generation of new ideologies – the examples and traditions and wider knowledge invoked – can show us which toolkits, strategies and repertoires were available and which were considered the right fit for a given set of situations and audiences.

We can also think of royal ideology and performance as being consciously concerned with furthering a supra-realistic discourse, since the development of imagery of royal power involved a symbolic projection of transcendence above the ordinariness of institutional realities.⁶⁵ In this line of thinking, ideology serves not as a foil or correction to the reality of how power is exercised or status is recognized, but rather as an attempt to create and embed new, idealized perceptions of the nature of the royal position, suggestively imagining the king's superior place vis-à-vis the political universe as a whole.⁶⁶ Thus not all imagery should be considered schematically propagandist in its aims, as a defensive response to contemporary socio-political features and dynamics. Instead, we should also be mindful of the capacity of royal ideology and performance to constitute a series of symbolically coded reflections on the nature of kingship,⁶⁷ and hence to possess an explanatory quality in ruler–subject relations, aimed at explaining – thus also concretizing – monarchic superiority and unassailability.⁶⁸ It might thus be said that, while ideological reactions to reality constitute a series of answers to the micro-questions of consensus and relational dynamics that underpin socio-political power, ideological creations of reality respond to the macro-questions of the institution's rationale and identity in a particular context in space and time.

This latter idea of micro- and macro-questions about kingship is compatible with a theoretical staple in royal studies, namely Kantorowicz's formulation of a king's 'Two Bodies', developed to capture medieval European political theology.[69] The 'body natural', namely the corporeal, mortal shell of the current royal incumbent, was transient compared with the 'body politic', the incorporeal, eternal kingly institution currently being incarnated. It has been further suggested, in Franko's study of balletic performance by monarchs of the *ancien régime*, that the performative dimension of kingship was primarily directed towards representation of the immortal sovereign body of a king rather than his literal physical form.[70] Indeed, it is true that no matter how personalized and 'charismatic' the imagery and ideology of kingship are, they are fundamentally purposed to showcase the exceptional royal nature and character of the ruler, and hence might be considered referent to kingship rather than kings – the larger institution being embodied or aspired to, not simply the short-lived (would-be) occupier of the title. Set in an early Hellenistic context, this prompts interesting questions that are worth exploring further. Are royal ideology and its performances by the *diadochoi* constitutive acts, namely a construction of what *basileia* is in the post-Alexander world? Does early Hellenistic royal ideology define the institution itself and shape expectations of what it should look like? In basic terms, does the performance of royal ideology create the reality of kingship?

3.2. Meaning and effect: the performance of kingship

Inspired by Anderson's *Imagined Communities*, Parker suggests that '[p]erforming kingship is ... the creation, maintenance, and dissemination of imagined social differences'; further, this imagined social construction involves presentation to both the elite, who are the key stakeholders of royal power and authority, and a wider world of subjects (real and potential), who are necessary for the functioning of the royal state, especially the extraction of economic resources.[71] In other words, the performance of kingship is about rationalizing monarchic power and status through the setting and justification of boundaries that shore up the kingly regime. This categorical reflection on the royal institution is a helpful means of framing the development of early Hellenistic kingship.

We can productively regard kingship and royal power in the early Hellenistic period as performative – that is, as contingent on the creative force of the ruler's articulations of his own image and identity. This is not to take away from the praxis of power and its central importance in developing the royal institution; but we have to recognize that legitimacy did not take a solely pragmatic dimension, nor was it concerned solely with formal conditions of legitimation.[72] To borrow from Hekster's critique of Millar's well-known model of the Roman emperor, even though 'the emperor was what the emperor did', 'the emperor was also ... what he appeared and was perceived to be'.[73] In the early Hellenistic world, where the new kingships developed out of a collapsing empire, it could be argued that the kings *were* their own performances: their ideological schemes shaped perceptions by internal and external audiences, especially in contexts which allowed only limited experience of the royal person.[74] Put another way, the kingships created by the *diadochoi* were fundamentally dependent on the figures themselves, not on the title of king to generate authority for them. To borrow from Machiavelli's *Discourses*, '[i]t is men who give lustre to titles, and not titles to men'; or put more broadly, 'power may readily give titles, but not titles power'.[75]

In this line of thinking, the king *was* the royal state and the royal office in the early Hellenistic world, and so his ideology and performance of it inevitably conditioned perceptions of his kingship.[76] An image of strength and dynamism suggested a strong and dynamic state; by the same token, perceived weakness in the ruler implied the state's feebleness.[77] This 'personification' of the royal state in the form of the monarchic ruler makes the issue of royal ideology one of serious, continual concern. Although an advantage in some respects – for instance, the monarch's singular physicality enabled effective ideological communication through careful crafting of his images and staging of his appearances – this was also potentially a disadvantage, inasmuch as it was always open to perceived failure through any 'slipping of the mask'.[78] Nevertheless, in general terms, the associative capacity of the monarch's image – its potential to signify an ideological construction – means that '[i]n terms of visualising power, the monarch has a dramatic head-start'[79] over other forms of political organization which lack a discrete, clearly visible personification.

It is also likely that the wide spread of coinage under Alexander, effectively becoming a mass medium for top-down ruler–subject communication, enhanced the need for the circulation of a coherent and recognizable symbolism of kingship on a continuous basis.[80] As the inhabitants of an individual kingdom lived in an increasingly monetized society, so too was that society increasingly mediatized, and hence responding to public expectations became ever more necessary.[81] Under Alexander, iconographic designs were introduced and then standardized across his world empire, west and east. The coins themselves circulated widely throughout

Figure 1 Silver tetradrachm of Alexander, 336–323. Staatliche Museen zu Berlin, Münzkabinett 18254121 / Dr Karsten Dahmen. [CC PDM 1.0].

the empire, and even beyond its boundaries.[82] Moreover, the size of the issues was enormous: including those issued posthumously down to the end of the fourth century, approximately 40,000 talents of silver (Attic standard) were monetized into Alexander's imperial tetradrachms using approximately 3,000 obverse dies, in total potentially constituting almost 60,000,000 coins depicting Heracles, Zeus and Alexander's legend.[83] Notwithstanding the economic reasons behind Alexander's (and his Successors') drive for monetization, this represents an articulation of ideology on an unprecedented level. This enormous production and circulation continued in the early Hellenistic period, hence the mediatization of royal power in the Hellenistic states continued, too.[84]

The objective historical circumstances of the early Hellenistic period required, to borrow a phrase from a study of Toyotomi Hideyoshi and his creation of authority in late medieval Japan, 'extrovert performativity and self-fashioning on various stages of political action'.[85] Hideyoshi, like the *diadochoi*, was an upstart who progressed his own power and position through prowess in warfare, strategic skill, clever alliance-building, and selective committing of treason to his state and its nominal ruler(s). He, like they, also had recourse to manipulation of available media and investment in symbolism and ritual in order to build acceptance of the new regime, particularly from powerful elite classes, and to concretize its standing in the eyes of the world. Further, in addition to progressing the longer-term aim of stable sovereignty, the clever ideological performance of rulership was also a more immediate survival strategy given how contested his power base was and how brittle and insecure was his position in it. The cases of Hideyoshi and the *diadochoi* were certainly not exactly parallel by any means, but they are examples of broadly the same type in that they bear out how exigent historical circumstances – principally, the need to shore up and explain an unprecedented, illegal build-up of personal power and authority in the face of rivals disposed to contest it – resulted in similar solutions, namely performative ideology founded on a distinctive pastiche of existent models that appealed to multiple audiences while nonetheless capturing the uniqueness of the new ruling power's position. For the *diadochoi*, as for Hideyoshi, it is exceptionally important to bear in mind the fact that newly accumulated power and authority could not be conveyed as simple continuations of existing positions and institutions. Straightforwardly appealing to inter-generational continuity was not an available strategy.

Another way of framing the same idea is to consider the theatrical and spectacular nature of royal representation and display.[86] The model of theatrical kingship is well-developed in some of our literary sources, especially Plutarch's biography of Demetrius but also accounts of other kings such as Pyrrhus, which compares well with the same model developed by writers such as Shakespeare in reference to Elizabethan England.[87] In Plutarch (as in Shakespeare), the metaphor is extensively developed and given motifs of stage, masks and clothing, and explicit reference is regularly made to tragedy and its major themes.[88] Theatrical displays of monarchic power are nothing new in ancient Greece, no matter how they are represented as distinctive in relation to the Hellenistic dynasties by Plutarch,[89] but they become much more bombastic as the Macedonian state builds dominance on the international scene from Philip II onwards.[90] This model helps us to consider the trappings and costumes of royalty, the development of authored themes and narratives in ideology, and also the ruler's function as actor, performing his role to progress the narrative with a range of implicit and explicit signposting along the way. Furthermore, to borrow from a classic concise formulation of the stage model, when we consider A (the actor) performing B (the role), we inevitably also have to think of the direction of the performance to C (the audience).[91] Theatre, theatricality, thus also presumes audience.

Articulations of royalty – across the gamut of word, image and deed – are ultimately a form of engagement with audiences.[92] In addition to being determined by socio-political context and the relational dynamics with key stakeholders of power, the performativity of kingship also has to be attuned to the needs and expectations of royalty held by different strata of subjects and elites, internal or external audiences.[93] However novel or innovative, such performances are always informed by ingrained (pre)conceptions, and ultimately by a society's traditions and practices;[94] indeed, they are only meaningful and explicable as such. Hence the performance of ideology, especially where involving precise visual representation and arrangement, is not blind or unthinking: it may be considered, like the imagery on coins, a significant and deliberate representational choice.[95] In other words, conscious design and crafting inheres in royal ideology, amalgamating the aspiration behind the performance (what does the ruler want to convey?), the chosen mode of performance (how will it be conveyed?), the target audience (to whom will it be conveyed?), and an evaluation of potential appeal and resonance (why will the conveyed message be effective?).

Given the historical circumstances of fragmentation and usurpation in the early Hellenistic world, systems of royal ideology and performance had to be developed anew, over a long-term period. At a more fine-grained level, however, we can see how these new systems have borrowed from and synthesized a plethora of individual existent models and examples from different cultural backgrounds (see section 4, below). This is because although the political situation was unprecedented, ideological recognizability and resonance with target audiences remained crucial concerns. They were crucial in the foundational royal imageries of the *diadochoi* because too little grounding in precedents and established models might have rendered any new ideology unintelligible and thus ineffective.[96] In other words, ideology needed to be explicable to its audiences in order to be effective, and situation within existent traditions was a strategy for engaging audience knowledge. It could, moreover, carry significance beyond the single act of borrowing and constitute its own form of symbolic legitimation; however limited, participation in a specific existent symbolic discourse was an act of self-orientation, of belonging to and embodying an idealized character that was defined by a series of paradigmatic exempla rooted in the wider tradition.[97]

None of this is to suggest that early Hellenistic royal self-representation was uninventive, or that it did not develop new registers of meaning in the appeal to older traditions of monarchic eminence. But none of the ideology under discussion in this book is *entirely* new and innovative: it would have had little value and effect had it not been grounded in recognizable patterns of thought, customs and cultures. Accordingly, an approach to kingship and royal self-representation in the early Hellenistic world must be context-driven, contingent on determining specific conceptions of meaning according to contemporary contexts rather than on imputing static, unchanging and continuous registers of meaning.[98] As part of situating and interpreting clear historical contexts, this involves a further, more explicit study of the genealogies underpinning early Hellenistic kingship.

4. Genealogies

Ma outlines four 'genealogical strands' of the Hellenistic royal states: roots in Macedonian royal practice, inheritances from the Achaemenid empire, models offered by pre-Achaemenid Near Eastern states, and a shared Greek identity and culture.[99] Each strand carried different weight and influence in its appropriate local or supra-local contexts, and we might characterize Hellenistic kingship overall as consisting of selectively variable mixtures of some or all of these elements in different times and places.[100] Holding this quadripartite model in mind helps to explain the nature of Hellenistic royal practice, especially in terms of its structural flexibility and diversity, and the 'tertiary' forms of the Hellenistic royal states themselves, inasmuch as they combined models and were products of dominating regions which had their own multi-layered genealogical backgrounds.[101]

This situation is true of the Hellenistic period and the Hellenistic kingships in general, yet we need to consider how this situation came about. Alexander had kickstarted a process of marrying different royal models together, but as in so many other areas this work was time-limited and was cut short, and we are unable to determine its long-term direction.[102] Inevitably, it was left to his Successors – the founders of the Hellenistic royal states – to work out the dynamics and problems involved in such inter-cultural blending of ideology and performance, and to establish a longer-term model. In the immediate post-Alexander period, we can see how these issues are negotiated, which decisions are taken, and what the broader patterns of these processes are.

4.1. Achaemenid and pre-Achaemenid models

There is a stratigraphy of royal ideology and imperial structures that can be excavated once we recognize the importance of each level and how and where it underpins the operations of the Hellenistic kingships. All four genealogies, indeed, are significant, but the Hellenistic kingdoms are widely indebted to the Achaemenid imperial model in particular in many important structural respects.[103] The Hellenistic royal strategy of adopting particular acculturated guises in local environments controlled by them, for instance, conforms very closely with the previous Achaemenid practice of 'chameleon-like' royal adaptability in dealing with regional diversities.[104] Likewise, the Achaemenid feature of a 'dominant ethno-class' in overall imperial organization was maintained, though with Greeks and Macedonians replacing Persians in this top-tier role.[105] For the Seleucid state in particular, the exigent demand of governing a diverse, multi-regional Asian empire could be neatly solved by the Achaemenid imperial blueprint, not least (in adapted form) the continuation of the satrapal system.[106] Even for the other early Hellenistic states which, unlike the Seleucid, did not form empires territorially comparable to their Persian antecedent, traces of Achaemenid imperial frameworks are certainly visible, particularly in relation to tribute capture, the extraction of wealth, aulic composition, and ideologies of universal rule.[107] In addition to this, there are a good number of individual cases of 'Persianization' across the post-Alexander generation, probably founded on Alexander's own example.[108]

Thus even though Briant, and other scholars of the first millennium *longue durée*, regard the diadochan age as the real point of rupture from two centuries of Achaemenid rule – Alexander, in this model, was 'last of the Achaemenids', inasmuch as his reign effectively represented a continuance of the model developed by the Achaemenid empire – there are sufficient grounds to posit, even if not direct routes of institutional continuity in all cases, the influence of established imperial structures and strategies.[109] How and from what perspectives we construe these continuities remain contested questions. As the varied responses to Briant's 'last of the Achaemenids' formulation have shown, there are no easy answers.[110] Perhaps, as Bang suggests, the issue of whether or not Alexander was, ideologically or pragmatically, an Achaemenid is less significant that the repeated worry and anxiety in the source tradition that he might become one.[111] It is striking in this regard that despite the obvious structural inheritances, none of the early Hellenistic kings – not even Seleucus – ever explicitly identified himself as embodying an Achaemenid pattern.[112]

Models drawn from pre-Achaemenid Near Eastern states also played an important part in the establishment of, effectively, Graeco-Macedonian colonial regimes in regions with their own long royal traditions and complex experiences of empire.[113] The animation of these models in new Hellenistic state formations is indebted to the resilience and continuity of local customs and identities, but it was also partly enabled by the Achaemenids' own policies of local acculturation, which had seen the use of a plethora of local models in building regional legitimacies, whose effect was to preserve earlier traditions.[114] It is in no doubt, for instance, that there was an enduring relevance of the pharaonic tradition to the Ptolemaic state in Egypt, or that the Seleucids were actively mindful of the layers of Babylonian history in their operations in that region.[115] This relevance was articulated through direct enactment of local tradition by the ruling power, for which we have examples even from the very earliest post-Alexander years. Ptolemy's honouring of the dead Apis bull, for instance, in his first years after taking the satrapy of Egypt in 323, was an act of participating in a locally important religious discourse, and it ingratiated him with the Memphite priesthood of Ptah in a way that was probably indebted to Alexander's own example during his takeover of Egypt in 332/331.[116] The formulation of the ruling power's activities in these terms meant that a variety of monarchic traditions from the pre-Achaemenid Near East found renascence under the Hellenistic kingdoms, in concert with the endurance of a typically Achaemenid pattern for the Hellenistic rulers' behaviour.

There are further interesting historical observations that could be made on the basis of seeing these inheritances. For instance, an expansionist Egyptian polity in competition with a Syrian-/Mesopotamian-based one was a recurrent pattern in the ancient Near Eastern *longue durée*, into which Ptolemaic and Seleucid rivalry nicely fits.[117] Further, the Ptolemies actively engaged in internal state-building and consolidation in a way that was informed by Egyptian precedent and expertise, in addition to presenting themselves explicitly as Egyptian pharaohs with the full range of traditional titulary.[118] In all of this, however, we must recognize again a key difference between ideology and structure, or between image and practice. Even recognizing that practice generates image, structural borrowings were not always incorporated in wider ideological projections by the emerging Hellenistic royal powers. Features of their regimes were indebted to pre-Achaemenid models, yet there were no overt pharaonic representations by Ptolemy beyond Egypt, and no Babylonian representations by Seleucus beyond Babylonia.[119] In simple though not overly reductive terms, localized communities were engaged via regionally specific performances of royal ideology that deliberately linked into local systems of symbolism and tradition. But these were not naturally transferrable to an international stage.

4.2. Argead Macedonian and Greek cultural models

In that case, what were the supra-local ideological systems used in the early Hellenistic world? The Achaemenid imperial blueprint was certainly influential, and this had its share of impact. One notable case in point is the ideology of universal empire, which itself had been propagated by pre-Achaemenid Near Eastern states, so was possibly taken up from them by the Persians.[120] Temporally, we can see it in operation from the very earliest years of Hellenistic kingship down to the imagination of a new Ptolemaic world empire in the infamous Donations of Alexandria in 34 BC.[121] This was an exceptionally important inheritance for the Hellenistic states, in that it offered a working ideological model for structuring a wide world of different subject states and cultures cohesively together under a single royal power.[122] Moreover, perhaps somewhat paradoxically, universalist ideology in one imperial state was not undermined by the existence of the same in other states: in fact, it became just a way of framing competitive discourse between rival powers.[123] Hence it did not preclude mutual interstate recognition of sovereignty.

Such cases of Achaemenid influence should not be underestimated, yet in the wider picture of early Hellenistic kingship the Achaemenid genealogical strand was not dominant in international ideological discourse. There are good reasons why Greek and Macedonian symbolism, instead, was the early Hellenistic ideological lingua franca. We have already noted that a dominant Graeco-Macedonian ethno-class constituted the primary imperial bureaucracy and governing elite of all the Hellenistic royal states. This was true as early as the Babylon Settlement after Alexander's death in 323, which saw the division of satrapies to a majority of Greeks and Macedonians;[124] it had also already been anticipated in Alexander's administration, in the dilution of traditional satrapal authority after 331, when Persian nobility began to be brought into Alexander's imperial framework yet Greek and Macedonian financial and military officials were given control of the real levers of power in the empire's regional units of governance.[125] Moreover, the Macedonian military were spread throughout Alexander's former empire, especially in the period 323–306, and events showed that these men could be attracted and suborned, their loyalty transferrable to a new general able to communicate the viability and authority of his command.[126] Beyond this, Greeks and Macedonians were settled into the new city foundations of Alexander and the *diadochoi*, and the wider Greek world was an important audience for the latter in their drive to encourage continued streams of settlers to these communities, which was also important in turn as an investment in military capacity and courtly personnel.[127] Further, all the *diadochoi* and early Hellenistic rulers were eager to gain alliances with, or otherwise maintain power and domination over, systems of *poleis* and *koina* throughout the Aegean world.[128]

This wide supra-regional or international spread of Greek and Macedonian audiences converges with the structural and ideological backgrounds of the *diadochoi*, which were Macedonian and Greek, notwithstanding experiences gained in Asia and Africa during service under Alexander and the post-Alexander regencies. These are compelling reasons why Macedonian origins and Greek cultural characteristics can be seen widely at work in early Hellenistic monarchic discourse. The well-recognized pillars of Hellenistic royal power, namely 'king, friends/court, and army', for instance, clearly has institutional roots in Argead Macedonian practice, notwithstanding influences from the Achaemenid model also.[129] Another crucial example is the language of Hellenistic royal coinage – both symbolic, namely the iconography, and literal, the inscribed legends – which is fundamentally Graeco-Macedonian, and (in the case of gold and silver coinages, at least) circulated on a wide international stage.[130] This coinage adhered, as it did under Alexander, to an Attic weight-standard (with the exception of the Ptolemaic reforms of the 310s, which decreased silver tetradrachms to a peculiarly Ptolemaic measure – nonetheless, the Attic standard was adopted for approximately the first decade of Ptolemy I's satrapal rule),[131] and the iconography featured deliberate symbols of the ruling power's identity.[132] Likewise, the chronological systems of the Hellenistic royal states, notwithstanding local calendrical reckonings, was Macedonian on a supra-regional level. This both represented an institutional continuity and carried an ideological claim, namely that the world of the Hellenistic kingdoms was temporally structured in terms of the dynasties' existence and retention of power, most obviously in the case of the Seleucid era.[133]

Thus, the key constituencies that the *diadochoi* needed to communicate with across regional boundaries were spoken to in a symbolic language founded on Greek and Macedonian models, and some of the key ideological underpinnings of their new regimes were rooted in models drawn from shared culture and heritage. On the Macedonian side, there was a discrete royal tradition in the Argead dynasty that enabled these foundations to be laid down. Would-be competitors for kingship after Alexander's death, whose early claims to authority were tied up with the ability to bring Macedonian nobility and soldiers to their side, had recourse to the Argead model given its recognizability and value for their primary target audience. We see in Chapter 2, for instance, how the Macedonian marshal Craterus made use of this in his distinctive, though ultimately ill-fated, manoeuvrings for position in the very earliest years after Alexander's death. Various specialized ideologies of kingship present in the Hellenistic world have their roots in Argead practice, ranging from the Ptolemies invention of ancestry to the Seleucids' 'diasporic' imperial identities.[134] As a more concrete example from the earliest post-Alexander years, we may observe how stridently all of the major *diadochoi* competed for marriage alliances with female members of the Argead house such as Cleopatra;[135] we may also note how much power could be directly wielded in the post-Alexander struggles by established queens such as Olympias and Adea-Eurydice.[136] This last example underscores the power rooted in female members of the royal dynasty, including their role in building authority and legitimacy, that was so distinctive of Argead Macedon and which transferred into the dynastic set-ups in the Hellenistic world.[137]

Beyond the Macedonian homeland of the *diadochoi* and the paradigms of royal ideology and practice stemming from there, there were various models of kingship in Greek culture. Despite the common conception that it died out in mainland Greece at the end of the Archaic period, there was an enduring existence of monarchic rule, mostly tyrannies but a good number of *basileiai*, too, throughout the Classical and Hellenistic periods, such as the Spartan dual kingship and the tyrannies of Pherae in Thessaly.[138] Classical monarchies carried their own complex undergirding systems of values and ideologies, particularly centred around individual excellence or *aretē*.[139] Even without direct modelling on specific institutions, there was a wider cultural tradition of kingship, as embodied in the world of epic, tragedy, philosophy, and popular mythologies of heroic leaders.[140] Indeed, one primary referent for *basileus* in the Greek world, beyond the Great King of Persia, was probably the Homeric *anax* or the tragic rulers who were so ingrained in elite culture and education.[141] In fact, in Macedonian elite education, not least Alexander's well-documented tutoring, these models and literatures likely featured very heavily, and among this elite there was deep resonance as 'culture was often put to use to justify their traditionally violent ways'.[142] In hypothesizing the take-up from, for example, epic and tragic models of rulership in early Hellenistic royal ideology, we are dealing with a classic form of selective engagement with Greek literature and culture, structured along the lines of the appropriator's cultural interest and purposed to express something about the nature of their society in idealized terms.[143] In this respect, there is a compatibility between Argead royal tradition – which might itself already be characterized as somewhat 'Homeric' in nature[144] – and the multifarious Greek cultural models of kingship. All of this also leaves aside the extent to which Macedonian society was already Hellenic, Hellenized, or something else entirely – a controversy that need not detain our discussion.[145]

If we set the combined Graeco-Macedonian international ideological discourse of kingship, as found in the early Hellenistic period, into a longer-term history, we can frame it as the continuation of a trajectory that took a sharp upward turn in the earlier fourth century under Alexander and his father before him, Philip II.

Philip was a true 'impresario' in terms of developing his monarchic image,[146] establishing many of the features commonly observed in the Hellenistic states, such as an international coinage with symbolically meaningful imagery (often religious and epinician) and self-divinizing pretensions.[147] Alexander continued this upward turn, and although many of the specifics of his self-representation were indebted to his ancestral background, he engineered some innovative ideological associations, such as his liberal use of the Trojan War myth-schema and his mother's ancestor Achilles, plus his standardization of the figures of Athena and Nike, respectively, on the obverse- and reverse-types of his gold coinage.[148] Thus there was, under Philip and Alexander, a departure from pre-existing models of Argead ideology, or rather a magnification and expansion of these models; and in some cases a modification, via integration with non-Argead traditions that were nonetheless drawn from a common Graeco-Macedonian cultural heritage. That this was coterminous with the rise of Macedon as an international power under Philip, Alexander and the *diadochoi* is not surprising: the uptick in Macedon's status on the international stage necessitated a corresponding uptick in international performances of royal ideology.

One benefit of recognizing the importance of Greek and Macedonian ideological language at an international level is in enabling internationalizing perspectives and approaches to be built. We may unify the Hellenistic kingdoms in one conspectus, but more importantly unify Hellenistic kingship as an analytical category and typology, even while we preserve localizing perspectives and approaches where differentiation is needed. An additional benefit of this approach is that it provides a means by which to bring the kingdoms of Lysimachus and Cassander – often neglected in studies of Hellenistic kingship in favour of the more famous, more long-lasting Ptolemies and Seleucids, and to a lesser extent the Antigonids – back into the interpretative fold. With a view on the Graeco-Macedonian ideology and performances of kingships that were articulated in an international field of discourse, we can bring all the major *diadochoi* who founded kingdoms – Antigonus and Demetrius, Ptolemy, Seleucus, Lysimachus and Cassander – into a joint analytical framework, and so develop a unified approach to early Hellenistic kingship.

4.3. *Imitatio Alexandri* and genealogical 'bricolage'

The four genealogies discussed above encompass features that were both intrinsic and extrinsic to the background of Alexander and his Successors yet assembled to constitute a unitary and incorporated imperial system. Looking within any of the diadochan power bases *cum* early Hellenistic royal states, we can see different admixtures of these models, tailored to particular locales, communities and their historical traditions. Looking beyond these local spheres to an international view of the early Hellenistic states, we can see that there is less mixture, more concentration of Graeco-Macedonian models. These two realities, local and international, existed coextensively, and they constituted the imperial whole of Hellenistic royal discourse. The local ideological worlds of early Hellenistic kingship came in many cultural colours, but the international ideological world was more monochromatic. Such was the *koine* of kingship in the Hellenistic period, and this common discourse emerged in its very earliest years.

The other model worth discussing briefly, not strictly a genealogy but rather a shared experience and exemplar, is that of Alexander the Great. All of the *diadochoi* were intimately familiar with Alexander's model, regardless of their level of service with his Persian campaign, and his posthumous influence and legacy is so pervasive as to be considered ubiquitous in early Hellenistic culture and society. The early Hellenistic period was the first stage in the development of the long-lived – indeed, still-existent – trend of *imitatio Alexandri*, and saw the establishment of many of the reflexes and thematic preoccupations that would become defining parts of the tradition, particularly with respect to monarchic image-making.[149] To put the point more strongly, even though there was the predictable assimilation with Alexander's style at his court during his lifetime, the *diadochoi* themselves can be said to have invented the tradition of a dislocated *imitatio Alexandri* after his death and popularized the reflex whereby a constructed association with Alexander had significant capital attached to it, which could be utilized in the development of political, military and social power in more pragmatic terms.[150]

This is important in and of itself, as *imitatio Alexandri* can be considered a category that is individually distinct from the more generic Argead Macedonian and Greek cultural genealogies discussed above. Indeed, it is possible that the Alexander-model complicates our thinking in terms of separate genealogies, since in important respects he already blended them together in his royal ideology and practice: Alexander's 'Persianization' was well known, and indeed infamous, in his lifetime, and he also – although perhaps following the general Achaemenid paradigm of local acculturation – engaged with pre-Achaemenid traditions such as taking on the pharaonic mantle in Egypt and interacting with religious traditions in Babylonia.[151] Alexander's model by the early Hellenistic period, then, was a composite of different cultural models and traditions in itself, and it is clear that this composite model continued to have resonance and was the source of imitation by some of the diadochan elite, especially in the very early post-Alexander years. The image and model of Alexander could thus be a conduit for conveying different ideologies through a multi-layered referential mode.[152]

In other words, in addition to there being four distinct strands in the ideological genealogies of early Hellenistic rulers, there was also a shared example in the form of Alexander which showed a blending together of these genealogies. In the case of *imitatio Alexandri*, we seem to be dealing with 'bricolage', a model which has been applied to questions of cultural continuity and change in many Hellenistic contexts.[153] Versluys's use of the term is helpful for framing the idea here; in his study of Antiochus of Commagene, he defines the mixed style there in terms of bricolage as 'a juxtaposition and blending of discrete elements suggestive of different cultural traditions within a single, new style as the result of conscious appropriation'.[154] This certainly captures the phenomenon of imitating Alexander, and also of recreating Alexander, that we see in the early Hellenistic world, whereby Alexander is counterfactually depicted or narrated in ways that do benefit to the agendas of the *diadochoi*.[155] It also, potentially, describes the entirety of Hellenistic kingship, the formation of a new coherent model out of a series of discrete appropriations.

5. Competition

Imitatio Alexandri, and the conveyance of legitimacy and prestige that went with it, was an area in which we can see significant competition among the *diadochoi*, part and parcel of a wider competitive dynamic. Even without subscribing fully to a Realist model, it is clear to see that the world in which Hellenistic kingship emerged was fundamentally a competitive one.[156] The major players among the *diadochoi*, before and after the accessions of 306–304, engaged frequently – almost continually – in political and military conflict with one another, and their ideological apparatuses reflect and even further these continuing disputes. A competitive framing of diadochan activity has deep roots, with agonistic terminology and metaphors pervasive in the ancient literary evidence for this period. The most obvious example is Alexander's famous deathbed prophecy, after supposedly saying that his empire would go to 'the strongest' (or 'the best'), that he foresaw a great funeral *agōn* ('contest' or 'games') coming to pass after his death.[157] Diodorus, among many sources recording this tale, goes on to clarify explicitly that this *agōn* would be the struggles of the *diadochoi*. In Justin's retelling of the story, he likens Alexander's utterance to the casting of a *malum*

Discordiae ('Apple of Discord') – referring to the role of Eris, 'Strife' personified, in the Judgement of Paris and hence in causing the Trojan War – and characterizes the *diadochoi* in response as 'rising up in emulation against each other' (*ita omnes in aemulationem consurgunt*).[158] This mythic archetype for competition is an apt metaphor for the competitive activity that proliferated after Alexander's death.

Whether these accounts are apocryphal or real is less important than the fact that they reflect a deep-rooted analogy in ancient cultural mentality between politics and warfare, on the one hand, and competitive games, on the other.[159] This analogy, historically significant in its own context, is also marriageable with models from our own analytical toolkits. The idea of competition or agonism has been meaningful for modern scholars of Greek history across different periods, and it has been established as a critical impetus in a wide variety of political, social and cultural spheres.[160] Extended to this study of early Hellenistic kingship and the role played by royal ideology in its development, competition is a helpful way of framing and explaining four central issues: the field in which political ideology developed; the dynamics resulting in continued innovation in ideology; the causes of parallelism and 'sameness' between the royal ideologies; and the reasons for their longevity.

* * *

First, thinking in terms of competition helps us to conceptualize the field or environment in which the early Hellenistic monarchic discourse evolved. Although the uniqueness of Greek agonism is now (rightly) no longer assumed,[161] it remains undeniable that the Greeks and Macedonians were exceptionally agonistic in their world view, in their pursuit of cultural and intellectual achievement, and in the spectrum of their political and social activities and relationships.[162] In particular, it has been well-argued that competitions for prestige and status – various forms of capital, in Bourdieusian terms – were defining characteristics of earlier Greek institutions, as for instance Duplouy argues for Archaic *polis* communities.[163] In Duplouy's model, elite status and identity were open to inventive self-construction: attempts to win prestige and honour, and recognition thereof, were not determined by a static set of ideals and markers of a closed elite social category, but rather were developed in and shaped by a changeable social field that was open to creative, individualized attempts at self-definition. In this vein, innovation in socio-political representation was a key force in shaping aspects of elite status and identity, which, on account of continual collective and individual innovation, remained fluid and malleable constructs, and did not achieve permanence in any particular form.

Confronting the theatre of action in this way, as well as the actors themselves,[164] is equally important for the early Hellenistic world, for which a partly comparable picture can be envisioned. Pre-Hellenistic elite Macedonian culture already had been characterized by a rivalrous socio-political discourse, wherein the elite competed with the king, as institutionally enshrined in certain *loci* such as the hunt, and the king himself continually emphasized his pre-eminence through competitive displays of excellence.[165] From these roots we can trace the continuation of a competitive dynamic governing elite and royal behaviour into the Hellenistic world, a dynamic that paralleled – even fuelled – the continuation of the Macedonian state's expansionist trajectory.[166] The death of Alexander intensified elite competition, with the regencies of 323 onwards governing on behalf of two inactive royal office-holders: the insufficient authority of the kingship meant that there was no check on the agonistic drive of the elite, and in fact the regents themselves directly pursued internal conflicts to obtain greater power and standing. This situation was compounded by, and contributory to, the unprecedented emergence of multiple non-royal Macedonian power centres across the Aegean world and the Near and Middle East. This was a socio-political field that was wide open to creative programmes of self-orientation, where individualized performances of ideology could effectively express power and status in manifold forms. Put another way, the fragmentation of political power and control in the Argead Macedonian empire after Alexander's death created the conditions that allowed the *diadochoi* to engage in independent self-definition, at the same time as their own decentralizing political activities accrued them more and more *de facto* power and control and greater opportunities for ideological projection.

It must also be considered that, after Alexander's inventive representational example, there was no uniform categorization of the monarchic image that the *diadochoi* could easily capitalize on. There was no obvious traditional model in operation, and so the evolving monarchic discourse became subject to new influences, both internal and external, as part of a competitive drive for distinctiveness and primacy among the diadochan elite. Since the early Hellenistic world was inhabited by numerous ambitious political actors, each attempting to achieve and concretize a position of power and status, an agonistic ideological climate continued to flourish. This was constituted by ideological competition and one-upmanship, as the *diadochoi* attempted to further their aims and agendas, specifically a trajectory towards kingship on a permanent footing.

* * *

An emphasis on competition, secondly, is productive for further conceptualizing the dynamics that were responsible for individualization and continued innovation in the monarchic discourse. Even though it could also have negative corollaries, the entrenched Greek view of competition was that it could stimulate outstanding individual and collective achievement.[167] Modern scholars, too, have emphasized competition as a significant factor in stimulating innovation in various aspects of Greek political, social and cultural life.[168] An agonistic milieu, in this vein, results in continued innovation, in part because competitive impulses often result in novelty and experimentation – the need to do or be better resulting in attempts to stand out from the crowd.[169] Equally, however, competitive self-orientation entails responsiveness to, and distancing from, rival modes of self-definition: individualization supports the achievement of distinction and pre-eminence in a competitive field.[170] In the early Hellenistic context of multiple emergent royalties, ideological innovation and individualization had a clear place and important purpose.

A more specialized reason for the diadochan need to present their images in new and increasingly magnified fashions was the usurpatory basis of their regimes. As the oft-cited *Suda* definition of *basileia* reminds us, the *diadochoi* could claim neither *physis* ('nature', namely traditional legitimacy) nor *dikaion* ('law', legal legitimacy) as a basis for their royalty: rather, their personal qualities and competences qualified them for kingly status.[171] In this way, representational innovation, even in the earliest post-Alexander years, was partly compensatory, designed to highlight personalized prestige and status for usurpers wishing to cement rule in their power bases and, eventually, become kings on an individualized rather than dynastic basis. More importantly, however, it was necessary on account of the uniqueness of the contemporary context, and the inapplicability of any single pre-existing ideological template. In other words, the extraordinary political circumstances of the post-Alexander years necessitated – and so stimulated – extraordinary representational measures; and the coterminous development of new ideological structures by all the regal-aspirant *diadochoi* intensified this need on an individual basis.[172] This partially accounts for what we might call the experimental nature of early Hellenistic royal ideology, namely the broad-ranging generation of multiple new representational modes, some of which were non-traditional in their design or arrangement.[173]

The performance of early Hellenistic kingship involved the invention of some entirely new ideological apparatuses, but also the creative and selective redeployment of some pre-existing monarchic models. Some of these existent models had a clear and obviously determined place in an ideological pastiche, such as the Argead Macedonian or Achaemenid Persian models explored above. Here it might be said that, although representational innovation was both necessary and contextually determined, a representational programme constituted solely by new ideology ran the risk of unintelligibility and thus ineffectiveness.[174] Hence, there was recourse to recognizable models that had been proven to work and resonated with stakeholder knowledge and expectations. Individualized forms of royal ideology, then, were indebted to an agonistic ideological environment and to the concomitant search for modes of self-expression that were, on the one hand, sufficiently recognizable and so meaningful, yet were, on the other, uniquely attuned to the claimant and, as far as possible, irreplicable by his rivals. Such competition was for pre-eminence and superiority in the political field more than it was for making gains in an environment scarce of resources, and as a result there was no predetermined end in sight:[175] as rivals developed new forms and configurations of self-representation, the opportunity and the impetus to be more distinctive were omnipresent. In this way, ideological escalation, in part manifested in areas such as iconographical specificity (for example, the depiction of deities with specific attributes and in specific guises on coinages), was potentially boundless.

* * *

Thirdly, a competitive perspective helps to explain the ideological parallelisms found across diadochan programmes of self-definition. In the ever-shifting ideological landscape of the post-Alexander years, adaptation and retaliation to new developments, and generation of further distinctive forms of self-representation, were imperatives for political actors seeking to maintain a competitive edge and a position of perceived primacy.[176] In this vein, the close symmetries that can be found across the early Hellenistic dynasties' imagery should not be imagined as simply osmotic, as an unconscious or passive product of permeation between proximate and coexistent states, but rather as the result of intentional practices and processes of inter-state ideological rivalry.[177] These are important testimonials for the interactive evolution of early Hellenistic kingship: common strategies developed not simply on account of mutually shared backgrounds and comparable problems in need of solution, but also because of interactive engagement with and borrowing from rivals' methods of problem-solving. In this way, the competitive dimension of the contemporary political field induced the *diadochoi* to replicate robust features of their rivals' representational configurations and so capitalize on their constructed meaning; and since they were actors with effectively comparable aims and positions, some co-opted ideological materials could be applied equally in relation to their own parallel agendas.

Moreover, in seeking to replicate and capitalize on a specific representational tactic generated by (one or many of) his rivals, equally a diadoch could diminish its uniqueness by redeploying it in his own terms. Accordingly, co-option of a particular ideology or performance could divest it of its original distinctive meaning, as constructed by a rival figure, at the same time as its general meaning remained open to exploitation. New ideological specialization could be, in turn, superimposed by the co-opting figure.[178] Because of this, certain types of royal self-representation in the early Hellenistic world owe as much, in terms of both impetus and meaning, to ongoing chains of conceptual redevelopment as they do to a single origin in terms of ultimate source roots. An excellent case in point has already been seen at the start of the chapter, the emergence of diadem and *basileia* after Salamis in 306.

Ideological parallelism via replication of form and content conceivably will have served to reify, at least partially, the basic terms and value of ideologies that were co-opted, and explains a major aspect of the convergent development of early Hellenistic kingship: over time, a coherent and mutually shared contemporary syntax of royal ideology developed, with the diadochan competitors both contributing to and drawing from a common discourse. Such a scenario will have reinforced the necessity, discussed above, of the diadochan search for an irreplicable mode of ideological self-expression that communicated their unique distinctiveness. It should be stressed that not all ideological parallelisms were competitively induced: there were certain obvious and clear choices of sources for ideological modelling that will have appealed to and will have been natural determinations for all the *diadochoi*, on account of their shared experience and backgrounds. Even here, however, the specific terms of the arrangement and deployment of these common models, and their specific emphases and stresses, could also be subject to competitive reformulation, whether through innovation or replication.

* * *

Finally, thinking in terms of competition for the advent of early Hellenistic royal ideology is valuable for explicating the longevity of certain ideological modes. Just as ineffective institutional forms do not survive indefinitely in competitive inter-state environments,[179] so too the ideological forms and modes of performance that survive and attain some permanence do so either because they are effective in achieving their aims, or because they come to serve another beneficial purpose. By the same token, competition could result in the abandonment of representational constructs, because they prove either ineffectual or otherwise insufficiently distinctive and unappealing in an ideological marketplace populated by a multiplicity of developments by rival players. It must be said that, given the tailoring of certain ideologies to a particular dynast's circumstances, not all forms of royal self-representation achieved equal success in terms of inter-dynastic take-up, and so some constitute divergent rather than convergent examples when viewed in terms of the international setting. Even across the *longue durée* of a single dynastic setting, however, the longevity or abandonment of a representational mode can be read as a reasonable indicator of the extent of that mode's effectiveness.

This is not to say that the extent of ideological effectiveness should in all cases be measured solely by the criterion of longevity. Rather, changing priorities and new developments in a dynast's personal socio-political context should also be factored into any assessment based on longevity or abandonment. In other words, although it is likely that the changefulness of a diadoch's ideology and performance of that ideology was importantly determined by their (real or perceived) robustness in an inter-state system of competition, we should not forget circumstantial factors driving their malleability. The meaning of any single form of royal ideology, at the same time as possessing a generalized tenor that made it viable for inter-dynastic appropriation, had a specialized construction in the hands of its developer. We should keep in mind, then, both the general and specific fields of meaning that were embodied in the conception and performance of ideology, as well as both contextual and discursive influences behind its generation.

2

The Performance of Status in the Early Hellenistic World: Craterus at Delphi

The so-called Year of the Kings of 306–304, which saw the establishment of five Hellenistic kingships across the Aegean and the Near East, had a profound and transformative impact.[1] Alexander's single empire gave way after protracted conflicts to new monarchic states that together stretched from the Balkans and North Africa to the borders of the Indian subcontinent. It is sometimes convenient to think of the newly regnant *basileis* as the prime movers in the process of creating a paradigm for monarchic power and status that would endure until the end of the Hellenistic era. It is true, from an institutional viewpoint in particular, that the imperialistic frameworks adopted by the new kings had an exceptionally long afterlife, whether through the direct continuation of the dynasties or through interstate transmission and renascence in different contexts, some much later in time.[2] Plutarch's reflection on the accessionary scenario of Antigonus and Demetrius after Salamis, or rather on the flatterer's word he sees as its instigator, thus seems to be apposite in many respects: it did indeed 'fill the whole world with such great change' (*Demetrius* 18.4: τοσαύτης ἐνέπλησε τὴν οἰκουμένην μεταβολῆς).

While the historical significance of these events should not be underestimated, adopting an entirely prospective view, which takes the Year of the Kings as its point of departure, obscures the complexity and variety that inhered in the accessions' original developmental context; such a view can also misconstrue the inception of Hellenistic *basileia* as the product of a single, linear and predetermined trajectory of progression.[3] Just as there was no straightforward *translatio imperii* from a unitary Argead state to the numerous Hellenistic states, so too formulations of kingship in the post-Alexander period were not suddenly emergent in 306–304, fully fledged and fully effective. Instead, the series of accessions must be understood as the product of longer-term processes to which the *diadochoi* contributed: first, of accumulating the political and military power and authority that were necessary preconditions of successful regime-formation; and secondly, of trialling the effectiveness and impact of modes for identifying and articulating superiority of status. In other words, as the Macedonian empire steadily degraded, fragmenting into disconnected power bases controlled by individual marshals, political behaviour among the *diadochoi* became more and more particularistic, as they attempted to enhance their own positions within, and eventually external to, a socio-political system which was unable, without an effective central authority, to keep firm checks on the upward mobility of a powerful elite class.

Such a process was, of course, circular and reciprocal. Although they may have promoted, as an ideological pretext, cooperative enterprise within a single imperial entity reigned over by Alexander's nominal Argead successors,[4] the incapable Philip III (r. 323–317) and the infant Alexander IV (r. 323–310/309), the *diadochoi* sought to forward their own singular agencies and public personas; as a natural result, finding ways of representing individualistic prestige became the subject of varied exploration. In addition to the *basileis* of 306–304, we can point to other diadochs whose attempts at generating distinction had been ultimately unsuccessful, whether by reason of failure or simply of premature death, but no less symbolically vocal and energetic. Prominent members of Alexander's former elite such as Leonnatus, Perdiccas, Craterus, Eumenes and Antipater are important examples of this early Hellenistic trend towards independent political aggrandizement, but we can also consider in the same light figures who are usually more neglected in modern scholarship, such as Peithon, Cleitus, Arrhidaeus, Asander, Ophellas, Neoptolemus, Alcetas, Peucestas and Archon.[5] To varying degrees, these figures were responsible for the creation and endurance of the political climate that ultimately determined the self-assertions of royal status in 306–304: a highly competitive, multi-actor struggle for prestige and status, international in outlook, increasingly complex and changeable in its operations, and inventive in its engagement and adaptation of existing models. When viewed in this light, the accessions escalated and intensified a much longer dispute about primacy of status, giving it a different complexion, via a magnification of nomenclature and formalization of non-dependent status: it did not resolve the conflict.

The emergence of this environment after Alexander's death, and how the competitive pursuit of eminent status was articulated in the very earliest post-Alexander years, is the subject of this chapter. As has been explored in Chapter 1, political status in the early Hellenistic world was, at its heart, performative: the *diadochoi*, lacking the ability to present positions of superiority in some of the more established terms of legitimacy, sought to exercise creative force on the political reality through a range of adaptable, culturally embedded representational strategies – aiming, in sum, to shape the socio-political field around them, and to determine the manner of their own perceptions by others. The specific frameworks and registers involved in this, the varying deployments of and balances between tradition and innovation, remain important issues to be examined, especially with regard to the early years after Alexander's death, in which royal status was still formally attached to the Argead figures Philip III and Alexander IV.

This issue can be understood in depth through examining the example of Craterus' monument at Delphi, commissioned by Craterus (d. 320) to commemorate his saving Alexander's life in a lion hunt. Consisting of a now-lost statuary and a still-extant verse inscription, this monument projects an image of Craterus' unique status and qualification for royal office. It derives power from its complex engagement with earlier discourses of commemoration and paradigms of monarchic suitability, yet also from its sensitive, targeted situation in contemporary political currents. While we should certainly also consider it to be meaningful in light of his contemporaries' attempts to project their own aspirations,[6] Craterus' monument at Delphi in many senses stands alone as an illustrative case in point for examining Hellenistic performances of royal status, exemplifying how they were developed, their complexity of meaning, and the earliness their post-Alexander development.

1. Craterus and the monument at Delphi

By the end of Alexander's reign, Craterus had risen to an almost unequalled seniority in the Macedonian ranks, and he is now recognized to have been a key player in the high politics of the immediate post-Alexander period.[7] In 324, after being married to the Persian princess Amastris at the Susa mass weddings, he became responsible for repatriating more than 10,000 Macedonian veterans dismissed after the Opis mutiny and for taking over command of European affairs from Antipater, who had managed them since the beginning of Alexander's Persian campaign in 334.[8] Although this command suggests a great deal of trust from his king, we might also assume that Craterus' sympathies lay with the agitators against the recent incorporation of Achaemenid elements (often called 'Persianization') within Alexander's court and armed forces, as he, too, is accounted as a Macedonian traditionalist:[9] in this, he was likely trusted by both

Alexander and the veterans. Affairs in the Cilician satrapy delayed Craterus' return to Macedon with the veterans, and Alexander's death in June 323 found Craterus still in Cilicia – halfway between the imperial power games that ensued in Babylon and the reins of authority over Greece and Macedon itself. Being temporarily touted for the *prostasia* in an early round of the settlement at Babylon in 323, in spite of his absence, was a marker of Craterus' high standing among the Macedonian armies and elite, but Perdiccas' subsequent capture of office of regent for himself left little in the way of a defined role for Craterus,[10] and the marshal was perhaps left without a clear, viable direction after Alexander's death. Was he to approach the new *epimelētēs* Perdiccas, either contesting the settlement or attaching himself to him? Or was he to fulfil his orders, given by Alexander before his death, and seek to install himself in Macedon, an arena long dominated by Antipater? An inability to find a solution to this quandary might explain Craterus' continued sojourn in Cilicia more convincingly than other reconstructions that have been proposed.[11]

A call for aid from Antipater, besieged and overrun by Leosthenes early in the Lamian War (323), determined that Craterus and his veterans should return to Greece, where he proved decisive in terminating the Hellenic revolt in 322.[12] Soon afterwards, in 321, he turned his attention, alongside Antipater, to subduing Aetolia, the remaining major party to be punished after Athens had been suppressed; he had also married Antipater's daughter Phila, widow of the late *sōmatophylax* and Cilician satrap Balacrus, to strengthen ties still further with the elderly marshal.[13] The arrival of Antigonus Monophthalmus, probably in the winter of 321/320, brought news of Perdiccas' machinations in Asia,[14] which catalysed Craterus' abrupt return to Asia alongside Antipater: the two generals could thereafter present themselves as attempting to put down a faithless regent and restore leadership of the empire. On his arrival in Asia in spring 320, while Antipater was to progress onwards to Egypt, where Perdiccas was attempting to dispossess Ptolemy of his satrapy,[15] Craterus attempted to neutralize Eumenes, who had been left by Perdiccas as a line of defence against Antipater and Craterus.[16] It was in battle against Eumenes in 320 that Craterus lost his life, the former having contrived to conceal from his Macedonian troops the identity of the opposing general, reportedly fearing that Craterus' great popularity would incite desertion from within his ranks.[17] For reasons that are not explicitly recorded, it seems that it was not until c. 316/315, after Eumenes' own demise at the hands of Antigonus, that Craterus' remains were returned home to Macedon, to his wife Phila (and their child Craterus, hereafter Craterus II), who had by then been remarried once again, this time to Antigonus' son Demetrius

Poliorcetes.[18] Such was the abrupt end to the career of Craterus, the figure whom, in a counterfactual hypothesis, we might consider the likeliest candidate for becoming the second post-Alexander *epimelētēs* of the Macedonian empire.[19]

The precise date has been contested, but it was probably during Craterus' last months in Europe, after the Lamian War but prior to his ill-fated Asian expedition of 320, that he began to make preparations for dedicating a grand monument to Apollo's sanctuary at Delphi.[20] This monument commemorated an event from Craterus' years of campaigning with Alexander that is not otherwise chronologically fixed in our historiographical sources: participating in a hunt with Alexander, and saving the king's life by killing a lion. It consisted of a bronze statue group depicting the lion hunt scene – Plutarch describes this as a *kynegion*, a hunting scene with dogs, in which Alexander grapples with the lion and Craterus comes to his assistance – and a ten-line dedicatory inscription commemorating the scene in verse.[21] The statuary, the work of Lysippus and Leochares, no longer survives, and we have no sufficiently clear comparative material to reconstruct it with any degree of accuracy.[22] However, the dimensions and location of the *exedra* in which it was housed tell us that the monument was

Figure 2 Exedra of Craterus' votive offering, Delphi. Wikimedia Commons / Dennis Jarvis. [CC BY-SA 2.0].

one of huge proportions, well-positioned in the Delphic votive landscape: slightly more than 15 metres long, 6 metres deep, 4 metres high, and overlooking the terrace of the temple of Apollo – in sum, a chamber 'so well adapted to receive an *ex-voto* of such great and general importance'.[23]

Although the statuary may well have been ready at an earlier stage, Craterus' premature death meant that the monument's ultimate completion was effected by his son, Craterus II, at some point after 320; this was most probably in the period *c.* 319–316, during the *epimeleia* of Polyperchon[24] – who earlier had been Craterus' second-in-command among the 10,000 Macedonians after Opis and had acted as stand-in European viceroy during Craterus' and Antipater's expedition against Perdiccas.[25]

Despite the non-survival of the statues, scholars have focused largely on the artistic aspects of the monument, especially its relative place vis-à-vis early Hellenistic art history; its perceived eastern influences have also, in recent years, somewhat dominated scholarly discussions.[26] Although it is well-recognized that this monument involved an outward-looking projection of Craterus' persona,[27] the ways in which it presents an image of Craterus in light of Graeco-Macedonian traditions of excellence and prestige have been underaddressed. Voutiras has made the important point, too, that the monument represents the first monumental evidence for *Alexandri imitatio* in the Successor period.[28] To address this feature productively, we must recognize that the configuration of Craterus' position in relation to the model of Alexander is more complex than a straightforward designation of *imitatio* might suggest; indeed, reconceptualizing the semantics of *imitatio* has the potential to illuminate the development of innovative modes of identity alignment in this period, especially in relation to their composite modelling and their multiform engagement with tradition.[29] As will be explored below, Craterus' monument can be seen as an early, perhaps prototypical manifestation of some concerns that would later predominate in Hellenistic royal discourse; it constitutes a substantial test case for examining how new paradigms of status performance were conceptualized in the early post-Alexander world.

Since the statuary no longer survives, the inscription of ten lines (five pairs of elegiac couplets), found on the rear wall of the monument's *exedra*,[30] should be our primary focus. As a point of methodological principle, as with all monumental inscriptions, this should also be the subject of detailed attention in its own right, owing to its function as 'a fundamental part of the material object, crucial for its mode of engagement with viewers',[31] and with its own mode of deictic referentiality in relation to the *ex voto*;[32] it was not, therefore, simply an ornamental aside to a primarily sculptural spectacle.

υἱὸς Ἀλεξάνδρου Κράτερος τάδε τὠπόλλων[ι]
ηὔξατο τιμάεις καὶ πολύδοξος ἀνήρ·
στᾶσε, δ' ὅν ἐμ μεγάροις ἐτεκνώσατο καὶ λίπε παῖδα,
πᾶσαν ὑποσχεσίαν πατρὶ τελῶν, Κράτερος,
ὄφρα οἱ ἀΐδιόν τε καὶ ἁρπαλέον κλέος ἄγρα,   [5]
ὦ ξένε, ταυροφόνου τοῦδε λέοντος ἔχοι·
ὅμ ποτε, Ἀλ[εξά]νδρωι τότε ὅθ' εἵπετο καὶ συνεπόρθει
τῶι πολυαιν[ή]τωι τῶιδε Ἀσίας βασιλεῖ,
ὧδε συνεξαλάπαξε καὶ εἰς χέρας ἀντιάσαντα
ἔκτανεν οἰονόμων ἐν περάτεσσι Σύρων.   [10]

Child of Alexander, Craterus, to Apollo he, an honoured and greatly renowned man, vowed this. / <But it was Craterus who established it, the child he begot in the halls and left behind, completing the entire promise for his father,> / So that his hunt for the bull-killing lion, O Stranger, might have fame that is both eternal and alluring. / At the time when he was following Alexander, helping to sack with that much-praised king of Asia. / This is the way he helped to destroy: he slaughtered what came into his hands, in the farthest bounds of the sheep-pasturing Syrians.

FdD III 4.2.137 = CEG II 878

Some clarification is required on the peculiar transmission history of this epigram. Since the first couplet refers to Craterus' vowing of the monument, the second couplet is immediately arresting because of its complicated clarification that Craterus the son (II) was the ultimate agent of the monument's dedication. It has thus been suggested, plausibly, that the inscription had been composed, but not yet inscribed, prior to Craterus' departure for Asia in 320, as part Craterus' initial dedicatory plans; and that lines 3-4, the couplet detailing the son's completion of his father's promise, were interpolated ahead of the act of inscription, to explain Craterus II's takeover and completion of the dedicatory duties.[33] This is an attractive solution to the couplet's syntactical oddities and to its overall strangeness in the flow of the poem: accordingly, it should be noted that pronominal οἱ of line 5 refers to the same subject (viz. Craterus) as lines 1-2,[34] and should be seen as a dative of possession (thus, 'his [Craterus']').

Even though the monument's history precludes any straightforward readings regarding intention – as is discussed below, in section 4, we must allow Craterus II, too, a role in the construction of its larger message in a way that is meaningful in his own context – we can nonetheless posit, on the likely basis that Craterus commissioned the inscription prior to his death in 320, that the discourses it engages with and the symbolism it evokes are commensurate with his political agenda in that context. In other words, the effects the elegy creates, and the responses it seeks to elicit of the reader/viewer, ought to be seen as deliberately politicized, as intentional components of an extremely public act of self-representation. Indeed, the mode and setting of the dedication should be seen as an extension of a representational strategy; it is therefore important that we scrutinize, first of all, the inscription's linguistic choices, its intertextual relations, its discursive models and its thematic constructions overall. Here, the chosen literary modes possess substantive political force.

2. Discourses of valuation and commemoration

In terms of the spatial context of Delphi, the Craterus monument partly mirrors the enclosure for the Daochus monument, established by the Thessalians in the 330s, on the western side of the sanctuary; this monument's inscriptions are also formulated in elegiac couplets, and its statues also sculpted by Lysippus.[35] Additionally, from the point of view of our analysis, it is symbolically significant that the Daochus monument was dedicated by allies of a Macedonian king (Philip II), who perhaps used this Delphic space to project a contesting of their position within the new political order created by that king.[36] There was a long history of using Delphic space to articulate a new envisioning of political relations in this way, and indeed to commemorate military achievement, strategies that converge most markedly with Athenian monuments at Delphi (and Olympia) in the aftermath the Persian Wars; the monumental landscape itself partially serves as an aid to informing, codifying and broadcasting dedicatory intentions. In this same regard, the choice of elegiac couplets for the Craterus monument's inscription is also apposite, given their tradition of use in dedicatory epigrams accompanying prestige-advertising statues of the kind found more widely in Delphi, not to mention in elegies of historical narrative[37] – both prominently foregrounding aspects of praise and celebration, and both concerned with materialized as well as verbalized forms of memorialization.

As the below discussion establishes, the inscription's language suggests that the dedication's purpose was not simply to memorialize its *laudandus* Craterus and broadcast his dynamic position to a wider world, but rather, through that project, to immortalize him and his exploits in line with older heroic traditions. In itself, this is nothing remarkable: heroic *comparatio* was a natural reflex in Greek culture, in the diadochan age no less than in the Archaic and Classical eras, as Chapter 3 explores.³⁸ But the Craterus monument seeks to achieve this aim with a singular blend of contemporary and archaistic as regards language and models, and of conventional and subversive as regards generic and referential norms. However peculiar or aesthetically distasteful to some modern readers the resultant pastiche may be,³⁹ its historical significance in terms of the evolution of a post-Alexander representational syntax should not be underestimated. We might also contemplate a place for the elegiac inscription in the longer tradition of political elegy employed in relation to Hellenistic monarchs and courtiers,⁴⁰ as well as the evolving Hellenistic culture of ruler-praise more generally.

In the opening couplet, in line 2, Craterus is described as τιμάεις καὶ πολύδοξος ἀνήρ, 'an honoured and greatly renowned man'. The word πολύδοξος is extremely rare in the straightforward sense that is signalled here, of an enormous extent of reputation,⁴¹ but it seems to lack any specialized semantic significance in its own terms: its meaning is drawn, rather, from its confluence with the inscription's broader emphasis on fame, renown and honour, as signalled particularly strongly via the term *kleos* ('fame') in the third distich. It does, however, seem to be connected with other Homerizing archaisms throughout the inscription, and to be part of an attempt to depict Craterus (and, later, Alexander) in a manner typologically similar to the Homeric heroes, especially Odysseus, via use of the adjectival prefix *poly-*.⁴² In this vein, Craterus πολύδοξος of lines 1–2 partially anticipates, and mirrors, Alexander πολυαίνετος ('much-praised') in lines 7–8 – the latter quite closely harking back to πολύαινος, a Homeric epithet for Odysseus.⁴³ In addition to participating in an archaistic heroizing schema, therefore, the linguistic choice of πολύδοξος reinforces the overall construction, of which we shall see much more, of closeness between Craterus and Alexander, as expressed by a likeness in how their characters and acclaims are externally esteemed.

Worth stressing is the sparsity of familial connection, discordant in a commemorative context, in the face of the overwhelming individual prestige that the original inscription seeks to emphasize. Although there is a definite rationale for the placement of Craterus' brief, suggestive familial identification as 'Alexander's son', as will be discussed in section 3, it remains clear that the epigraphic ideology here is that, rather than by his genetics, Craterus is far more meaningfully characterized by, and remembered for, the immensity of his fame and honour, themselves ultimately products of an association with Alexander's conquests.⁴⁴ This point has significant bearing on understanding the individualistic construal of status in the early Hellenistic world: it encapsulates the performative, prestige-driven nature of political self-orientation among the post-Alexander Macedonian elite, and it points to an early public engagement with a pathway of status enhancement that is determined by actions and behaviours resulting in external acclaim. This is a sentiment with which we are very familiar from its much later and more simplified codification in *Suda*'s definition of *basileia*, which asserts the lesser importance of genetic legitimacy in the face of demonstrable capability in more important areas, such as governance and military leadership.[45] In sum, although he is identified as 'Alexander's son', Craterus' stature is more importantly clarified, and proclaimed, as that of 'an honoured and greatly renowned man' – and it is on the latter that the subsequent characterization of his superiority rests.

This performative paradigm is borne out and enriched by further linguistic choices. A great deal can be said about the use of τιμάεις ('honoured') in particular, which signifies the type of characterization of Craterus that is forwarded in the inscription and the discourses which are invoked as models. A relatively uncommon word as an adjective (as opposed to a verbal form of τιμάω, 'to honour'), τιμήεις (Doric: τιμάεις), in Archaic literatures, is either a descriptor of value for materials of which inanimate objects are constituted – and, thus, a kind of 'worth' is ascribed to the objects themselves – or, relatedly, it signifies a state of honour attained or possessed by an individual. Of the former kind, it is noteworthy that often it is divine or royal property that is esteemed as valuable,[46] and that it figures in certain influential scenes with a fundamental tension between word and image – most notably, the gold which constitutes part of Achilles' shield at *Il.* XVIII 475, in the build-up to the great *ecphrasis* (XVIII 478–608). Both of these features suggest a materiality embedded in the word's meaning, and both are contingent on a valuation of the individual being granted a gift: the gift is τιμήεις in the sense that the honour of a costly gift is fitting for the chosen recipient on the basis of how their worth and status have been valued, whether reckoning according to the donee's achievements or by knowledge of his or her position, perhaps hereditary, in the established social system.

In a closely connected fashion, to refer to an individual as τιμήεις, as possessing honour, is contingent on some estimation of the designee's status and/or achievement;[47] it, too, is based on some socially validated proof of how the individual embodies contemporary standards around honour. On both readings of how the designation of τιμήεις is constructed, reciprocity is clearly determinant, for while the proof of honour inheres in the individual, or in the object, it also inheres necessarily in the esteem and recognition of that honour that stem from members of the social group to which the individual or object belongs, or aspires to belong.[48] Indeed, being τιμήεις seems dependent on continuing reciprocal valuation by others, evinced by word and by deed; thus even Poseidon, raw with anger that Odysseus has returned to Ithaca, laden with gifts, and that the Phaeacians should have aided him and granted great gifts of their own, demands of Zeus: '... will even I be no longer honoured (τιμήεις) among the immortal gods, since mere mortals give me honour not at all (ὅτε με βροτοὶ οὔ τι τίουσιν)?' (*Od.* XIII 128–129).

This Homeric terminology of τιμήεις, animated in the context of struggles between Alexander's Successors, conveys not just an 'archaic' mode for Craterus' memorialization (creating such an effect surely being an aim in itself), but also transfers with it an understanding of the basis and rationale for that mode: Craterus is an individual of high standing within his social system, receiving continuing esteem in relation to others, on the basis of his demonstrable character as a performer of extraordinary, honour-achieving actions – here, as is materially represented in conjunction with the epigraph, the saving of Alexander's life, but also, as we shall see is strongly suggested in a later line in the inscription, an instrumental role in destroying the Persian empire. The monument itself thus also participates in the performative drive for Craterus' status, serving to create and broadcast a perception of Craterus' superlative stature in the contemporary socio-political hierarchy but also more generally in terms of *ethos*. The Homeric discourse of honour valuation is invoked to inform the performative paradigm of status enhancement in Craterus' own agonistic milieu, and the monument's inscription serves a vital communicative role in that paradigm's construction. The Homerizing nature of the terminology and its deployment, then, has a more than simply a cosmetic dimension and is in fact an important architectural feature of the larger representational edifice.

The discourse of honour valuation found in the inscription can be illuminated still further through reference to other texts. In particular, a parallel may be found early in Pindar's *Isthmian* IV, where Melissus of Thebes and his family are described as Θήβαισι τιμάεντες ... λέγονται, 'spoken of as honoured among the Thebans'.[49] This parallel is temporally and linguistically closer to the τιμάεις of the Craterus epigram, dating perhaps to 474/473 and also using a Doric dialectal form of the word.[50] Semantically, the two usages are similar, inasmuch as both states of 'being honoured' are contingent on the perceptible, social actualization of esteem. For the Pindaric text, this esteem is orally articulated, with the many testimonials of the fame of Melissus' family, accruing from past and present victories and from political associations, being 'breathed about among men'. It is worth noting, too, that the death of four members of this *oikos* in battle, probably against the Persians at Plataea in 479, is a major milestone in their family history, as the subsequent lines go on to record. This particular designation of τιμήεις, overall, has its basis in vocalized indications of esteem, and more broadly belongs to an oral discourse of fame and memory creation.

When read against Pindaric usage, the use of the terminology τιμήεις to indicate Craterus' stature is a surprising one to find in an epigraphic text, which suggests that we are dealing with an intrusion of an orally minded model, one that is intended to enhance the commemorative agenda of a material text. This seems to be a complementary, inverse equivalent to the interest in materialist modes of commemoration that can be found in other areas of Pindaric epinician and indeed Archaic and Classical verse more broadly.[51] The *locus classicus* for this mutual interest, in fact, is Pindar's own poetry, and more specifically the opening lines of *Nemean* V, where Pindar asserts that he is no ἀνδριαντοποιός, 'statue-maker', to fashion motionless statues, locked to their bases; instead, his γλυκεῖ' ἀοιδά, his 'sweet song', will go forth into the world, the news of the victor he praises borne along on ships of various kinds.[52] At face value, Pindar asserts the superiority of his oral craft over its material counterparts. However, rather than exemplifying polarized distance between stone and song as commemorative modes, Fearn has argued that these lines attest to their complementarity, and mutual interest: Pindar is not asserting the primacy of song over stone, but rather is defining, using a materialist metaphor, the role of sung praise alongside the role occupied by stone memorials – themselves, it should be remembered, also containing textual components in the form of inscriptions, thus also constituting sites of 'art plus text'.[53]

A comparable insight can be garnered from the discursive opening of *Olympian* X (1–6), where the poet again acknowledges the materiality of his own text, describing the praise-song he will sing as written, or indeed 'inscribed', in his 'mind' (φρενὸς ... γέγραπται), so attesting to Fearn's suggestion of mutual interest between stone and song. However, Pindar also claims that he has 'forgotten' this inscribed song, and invokes the Muses, and Alatheia – 'Truth' herself, here in Doric guise – to aid him in recalling it. Even though these lines attest to the oral poet's deep interest in material models, to which his own self-definition is indebted, and we reject such as blanket criticisms of the ephemerality of inscribed verse, there remains, for the spectator, an ineluctable perception of distinction between stone and song: the poetic performance context, or the context of encountering verse, differs between the movable song and the immovable stone, the former illimitable in its reach owing to its potential for reperformance across different sites, the latter limitable owing to its single, static point of encounter for the reader. As Pindar implied in *Nemean* V, material commemorations are fixed ἐπ' αὐτᾶς βαθμίδος, 'on their same pedestals'.

As with Pindar's own songs, then, Craterus' monument can be seen to exhibit something of a more widely attested mutual interest between oral and material modes of commemoration. Given the presence of the Doric τιμάεις in the latter, mirroring the τιμάεντες of *Isthmian* IV, the Craterus monument seems to be engaging in self-conscious modelling on Pindaric terminology, incorporating in its own form of panegyrical presentation the Doric patina that had earlier characterized Pindar's language of praise. It may not be coincidental that *Isthmian* IV, distinctively among Pindar's odes for Isthmian victors, subverts a conventional model of glory entitlement that is linked to personal beauty, and replaces it with a performance-based model, by which 'deeds alone warrant glory'.[54] Although Craterus, unlike the aesthetically unfortunate Melissus of Thebes, is not known to have been ugly – in fact, his biographical entry in the *Suda* speaks rather approvingly of his physical stature – the essence of *Isthmian* IV's model, which is to change perceptions, and to habilitate a performer of great deeds within a social world to which he might not have had a clear or innate right to belong,[55] is one which has an obvious currency when transferred to the political culture surrounding Craterus' monument, even if the parameters of that culture differed; we see here, as Goldhill has observed, that 'there is no discourse of praise that is not an expression of the changing, normative discourse of what it is to be a(n outstanding) man in society'.[56] Creative reality alteration was an aim of both Melissus' song and Craterus' stone, and in both cases the adaptable, non-essentialistic nature of the larger prestige game is highly evident, to say nothing of the flexibility of the specific prestige-garnering strategies.

Certain other words employed in Craterus' inscription are also drawn from Pindaric epinician. The striking word ταυροφόνος, 'bull-killing', for instance, used in line 6 to characterize the lion killed by Craterus, has its roots in Pindar's *Nemean* VI (40–2); this is the only previous extant usage of the word, but it strikes the reader as a fairly distinctively Pindaric compound, even if cognate constructions can be found elsewhere Greek poetry.[57] The content of the parallel at *Nemean* VI – referring to bovine sacrifices to Poseidon – suggests that we are not dealing with a particularly meaningful intertextual reference; but the fact of parallelism confirms nonetheless the inscription's close interest in the vocabulary used by Pindar in his epinicians, evidently as part of a broader attempt to utilize praise poems like these as a model for its own commemorative vision. As with the Homeric language and framing, we are not dealing with a superficial, purely ornamental mode of referentiality, but rather an evident attempt to capture the likeness of a certain linguistic apparatus as part of the broader attempt to tap into the tradition of commemoration with which it was associated.

Taking a slightly different tack, we can note that the epithet of ἁρπαλέον, 'alluring', for Craterus' *kleos* also has Pindaric parallels: *kleos* ποθεινόν ('longed for' fame) in *Isthmian* V (7-8), for instance, and *kleos* ἐπήρατον ('entrancing' fame) in *Pythian* V (72-3). These uses, particularly ποθεινόν, refer to the social dynamics underlying agonistic contests, to a competition for the 'fame' that accrues to the athletic victor, just as the victory ode itself acts as a site for how that symbolic capital is afterwards negotiated.[58] It is this same competitive, envious dimension that is evoked in the Craterus inscription, though perhaps even more strongly: a *kleos* ἁρπαλέον is a fame that also signifies a 'grasping', 'devouring', 'consuming' drive, and in that vein is a needful thing. This links closely with the zelotypic nature of political interactions among the post-Alexander elite that we have seen asserted elsewhere, in relation to the royal accessions of the diadochs in 306-304.[59] The epinician discourse of fame and memorialization should thus be read as informing the epigraphic construction of Craterus' prestige, in a manner meaningful to, and revealing of, its contemporary milieu. Nevertheless, we should not neglect to note that it is also a *kleos* tailored uniquely to Craterus' deed, inasmuch as it puns on the action it memorializes and which is enacted in the statuary itself: the 'lion-grasping' (*harpa-leon*) *kleos* verbally commemorated in the inscription is rendered plastically in the artwork as Craterus meets with the lion.

Kleos itself is contingent on orality. Since the earliest Greek literature, it has a fundamental acoustic dimension, inasmuch as it is a 'fame' that is heard as a result of oral distribution:[60] in unequivocal terms, '[i]f *kleos* is not acoustic, it is not *kleos*.'[61] Its very presence here, in a material rather than oral mode of commemoration – and not a funerary epitaph, it should be stressed, for which preserving *kleos* was a more normalized epigraphic ideology, on account of implicating the passer-by in the (oral) act of reading[62] – is something of a peculiarity, even if we allow for an habitual diffusion of terminology and tropes across materialist-oralist lines. This is especially so when we consider that the monument's use of a secondary epithet, ἀΐδιον ('eternal', 'everlasting'), for Craterus' *kleos* consciously signals participation in an oral discourse of *kleos* that links with the archetypal Homeric *kleos* ἄφθιτον – the 'imperishable', or, perhaps, the 'unfailing' or 'unwilting' fame of a Homeric hero.[63] There are many variations of such epithets for *kleos* – ἄσβεστον, 'inextinguishable', and ἀθάνατον, 'immortal', to name just a couple[64] – but it is clear that Craterus' *kleos* ἀΐδιον is to be regarded as situated in this same discourse.[65] Craterus' monument is thus rooted in an Archaic model of fame diffusion, and its inscription has sustained influence from oral discourses associated with that model.

Important further touchstones to note include not just Pindar's and also Bacchylides' odes for athletic victors, in which we can see various types of *kleos*,[66] but Ibycus' hymn to the Samian tyrant Polycrates – which uses the Homeric *kleos* ἄφθιτον, in the construction of a conventional poet/patron dynamic, whereby the poet's fame, and that of his poem, supports the endurance of the subject's fame as much as his own praise-deserving acts and status[67] – and, notably, Simonides' elegy of the Spartan war dead at Thermopylae, which speaks of Leonidas' *kleos* ἀέναον, his 'ever-flowing' fame, a phrase that is perhaps drawn from Heraclitus' usage, the only other example in extant Greek literature.[68] Like in Archaic epic, all of these praise or commemorative uses remain inherently predicated on the orality of *kleos*, on the distribution and movement of the 'fame' through vocalizations to and among listening audiences. Simonides' Thermopylae elegy, in fact, consciously defines this *kleos* as ἀέναον, 'everflowing', in a way that is complementary with yet distinct from other, material modes of commemoration;[69] here, the convergence with Heraclitean terminology perhaps also evokes that author's major doctrine of *panta rhei* ('everything flows') to underline the point: *kleos* was ever in movement, unlike an unmoving stone monument. To recapitulate the point: an 'eternal *kleos*' offered by a commemorative inscription is a peculiarity, perhaps even more so than a stone's valuation of an individual as τιμάεις; this is because, to expand upon Pindar, inscribed verse stands still, generating comparatively little *kleos* via acoustic repetition, but an oral song moves, generating potentially unlimited *kleos*.

To explain this peculiarity, the reader has recourse to confront in more general terms the discursive framework on which the reference to Craterus' *kleos* rests. The monument was dedicated, as lines 5–6 assert, '[s]o that Craterus' hunt for this bull-killing lion, Stranger, might have fame both eternal and alluring'. The entire conceit, then, is the same as to be found in those earlier examples of a *kleos* discourse in epic, lyric and elegy: just as the epic poet, the lyric poet, the praise or commemorative poet designates and transmits, and so guarantees, his subject's fame, so too this monument offers for Craterus. It is the monument, particularly its inscription, that becomes Craterus' poet, responsible for ensuring his eternal *kleos*, in a way that blends notes from the poetic models that have been identified as influences behind it: the very assertion of a role in sustaining *kleos* strikes a distinctly Homeric note, even while the specifics of the inscription's phrasing – of an optative desire for Craterus *to have* fame – might be generically more familiar to the lyric poet's self-conscious creation of *kleos* by means of his poetry.[70] It might thus be said, in partial mirroring of the poet–subject dynamic common to epic and lyric, that the inscription becomes the lapidary poet of the heroic diadoch. All this constitutes a remarkable conceit, for an epigraphic ideology showing such a complete immersion in oral modes of praise must be, if not unique, at least extremely rare when stemming from a commemorative rather than funerary epigraphic context – even though we should remember that both commemorative and funerary spheres share a predilection for reflecting on the spread of *kleos*,[71] potentially any inscription functioning as 'a machine for producing *kleos*'[72] in the sense of forcing the (oral) reader into the completion of a speech act.[73] Indeed, the *xenos* ('stranger') invoked in the narration of the third distich effectively functions as the 'passer-by' most common to the realization of the speech act of funerary epigrams, showing another borrowing, here from a different epigraphic model, in order to achieve the quite singular dedicatory aim: the lithic spread and preservation of the living Craterus' *kleos*.

The Craterus monument continues to create a distinctive position in its strategy for projecting Craterus' *kleos*, especially in light of the Pindaric dimension of its discursive modelling. The dearth of familial information in the inscription, and the complete lack of any identification of patrial ties – *polis*, region – contrast with the centrality of *oikos* in the *kleos* drive found in Pindar's epinicia.[74] It also contrasts with the background ties to be found in other commemorative-epigraphic contexts, even from the same period. One can point, for instance, to the monument dedicated at Delphi in 321 by Archon, a former officer of Alexander and then Macedonian satrap of Babylonia between 323 and 321, which honoured Archon's whole family to celebrate Archon's own victory in the Pythia:

> In your sacred precinct, lord, famed for the bow, the pair of horses crowned with Delphic laurel the head of Archon, who was ruler of the sacred land of Babylon, and, when he was with the divine Alexander, established many trophies of the spear. For that reason he erected these forms of his parents and brothers, and his fatherland Pella bears witness to the fame of his excellence (κλέος δ' ἀρετᾶς Πέλλα σύνοιδε πατρίς).
>
> Rhodes and Osborne, *Greek Historical Inscriptions* 92, col. A

Even in 321, in the same probable context as the commissioning of Craterus' monument, epigraphic voices at Delphi were straightforwardly oriented in terms of an honorand's belonging to, and achievement of reflected glory for, family and homeland, just like in Pindaric epinician. Archon represents the culmination of his family line, but the primary effect of that acclaim is to enhance the prestige of the family line and Archon's position in it, rather than Archon's individualized position per se. The *kleos* discourse found here, too, aligns well with a Pindaric model: there are shadows of the model behind *Isthmian* IV's 'honoured among Thebans', namely of a status confirmed and enhanced not just by exceptional achievement but also by the collective memorialization of that achievement among the victor's peers and in the victor's homeland. Interestingly, however, even though in terms of a memorializing discourse the Archon and Craterus monuments differ, the two clearly share similar features: not just a broadcasting of military service under Alexander (discussed further below), which would become in turn something of a trope, across social strata, to enhance an individual's esteem and status – note here the pretender, satirized by Theophrastus in the ἀλαζονεία-lemma of his *Characters* (23), who claimed previous service under Alexander and, later, lucrative timber contracts with his deputy Antipater – but also the strategy of broadcasting a longer record of association with the conqueror in a monumental setting. Evidently such records had great force and appeal, not just within circles populated by a Macedonian elite but rather among a wider, Panhellenic audience.

We are again forced to recognize the unique attempt in the Craterus monument's inscription to generate its subject's *kleos* according to an epic-poetic model, in terms of reflecting primarily (though not exclusively) on his individual standing rather than on his position in a peer or family or civic group. Indeed, the individualistic nature of the bid for Craterus' *kleos* shows a closer alignment to a Homeric *kleos* discourse, namely the ultimate model signalled by the choice of ἀΐδιον as epithet: the primarily personal *kleos* ἄφθιτον of Achilles, the attainment of which is stressed by the Iliadic poet to be exclusive of the possibility of Achilles' *nostos*, his 'return home'.[75] The distant exemplarity of this Achillean *kleos* fits well alongside the other evocations of a Homeric world in the Craterus inscription, and although we should imagine such Homerizing to have be consciously done – the dialectal choices, for instance, are not consistent throughout, indicating a certain artificiality – we should still recognize that some basis for this may lie in the partially 'Homeric' nature of Macedonian society, observable from a range of practices – hierarchical, onomastic, funerary, to name just a few.[76] We should also imagine that the presence in the monument of Alexander, who is documented to have pursued his own fascination with Homeric texts and models,[77] was also a factor behind the linguistic presentation: Alexander's own ideological preferences were invoked in the act of memorializing one of that king's most favoured companions and his exploits alongside him.

* * *

The Craterus monument consistently forwards an allusive, outward-looking agenda that seeks deliberately to showcase its honoree, and Alexander in turn, as a character from the Homeric universe, with the ethics, stature and prowess appropriate to that world and to its systems for evaluating such. A further vision of this Homeric world, albeit by a different angle, is provided by the characterization of the relationship between Craterus and Alexander in lines 7–8: ὅμ ποτε, Ἀλ[εξά]νδρωι τότε ὅθ' εἵπετο καὶ συνεπόρθει τῶι πολυαιν[ή]τωι τῶιδε Ἀσίας βασιλεῖ ('Who once, at the time when he was following Alexander, helping to sack with that much-praised king of Asia'). While typologically the Homeric parallel is already suggestive, the linguistic choices again make the picture clearer, here utilizing vocabulary drawn from Greek tragedy to make the point. In particular, the unusual verb συμπορθέω, formed from an Archaic verb of city-sacking (πορθέω) with imposed collaborative emphasis via the prepositional prefix *sun-*, has only one earlier attested usage, in Euripides' *Orestes*:

> A herald arose and said: 'Who wishes to speak on whether or not Orestes should be put to death for slaying his mother?' Then arose Talthybius, who helped your father [*sc.* Agamemnon] sack the Phrygians (ὃς σῷ πατρὶ συνεπόρθει Φρύγας). And he spoke, this man forever under the power of others, on both sides of his mouth, wondrously admiring your father while not praising your brother, spinning out noble and base words together.
>
> Euripides *Orestes* 885–92

The intertextual reference seems to be a secure one, since precisely the same conjugation of the verb occurs in both the inscription and the play: συνεπόρθει. Notably, this is an imperfect form, referring to a time that used to be and now no longer exists, in which vein we should also note this couplet's use of ποτε ... τότε ὅθ': we are clearly dealing with a nostalgic, *post factum* frame of reference. Moreover, the intertext has a clearly identifiable purpose: to characterize Craterus' serving with Alexander in his Persian expedition in the same light as participating in the archetypal heroic invasion of Asia, namely the sack of Troy, through imposing a parallel between Craterus' relation to Alexander and Talthybius' to Agamemnon. Craterus' *hetairia* with Alexander is thus given a Homeric complexion by its suggestive similarity to Talthybius' attendance on the Iliadic *anax andrōn*, Agamemnon, while in larger terms the Macedonian destruction of the Achaemenid empire is assimilated to the Achaean sack of Troy. A tmesis of the verb συμπέρθω in Euripides' *Helen* (105–6),[78] where Teucer relates to the eponymous character his past participation in Troy's sacking, also supports this latter register of meaning.

As with the inscription's use of Homeric and epinician models, it seems likely that the inscription's use of the tragic characterization does not simply establish a terminological point of contact, and impute a rough parallelism, with a character from the Homeric world, but rather also transfers a greater degree of meaning and significance along its referential route. In particular, it is noteworthy that while Talthybius is a minor character with little agency in the story of the *Iliad*, appearing as a *kērux* ('herald') *and therapōn* ('attendant', along with Eurybates) of Agamemnon at a number of points,[79] in the realm of tragedy he has a greatly expanded role in relation to post-Iliadic events: again he appears as *kērux*, and in this role occupies a more important narratological function as the bearer of plot-influencing news (such as in Euripides' *Hecuba* and *Troiades*),[80] but he is also characterized as having been a stalwart attendant to the by-then deceased Agamemnon in the above-quoted passage in Euripides' *Orestes* – his sole appearance in the play, in a scene where various figures publicly debate Orestes' fate on account of his matricide. The temporal context of Talthybius' characterization as 'helping to sack' Troy is thus important: he campaigned, once upon a time, alongside Agamemnon, but now he inhabits a world in which the triumphant conqueror is dead. His characterization as a fellow fighter of Agamemnon reflects a mode of thinking of contemporary events in terms of their derivation from an earlier age – that age, by extension, is given primacy – while it also simultaneously functions to establish Talthybius' credentials as a man of substantial standing, and worthy of attention, in the present. These echoes of a post-heroic perspective on socio-political definition are strongly resonant in the monument's dedicatory context of 322–321, and find an echo in Craterus' stress on closeness with Alexander, which constitutes the focal point of his attempt to concretize his standing to an international world in the aftermath of Alexander's death.

The nature of this intertextual reference also highlights a mode of conceptualizing, and attempting to represent to the wider world, contemporary events in the light of a heroic precedent. Here, the framework for the idea of close companionship with Alexander and fellow-fighting with him in the destruction of Persia is informed by the tradition surrounding the sack of Troy: it enriches the significance of theme under narration, and gives it greater meaning for the reading audience. This point has its own intellectual-historical significance, especially considering the partially archaic nature of Macedonian society discussed above, but when interpreted in political terms, it shows Craterus attempting to utilize a prestigious model, universally valued in Graeco-Macedonian tradition, to articulate his contemporary bid to enhance his standing. We may repeat the point discussed above that emphatic claims to service under, and closeness with Alexander, are virtually omnipresent in acts of political self-orientation across the period of the *diadochoi*, and so constitute an important, albeit internally variable, strategy within a contemporary legitimating discourse. Yet, in Craterus' monument, we nonetheless see something distinctive with the attempt to construe Alexandrian companionship according to a model which carried a widely embedded cultural force, not just in a way that capitalized on its intrinsic significance or in terms of its place within the power dynamics of the Macedonian aristocratic system.[81] This constitutes, at this point in time, a unique formulation in the competitive international climate of early diadochan politics, and, in light of its earliness, is tempting to read Craterus' scheme as having wider influence on the later development of the *topos* as a whole.

Further linguistic choices reinforce this heroizing scheme. In the same couplet under consideration, the description of Alexander as πολυαινήτος, already discussed above in the sense of harking back to the Homeric, Odyssean epithet of πολύαινος, has an even closer parallel, as with συμπορθέω, in Euripidean tragedy. Indeed, the only extant usage of πολυαίνετος prior to the Craterus epigram is in the *Heraclidae* (760–1), where the chorus refers to the city of Mycenae as εὐδαίμονα καὶ δορὸς πολυαίνετον ('much-praised for its war strength'). This gives a further 'Mycenaean' echo to the construction of Alexander and Craterus as the latter-day double for Agamemnon and Talthybius, as well as providing a semantic link with Craterus' secondary epithet of πολύδοξος, found in the opening distich. As with the Homerizing tenor of the inscription, this orientation in terms of the myth schema of the Trojan War can plausibly be linked with Alexander's own symbolic engagements during his lifetime, particularly during his crossing of the Hellespont in 334.[82] At any rate, the terminological parallel confirms the inscription's broader attempt to utilize tragic vocabulary that refers specifically to a heroic world, in a way that is similar to the strategy that we have already seen in the use of Pindaric language.

The significance of the detail that Craterus once fought alongside Alexander is deepened in the closing couplet of the inscription: ὧδε συνεξαλάπαξε καὶ εἰς χέρας ἀντιάσαντα ἔκτανεν οἰονόμων ἐν περάτεσσι Σύρων ('This is the way he helped to destroy: he slew what came into his hands, in the farthest bounds of the sheep-pasturing Syrians'). In particular, the verb συνεξαλάπαξε (from συνεξαλαπάζω) functions as a synonym for συνεπόρθει, both meaning, fundamentally, 'helping to sack'. However, συνεξαλάπαξε is a hapax legomenon: it is nowhere else attested in Greek literature or epigraphy, of any date, and it is seemingly an invention of the epigram's author; it provides a metrically appropriate analogue for συνεπόρθει, not repeating the verb but reinforcing its sense while echoing its phrasing. The root ἐξαλαπάζω, even when decoupled from the collaborative prefix *sun-*, is rare enough prior to the Craterus epigram, occurring only in Homeric poetry, once in Hesiod's *Works and Days*, and once in Xenophon's *Anabasis*.[83] The meaning and frame of reference for ἐξαλαπάζω is fairly uniform across these uses, inasmuch as a *polis* is always the object of the verb, and in almost all the Homeric uses, it is specifically the city of Troy, as we may expect.[84] In the Craterus epigram, therefore, we see an unusual, innovative take on the 'city-sacking' sense of the verb: there is no objective frame of reference – Craterus simply 'helped sack' – but the inscription goes on to clarify that Craterus' assistance came in the form of his slaying of the lion, with his own hands. Therefore, while the lion stands in for the objective *polis*, it is clear to the reader that it is the latter-day Troy, the Achaemenid empire, that Craterus has slain, a strategy that also makes effective use of the long-attested metonymic potential of the lion symbol and Persia.[85]

This is, in sum, no simple *topos* of symmachy: Craterus, as the killer of the taurophonic menace, as the saviour of Alexander, is ascribed a definitive, instrumental role in the Macedonian destruction of the Persian empire, an achievement that is enhanced and given world-changing force through its analogy with the sack of Troy. When it is considered overall, the inscription provides a remarkable rendering of Craterus' career. Indeed, it is Craterus' life as a whole, or more particularly his years campaigning in the east with Alexander, that it seeks to memorialize: as the third couplet reminds us, it is not the slaughter of the lion but rather the ἄγρα, the 'hunt' or the 'chase' as a process, that is willed to possess eternal, alluring *kleos*. On the readings forwarded above, this *kleos* that the monument seeks to provide for its honorand is rooted ultimately in the active exemplification of high virtue by a τιμάεις καὶ πολύδοξος ἀνήρ. As will be explored further in section 4 below, how this *kleos* was also construed as hereditable, as transmissible from Craterus the initiator of the dedication to his son Craterus II as its completer, is an important further dimension that ought to be explored, especially for understanding how early Hellenistic modes of status enhancement were received and further adapted after Craterus' own context – that is, for ascertaining how individual attempts at garnering status contributed to the evolution of the broader culture of such. Before this, it remains to be seen how the discourses explored so far relate to, and are taken further in relation to, their other major models: Macedonian paradigms of royalty and Alexander's own ideological entanglements.

3. Paradigms of royalty and the imitability of *physis*

Ancient literary sources on the Macedonian royal house emphasize its contested identity, the Macedonian kings' struggle to be seen as truly 'Greek' in the eyes of their southern neighbours, who for the most part regarded them as uncivilized barbarians.[86] Notwithstanding the problems of the innate Hellenocentrism and broader cultural bias of this narrative, and of asking further questions about ethnicity on this basis which unproductively aim at absolute answers, it is clear that one of the earliest encounters with the Macedonians' own attempts publicly to define their position in a wider Greek world involves a discourse of cultural belonging and exclusion. In Herodotus' record of Alexander I's determination to participate in the Olympic Games in the early fifth century,[87] Alexander elected, in the face of the opposition articulated by his competitors, to provide proof of his ancestry to the games' adjudicators, the Hellenodicae, in order to be allowed to compete. He duly evidenced his Argive descent, probably by recitation of his lineage, before going on to win (jointly) the race that he had sought to enter. If indeed it is historical, the fact of Alexander's victory should probably tell us that his competitors' attempts to exclude his entry was rooted less in a pure-minded concern about cultural integrity and more in their own personal interest, namely by excluding an impressive competitor. In fact, the entire dispute attests to just how deeply manipulable in antiquity was the nature of the cultural discourse of Hellenicity, no less than it remains in modernity.[88]

This vignette commands significant attention for the scholar of Macedonian royal ideology. Not only is Alexander's demonstration emblematic of the performativity that inhered in the dynasty's outward-looking articulations of its royal identity,[89] it also homes in on the principal legitimating *locus* that would remain a common feature of Argead self-definition until Alexander the Great, namely Heraclean ancestry. Indeed, while for many the acceptance of 'Greekness' that stemmed from Alexander I's winning the right of participation was the most important outcome of this very public dispute, an alternative suggestion might be that the formalized recognition of the Argead dynasty's belonging to the Heraclid *genos* was the far more impactful and wide-ranging outcome.[90] In that vein, Alexander's agonistic victory could be seen to have further affirmed, again in performative terms, his genetic *physis*, his inheritance from his now formally accepted ancestor Heracles, who was well-recognized as the model of the athletic victor par excellence.[91] Alexander's proof of his Argive lineage in the Panhellenic setting of the Olympiad, therefore, was perhaps not simply a victory in a struggle to demonstrate Hellenicity – the kind of narrative to which we are habituated on account of later constructions in our extant sources, particularly the kind of ethnological invective found in Demosthenic oratory – but also a triumph in terms of obtaining formal, reciprocal and international recognition for the specific genetic identity of the Macedonian monarchy that he sought to emphasize.

Whether he foresaw this or not, Alexander I's gaining of recognition of the Argead family's Heraclean ancestry would become a recurrent source of inspiration for acts of ideological self-expression by later scions of the dynasty. Numismatic evidence in particular attests to sustained inter-generational stress. Under Alexander's grandson Archelaus I (r. 413–399), a portrait of Heracles began to feature on the obverse-types of some Macedonian silver obols and *tetartemoria* (1/4-obols), alongside reverse-types featuring an aggressive animal, sometimes a wolf devouring its prey or a lion's head with an open, gaping maw.[92] These issues very clearly refer to Heracles' exemplary position in Macedonian society as huntsman, a position venerated through the cult of Heracles *Kynagidas*, a popular object of devotion among the Macedonian populace, elite and even royalty.[93] The visual representation of this facet of Heracles' legend on coinage, chiming with the centrality of the hunt in Macedonian elite society,[94] articulates the close relations with the demigod that the Argead kings sought to impress to the world: their own roles as hunters implicitly assimilated to their ancestral model, suggesting that the hunt was framed as a site for the enactment of their Heraclean *physis*, just as the athletic *agōn* had been for Alexander I. This was important for the Argeads in underscoring their now-officialized pedigree; but it also develops wider connotations when viewed as the continual, performative clarification of *ethos* and identity – themselves potentially inheritable, but also, importantly, imitable and thus externally acquirable. In short, the suggestive comparison between Heracles and the Argead monarchs, via the *locus* of the hunt, is about more than just a stress on genetic legitimacy.

The ideological elaboration of the Argeads' own roles as hunters that occurs certainly in the reign of Archelaus, though perhaps begun even earlier,[95] seems to continue apace under his successors. Under Amyntas III (r. 392–370), for instance, we see further uses of a portrait of Heracles in lion scalp in certain obverse-types,[96] paired with various reverse-type iconography including an eagle clutching a snake, which possesses some resonance in relation to the mythology of Zeus – as the father of Heracles, this makes it, potentially, typologically coherent with the broader signification of ancestry – but which also features as a general *topos* in a variety of textual and artistic media.[97]

Figure 3 Bronze coin of Amyntas III, 392–370. Yale University Art Gallery 2004.6.1475. [CC0 1.0].

In a more remarkable silver series, Amyntas clarifies further the act of hunting as an area of central royal ideological concern: we can see a mounted hunter bearing a spear on the obverse-type, and the hunter's quarry, a lion, on the reverse. These two types of a single coin issue together constitute an iconographical narrative:[98] the obverse horseman's spear distinctively continues in its trajectory into the reverse scene, thrusting into the space before the attacking lion; here, the exergue line on the reverse-type perhaps has been introduced to ensure that the combined hunt tableau is stable in all outputs. This experimental use of the iconographical space of the coinage has parallels in some vase imagery – characters acting out scenes within, and against, the vase space[99] – but it is an unprecedented novelty in a Macedonian numismatic context, just as it is an escalation in the imaging of the Heraclean-derived ideological scheme of the hunt. Such innovation indicates the scheme's significance and illustrates that any single monarch had the perennial capacity for individualizing his mode of ideological self-definition, even if this occurred within the parameters of an already established dynastic scheme.

Into the early fourth century, then, we see the enduring valuation of the Heraclean roots of the Macedonian royal house, a connection that is continually 'reperformed', as it were, by the continued creation of individualized imagery. This sequence sees the cumulative strengthening of the semantic association between, and perhaps even the eventual synonymy of, the symbol of the lion hunt and the Macedonian kingship itself;[100] in bare terms, we see the lion hunt symbolic *topos* gradually come to function as a signifier of the Macedonian kingship. Reciprocally, the leonine and Heraclean components of Macedonian numismatic iconography grow more and more stylized as Macedonian power begins to wax large on the international stage. After some bronzes utilizing a Heracles/lion pairing under Perdiccas III (r. 365–360/359),[101] the demigod comes to be blazoned on the obverse-types of new gold coinages produced by Philip II after his acquisition of the mines of Mount Pangaeum in the mid-350s, there paired with some apposite reverse iconography, sometimes the forepart of a lion, sometimes a thunderbolt sometimes Heracles' distinctive *hopla*, the bow and club.[102] The probable function of these coins – like that king's more well-known Olympic 'Philippeioi' coinage about which Diodorus writes, censoriously, that it was introduced to 'raise a mercenary army of noteworthy size and coax many Greeks into becoming bought-traitors to their homelands' – was for military and diplomatic ends that extended beyond internal state-building ventures, and rather took place in an interstate sphere.[103] The Heraclean ideological emphasis in this context suggests that the *ethos*, identity and character of the king – both as an individual and as a dynastic representative – were the subject of communication to the wider world, and not simply the prosaic, internally significant concerns of legitimacy and right to rule. Nevertheless, whatever the precise symbolic intention, the noteworthy feature in Philip's iconography is the ever-increasing visibility of Heracles, and his legendary leonine entanglements, within the Argead monarchy's chosen modes of self-representation for both local and international worlds.

In this kind of context we can situate Isocrates' speech *To Philip*, delivered in 346, after the Peace of Philocrates brought (temporary) peace between the Athenian and Macedonian states. Although not the genitor of the Panhellenic idea, Isocrates had been, since at least his *Panegyricus* of 380, an advocate of a united Greek expedition against Persia, and was now urging Philip to take on the mantle of leadership in this project; he was perhaps also attempting to habituate the Greeks, and the Athenians in particular, to the idea of his leadership.[104] In a masterstroke of persuasiveness, he cast his wished-for idea of Philip's eastern expedition against Persia as a second fulfilment, a reperformance, of his ancestor Heracles' own sack of Troy in the generation before the Trojan War.[105] Whatever the rationale behind Isocrates' rhetoric – perhaps it was, among other things, to win Macedonian royal patronage for his 'school'[106] – we see in his project of persuasion an attempt to flatter his addressee, using Philip's favoured model of self-identification, both personal and dynastic, to achieve his effect. This can be considered a clear secondary indication of the well-established pattern of Argead emphasis on Heraclean ancestry and the ongoing symbolic recreation of that ancestry. It is also a creative characterization of a new aspect of Argead royal identity that would become enormously significant in the fullness of time, namely as the invader of Persia, Hellenic revenger against the eastern transgressor. In this respect, it is a selective reference to the Heraclean *exemplum*, foregrounding the aspect of the Heracles myth most applicable to contemporary political circumstances. This attests to the dynamism and malleability of the Argead royal paradigm – the multiform, almost universalistic nature of Heracles' legend in the Graeco-Macedonian world could be an effective tool in the hands of a representationally innovative Argead monarch, and indeed those of a resourceful flatterer – but in Isocrates' engagement with that model we are also arguably able to see the forerunner of dynamics well known later in time, in relations between Hellenistic kings and *poleis*: Isocrates' rhetorical selectivity is redolent of Hellenistic civic sensitivity to royal ideological projections, which often involved a deliberate repurposing of those representational choices within persuasive or petitionary communication.[107] That Heracles came to feature on the obverse-types of Philip II's silver coinages,[108] not just the gold, should tell us that Isocrates' rhetorical agenda was very well-attuned indeed; but the very agenda itself can testify to the wide international spread of the ideology. The ideological message was heard and rechannelled accordingly.[109]

Some of the numismatic choices of Alexander the Great are less radical when considered against this longer Argead tradition, at least with respect to iconography: his creation of a single imperial currency for his new empire, it should be stressed, remains innovative with respect to its institutional scope and transformative in terms of its long-term historical impact.[110] Specifically, the obverse-types of Alexander's silver tetradrachm and bronze coinages, which were probably developed first not in 336 (as previously thought) but in 333/332,[111] bear a dynamic portrait of Heracles clad in his customary lion-skin headdress, showing a clear derivation from the obverse-types of his Argead forebears, including Philip II; even the reverse-type of the bronzes, showing a bow and club along with Alexander's (non-titled) legend, are typical of his dynasty's numismatic history. Innovation is evident, however, in the reverse-type chosen for the tetradrachms, which depict a seated (possibly enthroned), eagle-bearing (*aietophoros*), sceptred Zeus along with Alexander's legend (Figure 1). Although clearly showing alignment with the Phidian model of Zeus popularised in the fifth century and dominant thereafter,[112] Alexander's silver Zeus is more closely modelled on the so-called Baaltar coinage produced in Tarsus under the Achaemenid satrap Mazaeus, whose reverse depicted the seated god Ba'al, a prominent Semitic deity conventionally understood in the prevailing syncretistic system to be the analogue of Zeus.[113] Alexander's silver reverse, then, presents a

Figure 4 Silver stater of Tarsus, 333–324. Staatliche Museen zu Berlin, Münzkabinett 18259497 / Dr Karsten Dahmen. [CC PDM 1.0].

blend of Tarsian Ba'al and Phidian Zeus, and the coinage possesses a symbolism recognizable to both near eastern and Graeco-Macedonian users, a quality that probably owes to the pragmatic economic consideration of creating trust for the new money more than it does to any rarefied ideological objective of fostering inter-cultural unity.

Within a Graeco-Macedonian symbolic world there is also a clear link between the obverse and reverse imagery of Alexander's silvers – Heracles the lion-slayer, son of Zeus the king – which might constitute Alexander's own contribution to the inter-generational elaboration of the heritage of the Argead dynasty. Whatever else they might offer for the modern-day interpreter, Alexander's Heraclean numismatic choices also follow Philip II's pattern of an increasing international emphasis on Heracles as Macedonian power itself gains more and more prominence on the world stage. It should be noted, though, that Alexander's imperial gold coinage – perhaps inaugurated as early as 336/335, substantially before the creation of the new silver and bronze coinages – bears no overt Heraclean imagery, instead displaying an obverse portrait of Athena and a reverse tableau of Nike bearing a *stylis* and a *stephanos*;[114] here, we perhaps see an attempt to create an image with Panhellenic appeal and anti-Persian animus, drawing on Corinthian coin-types for the obverse Athena, thus alluding to the League of Corinth, and on Nike's embedded cultural connection to the Hellenic victory in the Persian Wars of the early fifth century, and particularly to the Athenian naval triumph at Salamis in 480.[115]

Figure 5 Gold stater of Alexander the Great, 334–323. Staatliche Museen zu Berlin, Münzkabinett 18250205 / Lutz-Jürgen Lübke (Lübke und Wiedemann). [CC PDM 1.0].

This communicates something different to the Heraclean imagery found on the silvers and bronzes, yet it is not misaligned, especially in light of the kind of equations drawn by Isocrates, in which Heracles could also be understood as signifying victory over an Asian power.

Over time, then, Heraclean imagery became increasingly prominent in Argead imagery and came to be styled in different ways, though broadly conforming with a common set of ideological parameters. Moreover, just as we should not forget that Alexander's iconographical choices belong to a broader dynastic tradition, equally we should not view his forebears' ideological broadcasting as primarily individual attempts to connect with their ancestral exemplar: rather, in each case, we see one of a series of participations in an ideological paradigm, evoking a particular monarch's ancestral character yet also simultaneously situating his kingship within a broader royal tradition. In other words, through the continued deployment of Heraclean imagery, each Argead king stamped his position within the dynasty and connected himself with his entire chain of dynastic forebears, up to and including Heracles himself.[116]

It is true, however, that with Alexander we see a more intense and more frequent ideological entanglement with the Heraclean paradigm than is observable for any of his dynastic predecessors.[117] This regard for Heracles may be so strongly observable as a consequence of better evidence for Alexander than for earlier Argead kings, or indeed the ever-increasing mythologization (especially posthumous) of the conqueror; but it also surely preserves the deeply performative link with Heracles that he had, historically, sought to entrench via a variety of explicit and implicit modes of self-identification.[118] The very least we can say is that Alexander's reign represents a sharp uptick in the trajectory of the Argead tradition of *imitatio Herculis*, even though for some scholars this assimilation of the king to the demigod was a more singular attempt to construct a paradigm of lifetime deification on the basis of Heracles' apotheotic model.[119] For our purposes, this is a longer-term ideological mechanism for communicating character and identity through reference to a mediating ancestral *exemplum*. That is, through the customary Argead stress on activities like lion-hunting – even if not referring to any actual documented instances of such hunting, and instead simply showcasing an idealized, hypothetical prerogative in this area – the Macedonian kings habitually highlighted their Heraclean roots, encouraging contemporaries to perceive them in a Heraclean light. Alexander's relationship with Heracles can even be said, in its very exaggeration, to have further clarified the dynastic habit, especially when we consider the unprecedented step of standardizing the image of Heracles across all his silver and bronzes coinages after 333/332.

In light of this broader dynastic tradition, we should reconsider Craterus' emphatic stress on the significance of his lion-killing in a grand act of self-representation at Delphi. At its most fundamental level, the nature and conceit of the leontophonic votive expresses Craterus' aspirational self-positioning, his attempt to portray himself as the figure suited for the kingship after Alexander's death by virtue of his demonstration of a comparable Heraclean character. In lack of a genetic qualifier, then, we can see how Craterus has showcased his acquisition of a heroic *physis* via imitation of its signification: it is deliberately redolent of the Argead dynastic paradigm. Once the political ramifications of this mimesis are understood, we may reconsider the meaning of the peculiar opening identification of Craterus as υἱὸς Ἀλεξάνδρου Κράτερος, 'Alexander's son Craterus': 'heir', or 'successor' more broadly, may be communicated,[120] as is natural for the man who spectacularly demonstrates Heraclean valour through his lion-killing, signalling his parity with the ancestral character of the Argead family. The implied adjacency of Craterus' capability, and the parallelism of his ideological self-expression, leaves little doubt that the superiority envisioned by the monument has a deliberate political goal in a context of unstable leadership. Moreover, just as the Argeads had evidenced their own dynastic belonging through broadcasting an association with a Heraclean model, so now Craterus' act of self-identification performatively cast him as an incarnation of the same family. In other words, through the very act of Heraclean self-comparison, Craterus was performing an habitual ideological reflex of the Argead dynasty.

One could also emphasize here Alexander's intermediary status, as the node of connection between the non-Argead Craterus and the dynastic tradition with which he sought to enmesh himself. This is a phenomenon of which we shall see more, in Chapter 3, in relation to other heroic traditions with which the *diadochoi* sought to engage, in most cases attaching to Alexander's *exemplum* as the link to a longer chain of ideological schemes. Some of these habits are already seen in the Craterus monument, too: in the metonymy of the sack of Troy and the conquest of Persia, for instance, we see a capitalization on Alexander's own ideological habits of self-comparison with the Homeric world. For now, it is worth noting that the typological imitation evident here – of Alexander's modes of self-definition, not necessarily an explicit comparison with Alexander himself – carried its own substantive political force, and that this observation might prompt us to avoid overly simplistic readings of the semantics of *imitatio Alexandri*, and connectedly of heroic *imitatio* more widely.

4. Contexts of dedication and ideological valences

The reading of the monument forwarded above – on the one hand, rooted in a cultural discourse of honour and value, and on the other, exemplifying the ideological habit of a particular dynasty, both showcasing Craterus' superlative stature and ability – can be coordinated with what we know about Craterus in the brief period between Alexander's death in 323 and Craterus' own demise in 320, during which time he seems to have been actively pursuing various means of enhancing his status. A particularly illustrative anecdote is preserved in Demetrius' *On Style*, a work dating perhaps to the first century AD,[121] in the context of conveying the power of deictic references to censure tyrannical or violent men:

> Often, in conversing with a tyrant or any other violent individual and wishing to censure him, out of necessity we need to use a figure of speech, as did Demetrius of Phalerum with the Macedonian Craterus, when he was sat high above him on a couch of gold and in a purple robe, and received the Greek envoys with insolent pride; he addressed him, using a figure censoriously: 'We ourselves once welcomed these men as envoys, including this man, Craterus.' For in the use of the demonstrative 'this man', the whole arrogance of Craterus is indicated, and is censured in the use of a figure.
>
> Demetrius *De Elocutione* 289

Although the negative stereotype of the arrogant Hellenistic despot probably colours Demetrius' recounting here – the discussion of Craterus' ὑπερηφανία ('arrogance') certainly indicates this,[122] so we should not unthinkingly accept this portrayal of his character – we are nonetheless provided with some basic details that illustrate a conscious concern, even at a very early post-Alexander date, with deploying visual trappings of royal power. It is worth noting, too, that this is in a context of interstate contact in the Greek world, and more so that the terms of the display are geared towards an audience with a supplicatory party. Although a specific context is not singled out, in all likelihood the scene described here took place in the aftermath of the Lamian War, when Craterus and Antipater received the surrender of the Greek states and came to a post-war accord, probably before the attempted pacification of Aetolia, thus at some point in 322.[123] Even if the rhetorical *schēma* described is effective in puncturing Craterus' swollen pride, in more pragmatic terms we must imagine that this scenario nonetheless carried some weight in reifying the superior power of the Macedonian Craterus, on the one hand, and the inferior standing of the Greek states, on the other.

The parallel between this scene and the Delphic monument discussed at length above is instructive, since although neither example explicitly involves Craterus' laying a claim to royalty, in both instances we nonetheless see the deployment of the symbolic syntax – in one case linguistic and paradigmatic, and in the other case visual – with which the authority of monarchic status and superiority were semantically delineated and hence communicated: Craterus' higher placement in the embassy scene, plus the use of expensive status signifiers in the form of purple and gold,[124] are correspondent with the linguistic evocations of high status in the celebration of lion-slaying. It is arguable, in that sense, that the lack of explicit clarification for Craterus' drive for *basileia* did not limit his ideological self-expression, and that the performances in both cases were no less effective for the lack of formalization. Political expediency was probably also a factor here, as such displays would not compromise the outward show of fidelity to the Macedonian throne that Craterus was careful to adopt in his other dealings in this period, not least with respect to Macedonian tradition – a point discussed further below.

We can point, too, to Craterus' self-styling to the Macedonian armies in particular as another convergent example of quasi-royal ideological movement. The *Suda*'s long entry on Craterus, for instance, describes some features of the marshal's activity that are highly significant in this regard, which aside from the author's reflection on Craterus' βασιλικὸς ὄγκος ('royal bulk'),[125] in contrast with

Antipater's smallness – physical stature, it seems, conveyed socio-political standing or belonging; rulers were meant to be big men, bodily as well as hierarchically – may be unified under two headings: first, a deliberately crafted external appearance; and secondly, a carefully performed set of relations and exhibition of behavioural characteristics. In terms of the first category, his σκευή, 'garments', we are told, were distinctive in their λαμπρότης, 'splendour', and 'in his whole outfit dressed himself like Alexander save for the diadem' (παντὶ τῷ κόσμῳ κατὰ τὸν Ἀλέξανδρον ἔσταλτο πλὴν τοῦ διαδήματος). We might align this detail with the kind of invective against *tryphē* that we find in sources recording the indulgent luxury of Alexander's companions: for instance, Aelian recounts Leonnatus' and Menelaus' extravagant hunting nets, and Perdiccas' and indeed Craterus' own *stadion*-long exercising lifts made of animal skins; Leonnatus' own lemma in the *Suda* also records, similarly, that he cared much for the 'splendour of his arms' (τὴν τῶν ὅπλων λαμπρότητα).[126] Given the parallel with Leonnatus' λαμπρότης, and the fact that the majority of Craterus' entry focuses on Craterus' relations with the army, it is possible that the σκευή in question is military gear, so meaning dazzling arms and armour. This is a feature of Hellenistic representational display common enough slightly later in the diadochan period;[127] perhaps pertinent in the same respect is the account of Craterus' recognizable *kausia*, discussed below, which suggests that Craterus did in fact adopt a distinctive, conspicuous war dress.[128]

Equally, however, the rich clothing attributed to Craterus may mean garments worn in non-military contexts, especially associated with performances, whether in the context of entertainment or office holding:[129] here, 'dress' would convey something like 'costume' or 'outfit', where distinctiveness – in Craterus' case, a conspicuous λαμπρότης – was important for signifying the role being undertaken by the figure wearing it, as well as the fact that the ensuing behaviour was in fact a performance. In this vein of thinking, we may consider the relevance of Demetrius' account, above, of Craterus' donning a purple robe while seated on a golden throne in his reception of Greek envoys: Craterus' costume is here that of the ruling figure, about to pass judgement on embassies of inferior status seeking favourable terms of settlement, a costume no doubt informed by the performances of power seen at Alexander's court in Asia.[130] Craterus, perhaps, can be said to translocate Alexander's aulic style in an attempt to concretize his own standing, hence the further detail in the *Suda* that he dressed like Alexander save for the diadem. Whatever the specific circumstances referred to, a conscious concern with noticeably lavish clothing suggests Craterus' attempt to stand out, to be distinctive, in the early years after Alexander's death – itself, it must be considered, in service of the larger political aim of status enhancement.

Equally significant in this vein is the second category of presentation referred to in the *Suda*, namely the distinctive set of behaviours in relation to the Macedonian army. Craterus was characteristic for his ἐπιείκεια ('reasonableness', 'fairness') and he had σεμνός ('solemnity', or perhaps rendered better as 'gravitas'); there was also a widespread appreciation of him as φιλοφρονέστατος ('extremely considerate'), and he was 'exceedingly persuasive' (πιθανώτατος) on account of the rousing nature of his speech. Accordingly, the armies revered Craterus 'like a king' (οἷα βασιλέα), praised him, considered his military capability to be unparalleled, and they 'held him to be indisputably second in esteem after Alexander' (δεύτερον τῇ προτιμήσει μετὰ Ἀλέξανδρον ἀναμφιλόγως ἄγειν). All this suggests a conscious concern with a form of role enactment popularized by Philip and Alexander: Craterus' performative behaviour, signalling his stepping into the mantle of Macedonian royal leadership. It seems that this had its desired effect, since the recurrence of the verb θεραπεύω ('be attendant', 'perform service') in the description of the army's treatment of Craterus can be aligned with descriptions of court service found in accounts of Alexander's royal *aulē*;[131] in other words, they attended to him, paid court to him, as if he were king. This careful behaviour towards the troops also compares well with some other key moments in early Hellenistic elite rivalry, notably the conflict between Perdiccas and Ptolemy in Egypt in the summer of 320, after the latter had seized Alexander's body and fortified the Nile delta against the royal army. Diodorus here records Ptolemy's ἐπιείκεια and fostering of a culture of παρρησία (literally 'free speech', but more broadly an indicator of equal social rights), in contrast to Perdiccas' tendency to infringe the autonomy of his fellow commanders; Diodorus also calls Perdiccas φονικός and βίαιος ('murderous' and 'violent'), descriptors of tyranny elsewhere in the *Bibliotheke*.[132] The very least that we can draw from such accounts is that there were recognizable behavioural patterns for a Macedonian leader, themselves to be understood as relational dynamics between king and army on which consensus between the two rested, and that these behaviours were the subject of careful performance by the diadochan elite in the early post-Alexander years, not least by aspirant figures such as Craterus.

This good relationship with the army is nowhere stressed more clearly than in Plutarch's account of Craterus' ill-fated encounter with Eumenes in 320, which plays a prominent narrative function in his biography of the latter. Here we also see how Craterus' pose as a Macedonian traditionalist – however belied by the behaviour, noted above, suggesting that he, no less than the other *diadochoi*, immersed himself in the fruits of the Persian conquests – functioned as a clarion call to Macedonian veterans of the day, and thus as a strategy devised to elicit popular military support. According to Neoptolemus' report to Antipater and Craterus regarding Eumenes' troops:

> [T]he Macedonians longed for him exceedingly, and if they should only see his cap and hear his voice, they would come to him with a rush, arms and all. And indeed the name of Craterus was really great among them, and after the death of Alexander most of them had longed for him as their commander. They remembered that he had many times incurred the strong displeasure of Alexander himself in their behalf, by opposing his gradually increasing desire to adopt Persian customs, and by defending the manners of their country, which, thanks to the spread of luxury and pomp, were already being treated with contempt.
>
> Plutarch *Eumenes* 6.1–2, trans. Perrin

Craterus' supposed traditionalism also seems to be borne out by other accounts,[133] even in the context of Alexander's lifetime, which suggest that what we are seeing in the post-Alexander period is the carefully cultivated uptick of a characteristic for which Craterus had been well known over a longer period of time. The authenticity of this pose matters little here: what matters, rather, is that the Macedonian armies, across Alexander's former empire, seem to have responded so positively to it. This is thus another early indication of how a particular pose or set of behaviours were employed by Craterus to enhance political and military standing. Such was the power of Craterus' ὄνομα μέγα ('great name') that Eumenes reportedly concealed from his troops that Craterus was the figure commanding the army opposing his, and even chose not to array Macedonians against Craterus' line, for fear that the Macedonians would go over to the populist general on seeing him.[134] As has been explored above, this detail further confirms the distinctiveness of Craterus' outward appearance, so by extension its careful management.

Craterus' death in battle against Eumenes' army brought about an abrupt end to the personal power that he had been gathering, and the various strategies for status enhancement that he developed were thus ultimately in vain. This is not to say, however, that the iconic power of Craterus as a figure simply dissipated. Eumenes performed the customary funerary obsequies to honour the fallen general, and seems to have retained his bones and ashes until he met his own end, after a defeat at the hands of Antigonus at Gabiene in 316. Antigonus returned the remains to Craterus' widow Phila, now married to his own son Demetrius, probably in the same rough context as the final dedication for the Delphic monument celebrating Craterus' undying *kleos* was completed.[135] From these details we can speculate that Craterus' memory was potent as a source of authority for both Eumenes, in the context of sustaining leadership of an unstable coalition of generals and satraps over a long war with Antigonus, and then Antigonus himself in turn, in the context of restoring order to the Asian domains of the Macedonian empire after the destruction of Eumenes' faction: for both, a transfer of charisma and standing is implied by the enactment of certain stages of funerary procedure, which perhaps best understood as analogous with the successional power that is bound up in the burial of a late king by his heir.[136]

The capitalization on the latent power of Craterus' memory is also evident in the completion of the Delphic monument under the name of Craterus the son, in all probability in 316/315. Here we should recognize that Craterus II is in fact explicitly alluded to in the elegiac inscription, and so receives his own share of the lithic *kleos*. Even though Voutiras is right to note that Craterus II is rather in the background to the monumental presentation,[137] he is nonetheless subtly given great agency and esteem: if we accept that reading an epigraphic dedicator's name (aloud) was a precondition for generating *kleos* for that dedicator,[138] then the naming of a second Craterus as completer-dedicator, in addition to the first Craterus as initiator-dedicator, also generates a degree of secondary *kleos* for the son. This is not, therefore, a nameless and thus objectiveless act of dedication. Becoming participant in the recitation and act of encountering of Craterus' *kleos* will have had serious implications for Craterus II's own public name. Moreover, if we tentatively accept a date for the monument's completion as being during Polyperchon's *epimeleia* of 319–316, then we can suggest that Polyperchon's involvement may well have been motivated by a will to capitalize on this Crateran family *kleos* – to which he also had his own long history of connections, as noted above. This might make sense given the historical context of Polyperchon's struggles – both political-military and ideological – against Antipater's son Cassander, who made much of Antipater's own reputation and standing and sought to position himself as the inheritor of his mantle. We can suggest, then, that the magnification of Craterus' status via the Delphic monument had a posthumous legacy of its own.

Finally, it is worth noting that later writers seem to have placed Craterus' abortive strategies of self-representation in terms of a trajectory towards kingship. For instance, Athenaeus records that Craterus had paeans sung to him at Delphi by Alexinus of Elis, with a lyre-player in accompaniment, and then immediately goes on to transmit details about paeans for Ptolemy by the Rhodians, and for Antigonus and Demetrius by Hermippus of Cyzicus (sometimes thought to be author of the infamous *ithyphallos* of 291/290).[139] In other words, through Athenaeus' comparanda we are able to see paeans for Craterus within an evolving discourse of authority creation in the early Hellenistic world, in all the other instances adduced culminating in *basileia* itself. Of course, the relation between paeans and superior status was nothing new to the post-Alexander world, with earlier examples such as Lysander, and the honours delivered to him by the Samians after the end of the Peloponnesian War in 404,[140] perhaps constituting a pre-existing tradition and model for early Hellenistic usage; paeans would also come to be a normal parlance of poetic speaking to power in the Hellenistic kingdoms.[141] But, given the examples with which Craterus is paired, we might imagine that, had he not died in 320, the achievement of *basileia* would have the ultimate outcome of the trajectory on which he had set himself. Craterus thus represents an important, revelatory example of the evolution of the monarchic discourse in the early post-Alexander world, and a sign of things to come.

3

Heroic Paradigms of Rulership and the Politics of *imitatio*

In the autumn of 327 BC, Ptolemy was commanding a contingent of Alexander's army in the campaign to subdue the Aspasians, in roughly the modern-day Bajaur area of Pakistan.[1] On one expedition, he encountered a substantially superior enemy force yet nonetheless managed to achieve victory. Arrian's account of this engagement, probably derived from Ptolemy's own historical writings on Alexander's campaigns,[2] renders it in vivid terms and centralizes the single combat that took place between Ptolemy and the local Indian chieftain:

> When he saw Ptolemy approach, he and the hypaspists with him turned about to oppose him. The Indian struck with his long spear at Ptolemy's breast through his breastplate, but the breastplate withstood the blow. Ptolemy, striking straight through the thigh of the Indian (τὸν μηρὸν διαμπὰξ βαλών), cast him down and stripped his body (καταβάλλει τε καὶ σκυλεύει αὐτόν). When the men accompanying him saw their leader lying prostrate they no longer held their ground; but others, distressed at the sight of their enemies desecrating their commander's body, rushed down and engaged in a mighty battle over it beside the hill. Alexander was at that point drawing towards the hill with infantry who had dismounted from their horses. They came upon the Indians and with great difficulty forced them back to the hill and seized the body.
>
> Arrian *Anabasis* IV 24.4–5

The account underscores the personal heroism of Ptolemy and its contribution to securing a Macedonian victory against superior numbers. By contrast, Alexander's late arrival, not to mention his subordinate focalization, casts him in an ancillary role, unconnected with the exemplification of heroic ability in battle.[3] There are a number of features characteristic of epic narratives in this account, most prominently the single combat followed by the spoliation of the fallen enemy, then a fight over his body.[4] More particularly, Bosworth also sees in the specific manner of the Indian chief's defeat a reference to Patroclus' killing of Areïlycus in *Iliad* XVI:[5]

> First the strong son of Menoetius struck the thigh (βάλε μηρὸν) of Areïlycus, at the point he was turning about, with his sharp-pointed spear, thrusting the bronze straight through: the spear shattered the bone, and he fell to the earth facedown.
>
> *Iliad* XVI 307–11

Here, Patroclus drives his spear straight through his foe's thigh, shattering the bone, resulting in Areïlycus' collapse – face down into the earth, instantaneously dead.[6] As Bosworth notes, thigh wounds in formulaic battle scenes in either prose or verse are rarely immediately fatal,[7] so he is probably right to see a specific Homeric colouring in Arrian's account. Arguing that the 'primary inspiration for the narrative was undoubtedly Ptolemy himself', he goes on to suggest that the referentiality was intended to magnify Ptolemy's achievements and, through the allusion to Patroclus' *aristeia*, to cast him as the Patroclus to Alexander's Achilles.[8]

Taking this parallel a bit further, we might suggest that, just as Patroclus – donning Achilles' armour, leading the charge against the Trojan offensive and defeating many foes one on one – had become Achilles' substitute in *Iliad* XVI (the so-called *Patrokleia*, culminating in the defeat of Zeus' son Sarpedon),[9] so Ptolemy represented himself as having become Alexander's substitute in the context of narrating the Indian campaigns.[10] An implied likeness to Alexander of this kind, and the suggestion of embodying the same ability, has an obvious political importance in the years after 323, in the political world of the diadochan struggles, as we have seen already with Craterus.[11] Moreover, assimilating the conqueror to Achilles, however obliquely, is a recognizable *topos* in the Alexander historians – and, indeed, familiar enough from Alexander's own active self-identifications – even though Hephaestion is often the figure doubled with Patroclus;[12] perhaps we see here an attempt to redirect the point of reference for the Achilles–Patroclus partnership,[13] with Ptolemy becoming the closest link to – as well as approximation of, and stand-in for – the central figure of Alexander.

These features are significant considerations. What remains under-appreciated in general scholarship, and which will be explored in this chapter, is the wider extent to which the *diadochoi* developed their own heroic imagery and ideology. Ptolemy's self-aggrandizing account of monomachy, in other words, is but one example of a much more widespread trend of heroic *imitatio* in the context of the diadochan age, which formed an important part of how authority and status were claimed in the competitive world after Alexander's death. As we shall see, heroic *imitatio* was partly an extension of *imitatio Alexandri* and partly its own independent mythologizing drive, but in its entirety was aimed at the acquisition of greater eminence – itself a precondition for success in the power games among the *diadochoi* as well as for building concrete, lasting regimes. In short, heroic self-styling made the *diadochoi* far more than ordinary mortals, and far more qualified for the authority and power that they were accumulating through more prosaic means.

Before further reflecting on *imitatio*, it is worth emphasizing a couple more salient features about the practice of single combat. Monomachy is a fairly common feature in early Greek literatures, particularly epic and tragic poetry and other stylized narratives of war from the Archaic and early Classical period, all of which foreground the extraordinary individual and his determinative power to shape the course of a given battle.[14] Even in Diodorus' account of the monomachy of Eumenes and Neoptolemus in 321/320, he writes that 'they engaged one another and made the victory hinge upon the monomachy between them'.[15] These traditions inform Arrian's Ptolemaic-derived account, and they serve to magnify the historical achievement through creating parity with a mythic analogue. Yet we should recognize that the actual practice of monomachy is quite widely attested under Alexander and his Successors, and indeed was widespread enough that it might have constituted a common custom, or at least became a common trend.[16] In other words, while in literary terms monomachy was an archaism, in historical terms it was contemporary practice.

This convergence of myth and reality is very suggestive, and it captures a duality to the early Hellenistic practice. That is, just as we might see monomachy as a pragmatic form of legitimation for the Hellenistic dynast[17] – namely, an attempt to demonstrate suitability for power and authority, through a show of military ability in concert with a willingness to put oneself in the front line of combat – so too we might see it as a kind of ideological spectacle, showcasing the distinctive brilliance of the *monomachos* and his embodiment of heroic leadership. In other words, successful single combat communicated *aristeia*, in the specialized sense of impressive prowess in battle, and superlative *aretē* (excellence); who embodied these ideals could be imagined as especially qualified for higher authority.[18]

In addition, retaining proofs of victory, through spoliation – just as, we note, Ptolemy despoiled his fallen Aspasian opponent, taking his armour and weaponry – was presumably a complementary means of status enhancement, of gaining more socio-political standing, just as it was the case in the Homeric world that the taking of spoils enhanced the victor's *timē* (honour).[19] Such victory was ripe for memorialization in other ways, too, and thus the accomplishment, and its attendant influence on the distribution of symbolic capital, could be repeatedly invoked after the fact. This is certainly true in the case in Ptolemy's historical account of Alexander, as we have seen, but the same deliberate memorializing drive can also be found in operation in a variety of other media – not least in Hellenistic art, even group scenes such as the Alexander Mosaic and the Alexander Sarcophagus, reflecting perhaps an interest in seeing individual personalities and their individualized states of being and feeling.[20] Perhaps this, too, is an evocation of an archaic mode of conceptualizing individual achievement and its significance;[21] certainly it bears distinction from the Classical *polis*-centred ideology of cooperative warfare, which centred around the civic phalanx and largely discouraged individualism in the representation of specific victories.[22]

1. Complexes of imitation

Even while recognizing that much of the mythologization occurred later, as literary and cultural traditions (not to mention political agendas) grew, a heroic mythology in reference to Alexander nonetheless seems to have developed to a significant degree in his own lifetime.[23] He seems to have actively attempted to present himself as a latter-day combatant in the Trojan War, as a new Heracles or Achilles, or simply as a distillation of outstanding heroic *aretē*. The difficulty for the modern interpreter of Alexander's *ante mortem* self-mythologization lies in the analytical disentangling: should we see these heroic identifications as alternate and discrete, or cumulative and overlapping? Were they contingent on particular contexts, or were they meaningful beyond them? Absolute general answers are not possible; but given the interconnected and (in some ways) essentialistic nature of Greek mythical tropes and schemes,[24] it is perhaps more prudent to keep open the possibility of an entanglement of models, namely the invocation of a series of connected models in a single act of self-mythologization. In other words, it is helpful not to conceptualize an act of *imitatio* as restricted to a single object of imitation but rather see it as linked to a number of different referential points.

Conceiving of *imitatio* as a semantically expansive complex of multiple associations, rather than a restrictive unitary link between one model and one imitator, is particularly productive for approaching the emergence, evolution, and longevity of the phenomenon of imitating Alexander – *imitatio Alexandri*.[25] We have seen one case already, namely Ptolemy's self-modelling on Patroclus. In this case, Patroclus is not the end link in the constructed chain of referentiality, even though such a unitary link could doubtless possess its own power. Rather, it is the fact of Patroclus acting as the stand-in for Achilles that is subject of the allusion, which resonates contextually with Alexander's own self-modelling on Achilles, and in sum symbolizes Ptolemy as a stand-in for Alexander. Here the complex web seems to be deliberately established, the parallels neatly aligned. Yet even in cases without such conscious design, it is arguable that already existent symbolic and referential worlds conditioned the generation and interpretation of an imitative act. As it has been suggested in intertextual theory, especially on the embeddedness (or 'situatedness') of a text:

> The textual system exists before any text, and texts are born always already situated within that system, like it or not. Just as no person can escape her or his historical situatedness, so no text can exist except against the matrix of possibilities created by those pre-existing texts.[26]

As Fowler argues for texts, so we may argue for cultural symbols deployed for political means. A symbolic system antedates the generation of a new symbolic output, and the design and interpretation of an ideological construction is conditioned by that situatedness. There is not necessarily a single correct intertext, but rather a wide multiplicity of potential allusions, and the reader (and their ideology) is the important factor in determining which have validity; further, part of that determination is about how special, significant and singular the allusion appears to be.

Originality is another important issue. Far from being moribund, a culture of *imitatio* in the early Hellenistic era would seem to suggest sustained creative reflection on the significance and meaning of a new political world.[27] Taking this thought further, we may regard *imitatio* as a constructive and innovating practice, with reimagining and redeployment of the model, not simply unthinking repetition, inherent in the imitative act; further, *imitatio* is conducive to, and in alignment with, processes of change at work in contemporary political and cultural realities. Moreover, *imitatio* possesses its own traditionalizing or conventionalizing force, with a capacity to cement the exemplarity of the model imitated and thus further embed its cultural significance (and thus continuing potential for future *imitatio*).[28] A good example of this is the poetic literature produced in the early Hellenistic period, most prominently the poems of Callimachus, Theocritus and Apollonius Rhodius. In these writers, there is a renewal of interest in and reflection on the heroic individual, in concert with a close reading of archaic literature – prominently (but by no means exclusively) Homer, Hesiod and Pindar.[29] There is even a form of linguistic *imitatio* that supports the evocation of a heroic age, inasmuch as these same early Hellenistic authors all experimented with an artificial importation of Doric lexica into their poetry:[30] here, we must imagine that their poetic renditions even *sounded* like they were call-backs to a different age. In turn, of course, a reciprocal effect might have been that future would-be imitators would perceive the specific imitative mode – Doric dialectal choices – as a major criterion in their own mimetic projects, especially if it was seen to be validated by external esteem from a sought-after audience, leading to its further profusion: an imitative novelty can become a trend and then a convention or tradition.[31] In this particular example, it seems logical to suggest that an archaistic drive in poetry was linked to the same in royal political presentation, and that the two were in circular service. However, poets like Pindar were themselves archaizing in their constructions, making the contemporary tyrants whom they hymned recreate conditions of kingship found in epic *exempla*.[32] In our example of Hellenistic literature, then, there is a complex series of links involved in allusive characterization, a multi-referential strategy for evoking a model: an imitative complex, not just a simple reference.

None of this is to say that interpretation is not in the eye of the beholder: or, to put it in postmodernist or poststructuralist terms, that the author is alive in all cases. Yet when we encounter cases of innovative self-representation, such as the examples that are discussed in this chapter, which have consciously designed schematics of symbols and references – particularly in numismatic iconography, in which novelty in imagery is never accidental or meaningless to the issuing authorities[33] – we have the ability to pursue at least some of their multivalent chains of meaning and significance. These chains can in turn be historically situated, and thus the projects of *imitatio* can be used to reveal something of the attempts being made to represent and shape contemporary realities, and indeed others' perceptions of those realities. In the case of the *diadochoi*, we can see how heroic *imitatio* was developed for political ends in the years after Alexander's death, and in tracing the complexes of imitation that inhered in these projects we can find out more about the evolution of royal power and authority in the early Hellenistic period, especially prior to the existence of the Hellenistic kingships that came about in 306–304.

2. Ptolemy *Aegiochus* and the body of Alexander

Arrian's account of Ptolemy's battlefield heroism against the Aspasians in 327, discussed at the opening of this chapter, is very similar in some respects to

Diodorus Siculus' presentation of Ptolemy's outstanding *aretē* when fighting against Perdiccas in 320:

> The troops of Perdiccas . . . boldly assaulted the fortifications. At once the shield-bearers set up the scaling ladders and began to mount them, while the elephant-borne troops were tearing the palisades to pieces and throwing down the parapets. Ptolemy, however, who had the best soldiers near himself and wished to encourage the other commanders and friends to face the dangers, taking his long spear and posting himself on the top of the outwork, put out the eyes of the leading elephant (τὸν μὲν ἡγούμενον τῶν ἐλεφάντων ἐξετύφλωσεν), since he occupied a higher position, and wounded its Indian mahout. Then, with utter contempt of the danger, striking and disabling those who were coming up the ladders, he sent them rolling down, in their armour, into the river. Following his example, his friends fought boldly and made the beast next in line entirely useless by shooting down the Indian who was directing it. The battle for the wall (τῆς τειχομαχίας) lasted a long time, as the troops of Perdiccas, attacking in relays, bent every effort to take the stronghold by storm, while many heroic conflicts were occasioned by the personal prowess of Ptolemy and by his exhortations to his friends to display both their loyalty and their courage (αὐτὸς ἀριστεύων καὶ τοὺς φίλους παρακαλῶν ἐνδείξασθαι τὴν εὔνοιαν ἅμα καὶ τὴν ἀρετήν, ἡρωικοὺς ἀγῶνας συνεστήσατο) . . . Perdiccas gave up the siege and went back to his own camp.
>
> Diodorus Siculus XVIII 34.1–5, excerpts, trans. Geer

In this account, Ptolemy's quick thinking and martial ability form an example for his troops: his leadership, and their following of his actions, turn the tide of the battle and ensure Perdiccas' defeat at Ptolemy's hands. That there is a heroic tenor to this account is clear through the dramatic nature of the narrative, but it is more explicitly signalled by the description of the battle as a series of 'heroic contests' (ἡρωϊκοὶ ἀγῶνες) and by the description of Ptolemy as ἀριστεύων – literally 'the one who is best [at fighting]', but more broadly communicating that he is the hero of an *aristeia* scene.[34] The account, obviously highly favourable to Ptolemy, memorializes his heroic combat in terms similar to how Ptolemy himself had narrated his Aspasian exploits: a pro-Ptolemaic source probably underpins Diodorus' composition, perhaps composed in the early Hellenistic period with a clear political agenda.[35] Beyond establishing Ptolemy's isolated brilliance, the account also evokes his mimetic power, his capacity for inducing transformation in others: the tide of the battle is turned by the troops' replicating Ptolemy's actions, by their becoming like Ptolemy. In other words, their collective valour cements Ptolemy's individual exemplarity, and so the troops become vicarious stand-ins for Ptolemy's greatness. Another overall effect is to cement the potency of Ptolemy as a model and inspiration for heroic action.

A distinctive heroic feature of Ptolemy's *aristeia* was the titanic size of his bestial opponent, an Indian war-elephant. An impressive act in its own right, and comparable with a range of heroic animal-slaying narratives (not least by the Argead dynastic genitor Heracles),[36] this was also an area for which Ptolemy could claim some parity with Alexander's exploits in India, as had been celebrated most notably in the form of the so-called Porus Medallions.[37] One particular issue of this enigmatic coin series depicted a Macedonian cavalryman – identified by scholars as Alexander himself – spearing a retreating Indian elephant, ridden by two mahouts, perhaps one of which was meant to represent Porus. In a sense, elephant-slaying represented conquest through military victory, similar to the lion-slaying metaphor utilized in the Craterus monument.

We see this same symbolic power capitalized on in coin-types produced by Ptolemy in the aftermath of defeating Perdiccas. While retaining Alexander's imperial reverse-type of enthroned Zeus *aietophoros*, Ptolemy's silver tetradrachms from 320/319 develop a dynamic new image of Alexander wearing an elephant-scalp in place of Heracles in lion-scalp.[38] Alexander is also adorned with a headband (most likely a diadem) in some types of this series,[39] plus an *aegis*, and a ram's horn protrudes from his temple. Although this does not straightforwardly feature Ptolemy's slaughter of the elephant, the image nonetheless invokes its recent memory in the new construction of Alexander as patron of Ptolemy's authority.[40] Put slightly differently, Alexander's representation on Ptolemy's new coin has been adapted to fit the circumstance of Ptolemy's achievements, and so it should be considered to symbolize them. This does not exclude other interpretations,[41] but it is important not to ignore the explosive events in the contemporary context that resulted in significant changes to wider power dynamics.

A boyhood friend then *sōmatophylax* of Alexander, Ptolemy had received the satrapy of Egypt in the Babylon Settlement of 323. Soon after his appointment, he greatly expanded his remit, intervening in the Cyrenean *stasis* on the oligarchic side to gain a position of *strategos* in perpetuity; he also did away with Cleomenes of Naucratis, the financial overseer of Egypt employed by Alexander and then kept on, as a watchful pair of eyes on the new satrap, by Perdiccas.[42] Aside from conspicuous remembrance of service together during the destruction of the Persian empire, Ptolemy's unique connection with Alexander's authority centred around his hijacking of Alexander's funeral carriage in 321, then its transportation from Damascus in Syria (in collusion with its overseer

Figure 6 Silver tetradrachm of Ptolemy, *c.* 316/315. Staatliche Museen zu Berlin, Münzkabinett 18203058 / Dirk Sonnenwald. [CC PDM 1.0].

Arrhidaeus) into Egypt with an entourage of thousands of armed troops.[43] This armed procession heralded the transfer of Alexander's remains into Ptolemy's Egypt as well as guarded it from recollection, and soon after Ptolemy seems to have used his control of the body to attract further armies and settlers into his power base:

> Entombing him in this and honouring him with sacrifices such as are paid to demigods and with magnificent games (θυσίαις ἡρωικαῖς καὶ ἀγῶσι μεγαλοπρεπέσι τιμήσας), he won fair requital not only from men but also from the gods. For men, because of his graciousness and nobility of heart, came together eagerly from all sides to Alexandria and gladly enrolled for the campaign, although the army of the kings was about to fight against that of Ptolemy; and, even though the risks were manifest and great, yet all of them willingly took upon themselves at their personal risk the preservation of Ptolemy's safety.
>
> Diodorus Siculus XVIII 28.4–5, trans. Geer

Here, Diodorus tells us that the symbol of Alexander directly translates into political and military authority, or at least appeal for the soldiery, who were adrift on a rudderless ship of state. In this context, Ptolemy's victory over Perdiccas, the act of protecting and then retaining Alexander's body, further cemented the loyalty of the troops. There is heroic resonance here, too, inasmuch as Ptolemy's protection of Alexander's body from Perdiccas' invasion neatly maps onto the epic motif of a fight over the body of a fallen hero, and loyal protection by companions against enemies threatening to despoil the body and take up its earthly remnants of status – armour and weapons, which could be displayed afterwards to enhance the victor's *timē* and memorialize his superiority.[44] In the context of the early Hellenistic politics of the *diadochoi*, this could quite easily be seen as fideistic protection of Alexander's legacy from somebody who wished to take up his mantle, a latter-day *hoplōn krisis* from which Ptolemy emerged as the rightful victor.

In this symbolic register, one particular feature of Ptolemy's new numismatic portrait of Alexander that is worth investigating further for its heroic links is the *aegis*. In Graeco-Macedonian numismatic history to this point, depicting an *aegis* on a real historical individual (as opposed to a deity or other mythological figure) is entirely unprecedented: there is no single numismatic issue by any authority that deploys the *aegis* on a mortal human. This is mirrored in Greek literature, too, with one exception: in all previous extant Greek literature, there is only one instance of a living mortal man wearing the *aegis*, namely Achilles in the eighteenth book of the *Iliad*:[45]

> [B]ut Achilles, beloved of Zeus, rose up, and Athene
> swept about his powerful shoulders the fluttering aegis;
> and she, the divine among goddesses, about his head circled
> a golden cloud, and kindled from it a flame far-shining.
> *Iliad* XVIII 203–6, trans. Lattimore

This scene occurs as part of Achilles' re-entry to the struggle against the Trojans, at a time when his own armour had been lost and his divine-made armour had yet to be delivered. So Athena temporarily wraps Achilles in her own *aegis*, imparting her divine protection, and encircles around his head a golden, flaming cloud, giving him the ability to drive fear into the Trojan force.[46] Achilles' reappearance in this guise inspires the Achaeans, devastates their enemies, and results in a successful rallying against the enemy onslaught.

While the language here is adapted from standard Iliadic arming scenes,[47] and Athena's protection parallels the scheme of divine rescue that occurs at various points in the *Iliad*,[48] the particularity of Achilles' wearing the *aegis* remain distinctive and unique in all Greek literature.[49] The signification of Athena's divine protection is clear from context and from other scenes involving the *aegis* in the Homeric poems.[50] In this respect at least, there is something in common with Greek mythology as a whole, inasmuch as Athena performs the role of protector for a multiplicity of heroes – such as Perseus, Odysseus, Bellerophon, and of course Heracles – such that one might even say that Athena's support is a defining precondition of a Greek heroic protagonist.[51] Indeed,

Achilles in the *Iliad* has this support from Athena, right from her invisible appearances to him while he is in assembly with Agamemnon;[52] this association is also borne out in artistic renditions of Achilles' career, such as the famous scene of Achilles at a board game with Ajax.[53] She also evinces a concern or protecting the bodies of dead heroes, such as in *Iliad* XVII, where she mimics the voice of Phoenix to encourage Menelaus to protect Patroclus' corpse from Hector's and Aeneas' attempts to despoil it.[54]

Given its symbolic history, especially in 'one of the most impressive scenes' in the *Iliad*, as Achilles' *aegis*-garbing has been called,[55] the *aegis* on Ptolemy's new numismatic portrait of Alexander in 320 could thus be interpreted as a deliberately epicizing symbol, signifying divine protection for Alexander in both life and death – perhaps even a divinizing symbol, given that Achilles' appearance in an *aegis* in *Iliad* XVIII approaches an epiphanic scene.[56] Achilles' temporary protection, memorable in the *Iliad*, becomes a fixed iconographic feature of Alexander. As well as reflecting contemporary circumstances, namely Ptolemy's securing and memorializing the body under his protection, this reading is underscored and informed by Alexander's own imitative fixation on Achilles, which garnered publicity in his lifetime and remained a recurrent mythologizing touchstone in the myriad post-mortem recountings of his life and career; indeed, Diodorus and Plutarch both begin their accounts of Alexander with reference to his heroic lineage, Diodorus in particular noting that he inherited both *physis* and *aretē* from his Aeacid and Heraclid ancestors.[57] It is also worth noting that Athena's standardized presence on obverse-types of Alexander's imperial gold coinage had created a scheme of divine sponsorship which Ptolemy now seems to be additionally evoking (see Figure 5).[58]

In other words, Alexander's self-mythologizing reflexes are now deployed in Ptolemy's imagery to amplify his own role as protector of Alexander: he capitalizes on the latent equation between the hero and the conqueror to pronounce his own unique part in Alexander's legacy, here connected firstly to his historical involvement in taking, defending and preserving the body of Alexander against the invasion of Perdiccas, and secondly to his own evident attempts to create an independent power base and a mythological imaginary to rationalize its foundation. It is not coincidental that a statue of Alexander *Aegiochus* was developed contemporaneously, in the late fourth century, which depicted Alexander draped in a snake-bordered, scaly *aegis*, and which was located at the site of Alexander's tomb – clearly connecting with the motif of protecting Alexander's body and cohering with the numismatic imagery.[59]

Figure 7 Bronze statuette of Alexander with silver inlay, 1st–3rd centuries AD. The Walters Art Museum, Baltimore 54.1075. [CC0 1.0 Universal].

In larger terms, this shows a concern and a capacity to deploy heroic imagery in the diadochan period in pursuit of political goals, in part in mimicry of Alexander's heroic *imitatio* but with sufficient innovation that rules out a simple, unthinking immersion in Alexander's model without further political individuation.

These new images of Ptolemy's standing, an obverse-type of *aegis*-clad Alexander, continued to be manufactured in Ptolemy's coinage in the coming decades, even past his own accession in *c.* 305.[60] In fact, all features in the Alexander portrait in the obverse-type grew more prominent and more stylized over time: the snakes tying the *aegis*, plus the scaly make-up of its main fabric, and indeed the elephant-scalp headdress, the diadem and the ram's horn of Ammon all became more conspicuous and clearly delineated. When Ptolemy's own portrait appeared on gold and later silver obverse-types of his coinage (the gold perhaps as early as *c.* 305/304 or as late as *c.* 297/296, but at any rate after his accession),[61] it was noticeably different in some respects – it is veristic in style, with a receding hairline and distinctive physiognomy with respect to eyes, nose and chin[62] – yet it retained two unmistakeable symbols: the diadem, now with free-flowing ties near the nape, and the *aegis*, which remained scaly and tied with snakes.

Alexander's symbols become Ptolemy's. Of the diadem's further significance, we shall see more in the next chapter, but the fundamental connotation of succession from Alexander that it signifies is clear. Regarding the *aegis*, succession is similarly symbolized – a transference, or duplication, of a unique symbol from one king's portrait to another, instantiating a hierarchical similarity and likeness of esteem between the two wearers – but it is significant that this is an entirely invented tradition of representing the linear passage of power: Alexander *Aegiochus* becomes, or is joined by, Ptolemy *Aegiochus*. Not only did a newly developed image of Alexander come to have force in symbolizing political power, but a continuing heroic *imitatio* as a general activity could flexibly serve a variety of political goals as time and circumstances evolved. Moreover, we see again – as we saw with Craterus' construction of heroic superiority in Chapter 2 – how Alexander's heroic entanglements serve as an intermediary model for the elaboration of a diadoch's own extraordinary standing.

It is worth reflecting on the broader messages and the representational mode inherent in Ptolemy's creation of, and succession to, the heroic image of Alexander *Aegiochus*. In some respects Ptolemy's take-up of Alexander's remains and utilization of their talismanic appeal parallels the broader Greek tradition of the recovery and interment of a hero's bones for specific political and military (not to mention religious) objectives.[63] The proliferation of an Alexander cult in Alexandria, perhaps ktistic in original pretext but significantly broader in the longer term of the city's social imaginary, certainly shadows the practice of heroic cult that followed the translocation of heroic remains.[64] We have seen above how Ptolemy exploited the supernatural power of the dead Alexander to empower his position, just as we have seen his numismatic imagery advertise this empowerment, culminating in Ptolemy's own *basileia*. This should be regarded as a message to the other marshals of Alexander's empire, but also an attempt to concretize Ptolemy's standing in the specific region of Egypt and among the Graeco-Macedonian soldiery that were drawn there. A hero's bones

Figure 8 Gold stater of Ptolemy, *c*. 290. Staatliche Museen zu Berlin, Münzkabinett 18200178 / Lutz-Jürgen Lübke. [CC PDM 1.0].

have significant linkage to the religion and identity of the receiving or appropriating state, in addition to being an ideological concoction for external states.[65] In this sense, quite apart from framing his own unique personal connections and successional linkages with Alexander, Ptolemy was constructing a unifying point for the identity of a new regime and the local societies it ruled over, and an image to act as a blazon on his own road to kingship.

3. Lysimachus, lions and kingship

As Craterus had highlighted with his Delphic monument, imagery of lions and lion-slaying could be utilized in an activity-based mode of status enhancement, creating (among other things) a performative connection with the Argead dynasty and its ultimate heroic progenitor, Heracles. In time, other *diadochoi* appropriated this strategy, in a way that was just as specific to their individual contexts and persons: they did not necessarily always imply dynastic equation with the Argeads, but they nonetheless participated in a steadily evolving and mutually reinforcing typology of royal self-representation. In other words, through (re)deployment in various contexts, the dynamic imagery of lions and lion-slaying emerged as shorthand signifiers of kingship, or at least of aspirations of royalty, founded on the idea of an individual's exceptional, heroic, community-benefiting, authority-justifying achievement.

Lysimachus is a significant figure to examine in this regard, and it is worth supplying some context on his position. Although he was one of the principal powers that survived after the attrition of the first diadoch wars, becoming king in the Year of the Kings in 306–304 and then instrumental in Antigonus' downfall at Ipsus in 301, in early years after Alexander's death Lysimachus makes little impact on the international scene.[66] As a royal *sōmatophylax*, perhaps since prior to the death of Philip II in 336,[67] Lysimachus had been in the first rank of Alexander's generals and companions, alongside Perdiccas and Ptolemy, but received in the Babylon Settlement of 323 what was probably a mixed prize in form of the governorship of Thrace (reconfirmed at Triparadeisus in 320).[68] There, he spent many years involved in internal military activities, suppressing Thracian populations under the leadership of native rulers such as the Odrysian king Seuthes.[69] There is little direct evidence of these protracted and complex internal disputes, but his preoccupation with them probably explains why there is no evidence of his participation in Antipater's excursus in 321/320 to strip Perdiccas of the *epimeleia*.[70] Even so, as well as being his son by marriage (married to Antipater's daughter Nicaea, widow of the fallen regent Perdiccas), Lysimachus was clearly in Antipater's favour when the latter became regent at Triparadeisus in 320, since his brother Autodicus was made a *sōmatophylax* of Philip III at that juncture.[71] This also gave Lysimachus a close connection with the regency and royal power centre, and it aligned him publicly with Perdiccas' replacement and the major power in the European domains of the Macedonian state. This was clearly a strategic necessity, and it testifies to Lysimachus' political nous. Equally, it also illustrates a strategic need on Antipater's part to bring Lysimachus into the fold of the new regime.

Although apparently he did not stridently choose a side in the conflict between Polyperchon and Cassander after Antipater's death in 319, there are signs that he was at least cooperative with Cassander, and that measures of support were forthcoming in certain contexts, particularly regarding territorial access to his strategically important Thracian lands.[72] Certainly, after the death of Philip III in 317, and with the intensification of the diadochan struggles and the crystallization of power in the hands of fewer key figures that followed, Lysimachus' continuing tenure as de facto ruler of Thrace, and master of the crossing between Europe and Asia, left him in a significant role in diadochan international geopolitics. He was included in the so-called peace treaty of the diadochs in 311, which guaranteed peace between the major players – Antigonus, Ptolemy, Cassander and Lysimachus – and which handed over *prostasia* of the young Alexander IV to Cassander, who reneged on his charge and had the young heir murdered in *c.* 310/309.[73] He was also ambitious and internationally minded enough to seek the hand of Cleopatra, Alexander's sister, in *c.* 308 – as did in fact Cassander, Antigonus and Ptolemy, plus 'all the leaders who were most important after Alexander's death' – before she was terminated by Antigonus on account of the threat presented by the prestige she could bring to any of his rivals.[74] All this suggests that we should be not be surprised to find Lysimachus building up his own rationale for superior status and authority, even if we lack evidence from the early years after his Alexander's death. Indeed, Lysimachus in time found his own route to kingship, taking the diadem and the royal title in the Year of the Kings in 306–304 (discussed in Chapter 4).

One of Lysimachus' claims to fame was a story of his involvement in a lion hunt of Alexander. Indeed, so much did this story become bound up with Lysimachus' persona of authority that Justin relates that he was allotted Thrace at Babylon in 323 because of it: '[T]he most warlike (*ferocissimae*) nations were assigned to Lysimachus as the bravest (*fortissimo*) of them all.'[75] There are great variations in the retellings of this particular story, which attests to its popularity, not least among later authors and compilers but probably also within Lysimachus' lifetime, too. The simple version, provided by our earliest source Curtius Rufus, is that Lysimachus killed a lion while hunting in a Syrian *paradeisos*,[76] in the course of which the lion mauled his arm. At a later date, Lysimachus tried to intervene in Alexander's lion hunt near Samarkhand, placing himself between the king and the lion to protect the king,[77] for which he was rebuked by Alexander who then slew the lion in a single stroke.[78] The elaborate version of the story, related by later authors with varying degrees of embellishment,[79] is that Alexander's rebuke to Lysimachus resulted in the punishment of being locked in a cage with a lion, a scene which ended with Lysimachus killing the lion with his bare hands. Lund rightly questions the authenticity of this elaborate version, both on the grounds that it seems to be a *topos* of a king's barbarism and that Curtius himself mentions it but already rejects it as a distortion.[80] Even though we might agree with the assessment of this version as spurious, it is worth bearing in mind that even the development and elaboration of the tale is an interesting historical phenomenon, not least for reaffirming the intimate connection between the figure of Lysimachus and the activity of lion-killing, both in his own context and over the centuries of the story's (re)elaboration.

One explanation for the story's continued appeal was the leonine imagery employed in Lysimachus' own self-representation. He regularly employed various forms of lion imagery on reverse-types of coinages minted at his eponymous city-foundation Lysimachia, which is testimony to the valuation of the lion symbol within the scope of his own regime: indeed, not just the frequency but also diversity of separate lion images found on his coinages give a sense of its wide significance, including in the left field of his reverse-types.[81] Some scholars have even argued that this prominence might be rooted in in the use of a lion as Lysimachus' seal device.[82] Although there is no evidence that Lysimachus used a particular seal, the later continuation of the image on coins by his son Ptolemy, at Telmessus in the mid third century, could corroborate the hypothesis that the lion was effectively Lysimachus' sigil.[83] De Callataÿ and Kan suggest that the lion symbol appears on Lysimachus' coins as early as 306/305, perhaps alongside a lambda, notably before he struck any coins in his own name,[84] which would imply not just that the symbol was developed on Lysimachus' road to kingship, and so became associated with his persona very early indeed, but also that the lion symbol was a stand-in for Lysimachus' identity (Λ for Lysimachus, Λ for *leōn*). In other words, the lion perhaps signified Lysimachus himself and hence advertised his authority in the land he ruled.

There are some further connections that may ramify from this point. It is possible to relate Lysimachus' usage to the story that Philip II, Alexander's father, possessed a seal device with the image of a lion, which might thus connect Lysimachus' usage with Argead practice; but the story of Philip's lion seal is far from straightforward, included as it is in Plutarch's recounting of Alexander's birth mythologies.[85] Likewise, there is no evidence that Alexander used a lion seal device.[86] However, we might point to the fact that the Belevi tomb, probably

Figure 9 Silver tetradrachm of Lysimachus, *c.* 301–297. Staatliche Museen zu Berlin, Münzkabinett 18249715 / Lutz-Jürgen Lübke. [CC PDM 1.0].

built for Lysimachus but never his final resting spot, had an exterior decorated with lion-heads,[87] harking back to the lion-heads which decorated the lavish funeral carriage of Alexander.[88] Lion imagery was also prevalent in artefacts and architecture from Macedonian royal funerary culture, not least the well-known and controversially identified kingly tombs from Aegae.[89] Potentially, then, we are seeing imitation of Alexander, or even broader Argead dynastic imagery, in Lysimachus' symbolic choices.

Lysimachus' self-identification with the lion image, and use of it as a symbol of his power and authority, can be seen in another case, too. Memnon of Heraclea Pontica provides an interesting report of a capital ship named the *Leontophoros* ('Lion-carrier'), which was part of Lysimachus' fleet and had perhaps been built in the early 290s.[90] This was a behemoth of a ship that had eight banks and carried 1,600 rowers and 1,200 soldiers. The peculiar name suggests that Lysimachus did indeed identify his royal image – and indeed his power, represented here in gargantuan dreadnought form – with lions.[91] Alongside the coinage and the stories of the lion encounter from the time of Alexander, we can confirm that leonine imagery was a prominent part of how Lysimachus created a distinctive, personalized image of authority, which in turn underpinned his royal image.

One final anecdote is worth relating on the connection between lions and Lysimachus, told by Plutarch in connection with an embassy from Demetrius Poliorcetes, probably in the 290s:

> At all events, some ambassadors from him once came to Lysimachus, and Lysimachus, in an hour of leisure, showed them on his thighs and shoulders deep scars of wounds made by a lion's claws; he also told them about the battle he had fought against the beast, with which he had been caged by Alexander the king.
>
> Plutarch *Demetrius* 27.3

The context of this anecdote in Plutarch is humorous and satirical: Demetrius' own ambassadors jokingly juxtapose Lysimachus' scars with wounds inflicted on their own king by a Lamia, a mythological beast whose name was shared with one of Demetrius' consorts.[92] Although there is probably significant distortion in the tradition of this story, there is perhaps a historical kernel in Lysimachus' advertising physical marks of his encounter with a lion in Alexander's time to foreign dignitaries. This might suggest another area of political life in which lion imagery was used by Lysimachus, and in this context it is not too much of a

Figure 10 Lion-head from the Belevi Mausoleum, c. 285. Selçuk, Museum of Ephesus / Jona Lendering. [CC0 1.0].

stretch to imagine this as a broadcasting of Lysimachus' might and authority. In that sense, not just the lion symbol itself but the lion-struggle narrative were proxies for Lysimachus' power.

The implications of Lysimachus' self-identification with the lion symbol, and possible rationales for its use, are worth exploring. We have seen in the previous chapter the deep connection between lion-killing and the Argead royal paradigm, not to mention the ultimate dynastic progenitor Heracles, that was evoked by Craterus. It seems likely that Lysimachus was capitalizing on the same paradigm to a certain extent; indeed, Bosworth has suggested that, after Craterus' death, Lysimachus would have been able to 'bask in his reflected glory' of the lion-slaying message in the monument at Delphi.[93] In Lysimachus' case, however, there is some differentiation, in that Lysimachus seems not just to have underscored his triumph over a leonine foe but to have equated the lion with his own image. In other words, the lion symbol is a metonymous substitute for the lion-slayer, which is not just a variation on Craterus' paradigm but a new ideological specialization in its own right. Given its standing in Graeco-Macedonian culture, it seems likely that this is related to the widespread equation between Homeric *anaktes* and lions in epic poetry,[94] but perhaps also to the parallelism between lions and kings observable from Achaemenid Persian ideology.[95]

There is probably also a regional significance for Lysimachus' lion symbolism. Lions were noted to have been present in Thracian regions to the extent that they ravaged Xerxes' supply train to Greece during the Persian Wars, with a particular fondness for the taste of his camels.[96] Pulydamas, a famous fourth-century bodybuilder whose exploits were memorialized at Olympia, was famed for killing a lion on the slopes of Mount Olympus, after it had ventured across from the Thracian mountains.[97] Scholars have debated extensively whether or not lions existed in Iron Age Greece,[98] but at the very least we can state that there are testimonia supporting the notion that they did inhabit certain regions of northern Greece, Macedonia and Thrace.[99] Even if some stories of lion encounters are paradigmatic rather than historical, this does not negate their existence *in toto*.[100] If they ranged into human view only rarely, Thrace was seemingly one place of encounter. This rarity, however, would have added to the prestige of Lysimachus the lion-slayer and enhanced his force and mystique. As with any extraordinary heroic activity, it was only special because it was so unusual and beyond common experience. But even if lions were long-gone from Thrace, the memory of lions – real or invented – was enough to underpin Lysimachus' choice of imagery and self-identification. A 'real' lion-slaying encounter was not strictly needed.

Finally, it seems likely that Lysimachus' choice of lion imagery across various media and self-representation as a lion-killer was also a form of *imitatio Alexandri*, just as was implicit in Craterus' Delphic monument, too. Not only did Alexander participate in lion hunts throughout his time in Asia, he involved many of his upper-tier companions and bodyguards in the hunt. Lysimachus' repeated use of leonine symbolism, then, not just put Lysimachus in the mould of Alexander, it recalled Lysimachus' connection with Alexander, the special personal point of contact that could serve political purposes even decades after the latter's death. There is some similarity here, as we shall see in the next chapter, with the story of Lysimachus' receiving a diadem from the hands of Alexander himself. We should also not forget Alexander's repeated self-comparison against the yardstick of his distant heroic ancestor Heracles, the lion-killer par excellence. On this point, we should consider that Lysimachus' referential mode, of mediation through Alexander's image and own reflexes of self-mythologization, has a lot in common with the example of Ptolemy discussed earlier in this chapter: Lysimachus implying Alexander's Heraclean connections in suggestion of his inheritance of them, Ptolemy recalling Alexander's Achillean obsessions with the same goal in mind.

4. The bivalent paradigm: Pyrrhus of Epirus

Pyrrhus of Epirus is an interesting figure in a study of early Hellenistic kingship. On the one hand, he succeeded to his kingship as the scion of an established dynasty (the Aeacids, rulers of the Molossian realm of Epirus), rather than creating a power base and legitimacy *ab initio*; he also stood outside of the experiences of Alexander's Persian campaigns and the primary struggles of the *diadochoi* that led to the Year of the Kings. On the other hand, he was linked by blood to Alexander (first cousin once removed: Pyrrhus' father, Aeacides, and Alexander the Great were grandsons of Neoptolemus I), and he played the international power games of Hellenistic kingship, forming close alliances with key figures of the age, both the first and second generations of Hellenistic dynasts.[101] It might thus be said that although in terms of experience and institutional background Pyrrhus stood apart, he nonetheless had enough of a connection to the interconnected post-Alexander system to warrant mention in wider discussion. Indeed, he seems to display behaviour and imagery that is similar to the other *basileis*, especially in the area of heroic *imitatio*, so there is a good case to make that some of his representational choices respond to broader schemes of ideological commonality – and hence, in turn, testify to their authority and power in the Hellenistic world.

Pyrrhus is also valuable as a case study in early Hellenistic history for the quality of some of evidence available, in particular numismatic. For some of Pyrrhus' coinage, we can connect the iconography to important points in his career. For instance, gold staters produced at some point in the 290s–270s display an obverse laureate portrait of Zeus and a reverse image of seated, enthroned Dione.[102] The latter is a variation of the 'enthroned deity' visual schema that was significant in advertising divine sponsorship for the early Hellenistic kings, and which the kings themselves occasionally adopted, too.[103] We can connect this issue with Pyrrhus' sponsorship of and benefaction to the oracular sanctuary of Dodona, the only major religious site in the Greek world which involved the worship of both Zeus and Dione.[104] Pyrrhus' relationship with the sanctuary, moreover, continued over his career, as we know from several dedications. Remains of a bronze shield, probably dedicated after the battle of Heraclea in 280, show the fragmentary inscription:

> King Pyrrhus and the Epirotes and the Tarentines [dedicated this], [taken] from the Romans and their allies, to Zeus Naios.[105]

This testifies to the sending and publicizing of spoils from military victories, even overseas. Another notable instance is found in Pausanias' record, that Pyrrhus dedicated to Zeus Macedonian shields taken after a victory over Antigonus Gonatas, probably in 274 – and remains of this dedication, too, have possibly been found, in a shield fragment from Dodona bearing the inscription ΒΑ[ΣΙ]ΛΕΥΣ ('King').[106] The numismatic evidence confirms the Dodonian sanctuary's wider importance to Pyrrhus, while additionally suggesting that he broadcasted his relationship with it widely and integrated it into his public image. This is thus a good example of a king showcasing his support for a temple – temple support itself being a widespread area of royal practice among Alexander and the Hellenistic *basileis*[107] – in other representational media, drawing our attention to the significance of royal benefaction in public relations.

More strikingly, Pyrrhus produced a series of silver coins across mints in Epirus, central Greece and southern Italy which depict heroic and divine figures.[108] The obverse-type of this series depicts Achilles with a crested Corinthian helmet featuring a griffin symbol, whereas the reverse depicts Thetis facing left, on a hippocampus facing right, holding a shield. All examples of this coin-type bear the reverse legend ΒΑΣΙΛΕΩΣ ΠΥΡΡΟΥ, 'of King Pyrrhus'. Both obverse- and reverse-types are worth deconstructing fully, before turning our attention to the sequence of both images as a unified whole.

This portrait of Achilles shares similarities with the portrait of Athena popularized on Alexander's coinages, particularly the Corinthian crested helm, though the figure here is masculine and not Athena. The short curls of hair underneath the helmet are striking, and they recall the depiction of Alexander's hair in portrait statues and posthumous numismatic imagery, which was in turn imitated by figures such as Ptolemy and Demetrius Poliorcetes in their numismatic royal portraits.[109] This is not an archaistic Achilles, then, but rather a hero whose features conform with contemporary signifiers of royal style set by Alexander and conspicuously imitated by the *diadochoi*. There is an analogy here with Alexander's depiction of Heracles on coinage, which mirrored his own unbearded look, rather than the older, grizzled, hirsute Heracles that was more common in some earlier iconographic traditions.[110] In Alexander's case, although

Figure 11 Silver didrachm of Pyrrhus, *c.* 280. Staatliche Museen zu Berlin, Münzkabinett 18203180 / Dirk Sonnenwald. [CC BY-SA 4.0].

Heracles was not a crypto-portrait of Alexander, it is clear that the representation conveyed continuity from the hero to his most recent dynastic descendant, which was underscored by Alexander's repeated invocation of Heracles' mythology and emulation of his example.[111] It seems plausible that Pyrrhus' depiction of Achilles was similarly motivated and constructed, given that, just as the Argead house claimed ultimate descent from Heracles via Caranus, so the Aeacid house claimed lineage from Achilles via his son Neoptolemus.[112] In other words, in advertising the figure of Achilles, Pyrrhus was drawing a connection with his heroic inheritances and asserting his own character by extension.

There is a kind of typological imitation of Alexander's example here, inasmuch as the numismatic issue features a semi-divine heroic progenitor of the dynasty represented in modernistic terms that conform with contemporary features of royal style. In both cases it is also likely that generational inheritance from the hero in question – of *physis*, character, ability – is a primary implication behind placing him on coinage. In Pyrrhus' Aeacid case, however, unlike Alexander's Argead, there is no existent numismatic tradition of depicting the ancestral hero, so the choice of the image is additionally significant as a representational strategy and more direct in its intended implications to contemporary viewers of the image. Additionally, in an era of competing claims to links with Alexander, it is possible that the choice of an emphatic link to Achilles served a secondary purpose, as a form of *imitatio Alexandri* premised on Pyrrhus' embodiment of the same inherited heroic qualities as Alexander. This would align with what we know from Plutarch's biography of Pyrrhus, where he claims that Pyrrhus was seen as most like Alexander of all would-be Alexander-imitators:

> For they likened his aspect and his swiftness and all his motions to those of the great Alexander, and thought they saw in him shadows, as it were, and intimations of that leader's impetuosity and might in conflicts. The other kings, they said, represented Alexander with their purple robes, their body-guards, the inclination of their necks, and their louder tones in conversation; but Pyrrhus, and Pyrrhus alone, in arms and action.
>
> Plutarch *Pyrrhus* 8.1, trans. Perrin

Plutarch evokes a wider pattern of *imitatio Alexandri*, plus a distinction between authentic and artificial modes of imitation, one based in deeds and the other in image. Pyrrhus was trying to link himself with a distant figure who had died before he was born, but whom the world of competing kings around him held as a recurrent touchstone – hence the necessity and appeal for him of an Alexandrian mode of self-definition. Yet he retained an added advantage of genetic similarity, which the numismatic image of Achilles surely underscored, in a way reinforced by memories of Alexander's own programme of imitation of Achilles and the same Achillean ancestry.

The image of Thetis in opposition to her son Achilles marks the genetic and familial theme, too. This maternal imagery is additionally significant given the appearance of Pyrrhus' own mother, Phthia, on some of his coinages, particularly those in Sicily.[113] Indeed, there is a similarity between the portrait of Phthia and the visage of the figure of Thetis from Pyrrhus' coins: both are veiled, and both have curled hair reminiscent of the portrait of Achilles. It may be that the 'mother-type' is being evoked here in general terms, yet it is also plausible that there was a deliberate equation being drawn between the Achilles–Thetis pair and the Pyrrhus–Phthia. This is also likely because none of the other Hellenistic kings of the diadochan generation placed their mothers on coinage: this was a Pyrrhic distinction, at least at this point in time.

Most significant of all is the shield held by Thetis on the reverse of the Achilles coins. This shield is the sole focus of Thetis' gaze, and she is seemingly entranced as she faces away from the direction in which the hippocampus is moving, occupied solely by the surface of the shield. This can only be read as the shield of Achilles, famously evoked in an extended ecphrasis in *Iliad* XVIII that remained highly influential in both political and intellectual contexts in the later Greek and Roman worlds.[114] The most direct reading of this reverse image is that Thetis is in the process of bringing Achilles his divinely made shield, a well-known scene in the *Iliad* which is a prelude to Achilles' *aristeia*.[115] The presence of a militaristic portrait of Achilles on the obverse-type strengthens this reading. Given that we may read the presence of Achilles and Thetis as communicating something of the generational character of the Aeacids – and of Pyrrhus, the coin's named issuer, in particular – the motif of heroic *aristeia* has a significant impact on how we should understand Pyrrhus' contemporary ideological projections. More particularly, the highly martial quality of the allusion – to the *aristeia* of Achilles – links closely with the real nature of Pyrrhus' career as a roving warlord, while at the same time it represents a specialized, personal variation of the more general phenomenon of Hellenistic royal stress on an ideology of military capability and success.[116] This general ideology was at heart of Hellenistic kingship, and we are seeing here a distinctive Pyrrhic brand of it.

* * *

Pyrrhus' stress on Achillean descent and, by extension, his own Achillean character is striking, and it is unique among the diadochan generation of *basileis* for its choice of heroic emphasis. No other diadoch could claim this kind of link, given their lack of crossover with the Aeacid bloodline. Yet, strikingly, Pyrrhus also seems to have engaged with the more prevalent Hellenistic royal ideology of linking his position to the heroic Heracles. This is a salutary reminder that, although the distinctiveness of a link to Achilles could be utilized broadly by Pyrrhus, relying solely on distinctiveness without sufficient participation in the prevailing ideological system was an ineffective strategy on the international scene.

One area in which Pyrrhus asserts Heraclean links is ancestry. According to Justin, Pyrrhus' ancestor, also named Pyrrhus (the alternative name of Neoptolemus, Achilles' son), once went to Dodona to consult the oracle but while there forcibly abducted Heracles' granddaughter Lanassa, eventually leading to a union that produced eight children.[117] He then narrates that the daughters among this eight were traded in marriage alliance to neighbouring rulers, and that the mythic Pyrrhus gained great influence abroad as a result. Although this is not a new model by any means – trading daughters for influence is widely attested[118] – its similarity with Hellenistic royal and elite practice suggests that the account is not an unadulterated retelling of myth without contemporary flavouring. Indeed, no other source transmits the story of Heracles' granddaughter, and thus Heracles himself, being an ancestor of the latter-day Aeacids. In addition to these points, we may suggest that the Hellenistic Pyrrhus was the source of this story because he, too, married a woman called Lanassa, daughter of the self-made Syracusan *basileus* Agathocles, in about

295.[119] It is through this levirate marriage that Pyrrhus was able to assert a claim to Agathocles' domain after the latter's death in 289, and it is on the same basis that the Syracusans appealed to Pyrrhus for aid in the face of Carthaginian aggression in 279.

The story of Achilles' son and Heracles' granddaughter provides a mythic analogue for the latter-day marriage of a Pyrrhus and Lanassa pair. One fundamental implication of the story is that King Pyrrhus himself is a descendant of Heracles. This, too, is a recognizable strategy: inventing or embellishing mythic genealogies and kinship ties is well-recorded feature of dynastic ideologies, especially Hellenistic, and sits in a context connected with the mythicization of kinship bonds in and between Hellenistic *poleis*.[120] Moreover, there are territorial implications to the use of such fictive genealogies, in this case connected with Pyrrhus' Sicilian takeover attempt. It is unsurprising, in the context of his activities on Sicily, that Pyrrhus begins to mint coins there with obverse-types depicting Heracles.[121] This was a portrait of the demigod in a lion-scalp, which seems to have been inspired by but not stylistically copied from Alexander's imperial-types (among other things, the portrait bust on Pyrrhus' types faces left, not right). On this basis, we may posit that the story of Pyrrhus' mythical Heraclean ancestry through Lanassa, reinforced by marriage to Agathocles' daughter Lanassa, originated in the context of Pyrrhus' occupation of Sicily; even further, that Pyrrhus himself was responsible for originating it, in order to provide a mythical precedent for his Heraclean association and Agathoclean inheritance, the former highly significant given Heracles' wide legacy and worship in Sicily.[122] We seem to see echoes of this discourse from Plutarch's narration of Pyrrhus' attempt to capture the city of Eryx: Pyrrhus reportedly promised games and sacrifices to Heracles should he be successful, specifically making the wish that he be made worthy of his *genos* ('family') in fighting against the Sicilians.[123] Eryx, reportedly, had been conquered by Heracles himself and was regarded locally as 'Heraclid territory'.[124]

Another instance potentially discloses Pyrrhus' Heraclean connections. Plutarch records that the Epirote king once intended to sacrifice a bull, ram and boar in order to ratify a treaty of peace between himself, Lysimachus and Antipater son of Cassander.[125] The sacrifice was never completed by Pyrrhus, as the ram fell dead of its own accord before the ritual began. This was considered a bad omen until one of Pyrrhus' seers proclaimed that it meant that one of the three kings would die soon; this prodigy then negated the possibility of a binding peace treaty between the three, so it was abandoned.[126] We can date this incident broadly to between the years 297 and 294, the deaths of Cassander and Antipater respectively, and possibly refine it further to c. 296–295, specifically before Demetrius' intervention in Macedonia, as Plutarch does not mention Demetrius' activities as having any bearing on the peace process.[127]

The intended sacrifice is clearly a powerful action: such a triple sacrifice – of especially expensive animals – is rare in the Greek world.[128] However, the triple sacrifice can more importantly be understood as Pyrrhus' veneration of Heracles. Diodorus records that Heracles was honoured by his friends (notably Menoitius, son of Actor and father of Patroclus) with 'heroic' (ὡς ἥρωι) sacrifices consisting of a bull, a ram and a boar,[129] thereafter annually repeating in Opus, in northern Locris. Was Pyrrhus sacrificing to Heracles to ratify the treaty with Lysimachus and Antipater, hence integrating Heracles into his public image and royal practice? We may suggest here that Heracles would have been a particularly important choice for Lysimachus and Antipater, too. Lysimachus, as already discussed, emphasized his Heraclean power and connections as early as 306/305, and Antipater was under immense external pressure in his attempt to continue the kingship inherited from his father Cassander, who had continued Argead traditions and imagery, including minting coins with notable lion designs on reverse-types paired with an Argead/Alexandrian Heracles obverse.[130] We lack specific and detailed information on Antipater's self-presentation, but it seems likely that he would have followed his father's example and adhered closely to Argead models and traditions. A sacrifice to Heracles to bind a peace for three rulers who outwardly venerated Heracles makes sense as the backdrop for the dramatic reversal in expectations delivered by the death omen: the peace was triply ill-omened, and the prophecy of one of the kings' death all the more significant. On the other hand, we must recognize that the profusion of dramatic animal prodigies in sources for Alexander and the *diadochoi* might mean we are dealing with the literary sensationalization of an actual event, perhaps also its politicization.[131] Even this, however, adds to the picture of Heracles' significance and potency in the imagery and stories surrounding the early Hellenistic kings, and rounds out the extent to which heroic imagery and ideology widely featured in the development of early Hellenistic kingship.

4

Diadem and *basileia*: A Zelotypic Model

After the death of their father, the eldest son, Aristobulus, resolved to transform his office into a kingship (τὴν ἀρχὴν εἰς βασιλείαν μεταθεῖναι): since he was decided upon this course, first he placed a diadem upon himself (διάδημα πρῶτος ἐπιτίθεται).

Josephus *Jewish Antiquities* XIII 301

The Hasmonean ruler Judah Aristobulus was the first of his family line to claim the title of *basileus*, king. His reign was a short one, between 104 and 103 BC, yet it transformed the Hasmonean family into a royal dynasty: all succeeding rulers, however brief their tenures, took the royal title, right up until the end of the dynasty's existence as a client kingdom of the Roman and Parthian states.[1] Significantly, this transformation of Hasmonean rule involved putting a royal structure on an existent theocratic leadership, the Judaean high priesthood, and it came in a context in which the last Jewish monarchs had died out nearly five centuries before.[2] Because of this, Aristobulus and his successors had recourse to deploying a new royal tradition.[3]

As Josephus describes this inauguration, Aristobulus took a diadem upon himself to enact and to signify the conversion of his *archē* ('rule', 'office') into a *basileia* ('kingship'). This is no mere historiographical formula: 'taking the diadem' is not here simply an idiomatic means of expressing 'assuming the throne'. Rather, this is a mechanical, factual reporting of a conscious strategy, a literal action, undertaken by a non-royal ruler who had decided to make kingship his institutional reality. He tied the diadem around his head, as the etymology of διάδημα (from διαδέω, 'tie around') suggests, and in so doing declared his kingship. Seizing *basileia* by taking up the diadem in this way is ultimately indebted to the paradigmatic accessions of the early Hellenistic period, those of the 'Year of the Kings' between 306 and 304, which we have seen in Chapter 1 and will be explored more fully in the next section.[4]

In addition to the mechanics of accession, this scene importantly points to embedded expectations of kingship. Evidently in this context, for Aristobulus to have *basileia*, first he had to have a diadem. The royal tradition that Aristobulus was importing was one that had become dominant by this point in the eastern Mediterranean and Near Eastern worlds, namely that of Hellenistic kingship. The model of Hellenistic kingship had an enduring impact, well beyond the temporal and geographic parameters of dynasties whose existence began in the early Hellenistic period, the period of Alexander's Successors. In local terms, it is entirely possible that memories or experiences of foreign domination in Judaea, Seleucid royal rule in particular,[5] had some force in determining Aristobulus' take-up of the Hellenistic model; but it is more likely that he deliberately sought to imitate established Hellenistic dynasties of past and present in order to performatively clarify his incipient *basileia*.[6] The choice of his terms for accession thus reflects the dominance and diffusion of the Hellenistic royal model, and points to the reality that it had become *the* archetype of kingship in cross-cultural, international discourse by this point – so much so that the act of assuming a diadem was explicable to its audiences in a Hasmonean Judaean context as an assertion of kingship.[7]

So what is a diadem, and where does it come from? As mentioned above, the Greek word for diadem, διάδημα, has its roots in the verb διαδέω, '[to] bind round'.[8] This accurately reflects the nature of the Hellenistic diadem, a simple headband of cloth tied around the head.[9] The colour of the cloth itself is described only by later sources, which describe it variously as white, white spotted with blue, and white spotted with purple.[10] Modern scholars often call it white, probably correctly,[11] but in reality we cannot be sure, for the simple reason that the best depictions of the diadem (especially in the early Hellenistic world) are in numismatic iconography, hence non-colourised images. Likewise, the material used for the fabric of the diadem is not known, despite speculations.[12] Attempts by modern commentators to distinguish the diadem from other, strikingly similar headwear and to proscribe a definition of a 'proper' diadem based on exact positions and knots of the binding are at best counter-intuitive, especially in the period 323–276, where the diadem is first used in a widespread fashion in connection with Hellenistic royal imagery.[13] Our best summary is: it is likely that the diadem was simply a plain headband, probably white, worn by the Hellenistic kings and depicted mostly with but sometimes without its hanging ties.

As a symbol, then, the diadem is stark and simple, curiously unimpressive and unostentatious, hardly reflective of great wealth and power or complex ritual use.[14] Possibly in compensation for this, scholars have assumed that the Hellenistic diadem has significant transferred meaning from diverse cultural traditions. Arguments have been made for Assyrian,[15] Achaemenid,[16] Argead

Macedonian,[17] Dionysian[18] and Hellenic epinician origins;[19] the possibility of a Pharaonic Egyptian provenance has been noted, too,[20] as has a connection to the headbands of Greek heroes.[21] Given the wide prevalence of headbands worn for different purposes across ancient Mediterranean and Near Eastern societies, some very similar despite lack of connection, overly focusing on origins is a counter-productive approach to take. Although there may be some valence deriving from these different traditions, and these may have informed perceptions of the symbol by diverse populations and stakeholder groups, this takes focus away from actual pragmatics of use and constructions of meaning in contemporary Hellenistic contexts.[22]

Another good illustration of the paradigmatic dominance of Hellenistic kingship in international spheres, along with its signification by the diadem, may be found in the events leading up to the death of Julius Caesar in Rome. Plutarch gives a detailed report of a scene involving a diadem at the Lupercalia festival on 15 February 44 – exactly one month before his assassination:

> Caesar was viewing these things as a spectator, seated upon the rostra on a golden chair, decked in triumphal attire. Antony was among those running in the sacred race, since he was consul. And then he rushed into the forum, and the crowd parted way for him, carrying a diadem around which a wreath of laurel was entwined (φέρων διάδημα στεφάνῳ δάφνης περιπεπλεγμένον); he stretched this forth towards Caesar, and there was an applause that was not booming, but rather slight and contrived in advance, yet when Caesar pushed it away the entire crowd erupted in applause; again when it was offered, few applauded, and yet once more when he did not accept it, everyone applauded. Since this experiment had been rejected (οὕτω δὲ τῆς πείρας ἐξελεγχομένης), Caesar stood up, and having ordered that the wreath be carried up to the Capitolium, his statues there were seen to have been bound with royal diadems (ὤφθησαν δὲ ἀνδριάντες αὐτοῦ διαδήμασιν ἀναδεδεμένοι βασιλικοῖς). And the two tribunes, Flavius and Maryllus, approached and tore them off, and on searching out those that had first hailed Caesar as king (βασιλέα), carted them off to prison. The people were following in applause, and they called these men Brutuses, since Brutus was the one who had terminated the succession of kings (καταλύσας τὴν τῶν βασιλέων διαδοχὴν), and from the monarchy had rendered power to the senate and to the people. At this Caesar became apoplectic, and deprived those aligned with Maryllus of their offices.
>
> Plutarch *Caesar* 61.3–4, trans. Perrin

What actually happened at this Lupercalia and why has been the subject of debate; but what is clear is that after the sacred races, Mark Antony offered

Caesar a diadem wrapped in a laurel wreath, which was proffered several times with negative reactions from the crowd informing Caesar's refusal.[23] Afterwards, statues of Caesar were found with diadems wrapped around their heads, which the assertive tribunes of the plebs Flavius and Maryllus tore off – evidently so stridently that Caesar punished them by attacking their patronage networks. On the face of it, this was another sign that Caesar was on course to revive the Roman kingship, transforming his role of *dictator* into that of *rex*, and that this was comprehensively rejected by the Roman public.

In this context, all sources are agreed that a diadem was offered: Plutarch is not simply using a preferred Hellenic terminology of διάδημα, but rather all our Latin sources, too, use the word *diadema* (a loanword into Latin).[24] This is not a *corona* or a στεφάνη or another similar band, then, and so must mean the band of cloth that symbolized Hellenistic royalty.[25] Moreover, as North argues, it is clear that onlookers understood the significance of this act, even when it was unspoken, for instance in Cicero's correspondence.[26] Thus, in Rome of the mid-first century, a diadem signified kingship, and all audiences knew this. But more extraordinarily, it signified kingship according to the expectations and traditions of the appropriating culture. Despite deriving from Hellenistic *basileia*, the symbol of the diadem was received by its audiences as symbolizing Roman *regnum*. In other words, the spectators of Caesar at the Lupercalia in 44 did not see in the proffered diadem a symbol of the Hellenistic East, but rather interpreted it according to its staging and construction at that individual moment.

This latter point has not been sufficiently explored, and the idea that the operative issue was *regnum* is generally assumed and accepted.[27] The wider significance, however, is that there is a disconnect between the symbol and what is symbolized. There is perhaps a connection of this episode to Cleopatra – her absent presence, as it were – and with contemporary rumours about Caesar's potentially moving his centre of power to Alexandria (or perhaps even to Ilium),[28] so in other words a connection to the 'Hellenistic' influence on his ideology and public perceptions of him. Whatever the case on that matter, we are seeing here the totalizing power of the diadem to signify royal status. In its original early Hellenistic context, as will be explored below, the diadem was something of an invented tradition, and was utilized in contexts of accession and succession: it signified and visually demarcated a new *basileus* (or *basilissa*, as the case may be), and thereafter became deeply embedded internationally as a symbol of royal status in the round. Centuries later, when we see it in Julius Caesar's Rome, at the Lupercalia of 44, it is interpreted in terms of the monarchic history of the operating culture, namely it is understood as symbolizing Roman *regnum*, hence framed as part of Caesar's quest to revive the hated Roman kingship. So there is a form of Hellenistic influence in operation, but Hellenistic royal ideology and symbolism had become so successful in defining the discourse of kingship at an international level that they could be detached from their original context, and the mechanics and staging in the receiving culture actually condition its meaning more than this original context.

How do we get to this point? How does the diadem become established as a symbol of Hellenistic *basileia*? Or more particularly, how does it become established as the *defining* symbol, with a capacity to signify the wider institution and status of kingship – so successfully that it becomes a metonymous substitute, and that the simple act of taking a diadem is immediately understood as a staging of accession?

1. The 'Year of the Kings' and the dawn of Hellenistic kingship

The diadem's first live (as opposed to pictorial) appearance in the post-Alexander period, excepting perhaps the 'Alexander throne' episodes involving Perdiccas and Eumenes (see section 3, below), is in the aftermath of the battle of Salamis in 306. As mentioned at the start of Chapter 1, Salamis was a great victory of Demetrius Poliorcetes over Ptolemaic forces under Menelaus, Ptolemy's brother, with Ptolemy himself acting as reinforcement. On the crest of this triumph, Demetrius' father Antigonus Monophthalmus declared himself king and took the diadem, and Demetrius himself was made king alongside him, also with a diadem. Within the next two years the other prominent marshals also became *basileis*: Ptolemy, Seleucus, Lysimachus and Cassander all declared themselves kings and took the diadem.[29] Although Alexander's heirs Philip III and Alexander IV had died in 317 and 310/309, respectively,[30] 306 saw the first public declaration of post-Argead kingship. The ensuing proliferation of multiple kingships across Alexander's former empire – the 'Year of the Kings' – was the watershed after Alexander's death that determined the evolutionary direction of the Hellenistic world,[31] and it solidified kingship as the dominant discourse of power in that international world.

Gruen's classic study of the diadochan accessions notes that Salamis was 'the first major military victory by any of the dynasts since the death of Alexander IV', and that this was part of the reason why it catalysed Antigonus' accession.[32] This is not quite true, as there were other major victories between 310 and 306. Demetrius' capture of Athens in late 307, for instance, led to a significant shift in the balance of power in peninsular Greece, in that it initiated the dissolution of Cassander's network of oligarchies and garrisons and the installation of a new framework of leadership in the Greek *poleis* under Antigonus and Demetrius, culminating in their re-establishment of a Hellenic league based at Corinth in 302.[33] Another example is Seleucus' decisive victory over Antigonus in August 309 in Babylonia, which put the final nail in the coffin of Antigonus' two-year effort to re-subject Babylonia to his own rule.[34] After this, Seleucus was able to undertake his own eastern *anabasis* in the period 308–305, leading to the consolidation of the eastern satrapies in his hands and successful diplomatic contact with the Mauryan king Chandragupta, which saw borderlands being ceded in return for a reported 500 war-elephants.[35] These elephants, in turn, would be strategically and emblematically significant in the expansion of Seleucus' empire and dynasty.[36]

Yet there remain differences between the outcome of Salamis and such other major victories in the interregnal period. The capture of Athens of 307, while under Cassander's control through an oligarchy led by Demetrius of Phalerum, was not a direct victory of Demetrius over Cassander, nor even a military victory per se given that the city surrendered without battle[37] – though it was, locally, significant enough that the Athenians gave Antigonus and Demetrius a royal honorific.[38] In a slightly different fashion, Seleucus' victory in August 309 in all probability took place only slightly after the assassination of Alexander IV, and it is not likely that the news was known in Babylonia by this point – whether because of ineffective communication networks and intentional withholding of the information by the Successors,[39] or more simply because of the sheer distance between Macedon and Babylon. It has been suggested, indeed, that Alexander IV's death was not known abroad until 309/308.[40] Moreover, the eastern front between Antigonus and Seleucus was not one in which the other *diadochoi* were involved, unlike the interconnected conflict zones in the Aegean and eastern Mediterranean.

In other words, Salamis was the first major military battle since the death of Alexander IV (i) in which one diadoch had directly and decisively defeated another; (ii) around which there was certain knowledge of an interregnum; and (iii) which took place in a highly visible international sphere. The first of these factors, the triumph over a great rival, gave the victory its primary symbolic draw, and accordingly the result was a competitive advertisement of superiority, which took the form of a ground-breaking declaration of kingship. It is in this context that we encounter the diadem. Diodorus and Plutarch are the principal sources here,[41] and it is worth reproducing them:

Antigonus, on learning of the victory that had occurred, and buoyant at the height of his superiority, put a diadem around his head and thereafter took the title of king (διάδημα περιέθετο καὶ τὸ λοιπὸν ἐχρημάτιζε βασιλεύς), consenting that Demetrius, also, should hold the same title and honour.

Diodorus Siculus XX 53.1

As bearer of his own testimony (Αὐτάγγελον) about the victory Demetrius sent Aristodemus of Miletus to his father, the flatterer par excellence among all courtiers (πρωτεύοντα κολακείᾳ τῶν αὐλικῶν ἁπάντων) ... Aristodemus instructed his men to weigh anchor that they should all remain quietly on board while he himself got into the ship's small boat, landed alone, and proceeded towards Antigonus, who was anxiously awaiting news of the battle ... Aristodemus, however, would make no answer to anybody, but step by step and with a solemn face drew near in perfect silence. Antigonus ... came to the door to meet Aristodemus, who was now escorted by a large throng which was hurrying to the palace. Accordingly, when he had come near, he stretched out his hand and cried with a loud voice: 'Hail, King Antigonus, we have conquered Ptolemy in a sea-fight (χαῖρε, βασιλεῦ Ἀντίγονε, νικῶμεν Πτολεμαῖον ναυμαχίᾳ), and now hold Cyprus, with twelve thousand eight hundred soldiers as prisoners of war.' To this Antigonus replied: 'Hail to thee also, by Heaven! but for torturing us in this way, thou shalt undergo punishment; the reward for thy good tidings thou shalt be some time in getting.'

After this, the crowd acclaimed Antigonus and Demetrius for the first time as kings (πρῶτον ἀνεφώνησε τὸ πλῆθος Ἀντίγονον καὶ Δημήτριον βασιλέας). Antigonus was straightaway crowned by his friends (Ἀντίγονον μὲν οὖν εὐθὺς ἀνέδησαν οἱ φίλοι), while Demetrius was sent by his father a diadem and a letter that addressed him as king (ὁ πατὴρ ἔπεμψε διάδημα καὶ γράφων ἐπιστολὴν βασιλέα προσεῖπεν.).

Excerpts from Plutarch *Demetrius* 17.2–18.1, trans. Perrin [adapted]

The same outcome is evident – Antigonus and Demetrius as diademed kings – but the two sources are compatible only to a certain point. Plutarch's initial record is perhaps plausible,[42] that Aristodemus marched through Antigonus' *basileion* (palace), refusing to give a hint of the outcome about Salamis to onlookers, before dramatically revealing the victorious *naumachia* and pre-emptively addressing the general as *basileus* Antigonus in front of a swell of onlookers. If we agree that this happened, then it was probably coordinated,[43] namely Antigonus had decided to take the royal title on the strength of the victory at Salamis, and Aristodemus' pre-agreed role was as messenger (presented by Plutarch as a theatrical messenger scene, revealing off-stage action)[44] – and possibly also as kite-flier for Antigonus' court, testing the waters in the inner circle before taking it public. Alternatively, following Diodorus' report, Antigonus simply declared himself king after hearing the news. We can certainly accept Plutarch's detail that Antigonus' new royal title was then immediately solidified, in public, through an acclamation by his (and indeed any diadoch's) primary power base, namely the army.[45] Equally, both sources agree that afterwards, Antigonus sent Demetrius a letter delivering the news of his royal status, along with an actual diadem. Yet, we cannot reconcile the difference in agency in the take-up of the diadem, nor the place of this take-up in the order of events. Diodorus writes that Antigonus took the diadem himself and called himself king, and we can speculate that a public acclamation followed. However, Plutarch writes that Antigonus was proclaimed king by Aristodemus, the army agreed this publicly, and then his *philoi* crowned him.

On balance, I would contend that the staging of Antigonus' accession makes far more sense if we discount the king-making agency of the *philoi*, strip out Aristodemus' theatrics (which are potentially historical, but do not substantively alter the reconstruction), and piece together the event as follows:

1. Antigonus learns of the victory at Salamis;
2. Antigonus takes the diadem himself, and the royal title;
3. Antigonus receives a public, military acclamation;
4. Antigonus sends Demetrius a diadem and notification of his royal title.

This is certainly more plausible than the notion that Antigonus' Macedonian armies convened as an assembly and elected the two kings.[46] I also find it more convincing than the curiously defensive argument that Antigonus was striving to avoid the appearance of being a usurper, and so allowed his *philoi* and army to appoint him to the kingship and give him a diadem,[47] especially given that Salamis had broken a military as well as ideological deadlock and the magnitude of that victory – and by extension Antigonus' (and Demetrius') power and standing – were being celebrated with no shyness about perceptions. Moreover, my proposed model agrees with Strootman's reconstruction of Hellenistic royal inauguration, inasmuch as the new king took the diadem before appearing in public, but it does require taking Plutarch's account as inaccurate.[48]

Disregarding Plutarch's theatrical staging – without necessarily rejecting it – also minimizes the biographer's evident moralizing agenda of ascribing world-changing agency to Aristodemus (whom he calls πρωτεύοντα κολακείᾳ τῶν αὐλικῶν ἁπάντων, 'first in flattery of all the courtiers'), and to a lesser extent to all royal sycophants. Plutarch ends his account of the accession, and the changes this wrought in the demeanours of the new kings, including their transformation into 'tragic actors', by declaring: 'so powerful was the voice of single flatterer (τοσοῦτον ἴσχυσε κόλακος φωνὴ μία), and with such great change did it fill the whole inhabited world'.[49] In other words, Plutarch was interested to explicitly give Aristodemus and other such *kolakes* (flatterers, parasites) at the royal court substantial agency, so that their deleterious influence could be critiqued. This is almost a re-envisioning of the 'bad advisor' trope that sets flatterers (bad friends) in opposition to philosophers (good friends).[50] For Plutarch, indeed, flatterers attached to rulers were far more dangerous than those attached to private individuals, because their corrupting influence and friendship had the capacity to negatively impact on the wider communities controlled by rulers.[51] Hence, Plutarch points to how Aristodemus' theatrics have a negative and corrosive influence on Antigonus' and Demetrius' kingships, but more broadly on the culture and practice of Hellenistic kingship. For that critique to work, Hellenistic kingship needs to be inaugurated by the conspicuous stratagem of a *kolax*.

There is an essential point of distinction between Diodorus' and Plutarch's account, namely the qualitative difference between coronation and self-coronation and its attached consequences for interpreting political agency, which will be explored more fully in section 2. Returning to the pertinent issue of the diadem, the band was assumed immediately at the point of claiming *basileia*, which itself was claimed after momentous military victory. This is more specific than the generally accepted truth that military activity underpinned and legitimated the Hellenistic kingships.[52] As an extension, the diadem may be taken as an inherently agonistic symbol, signifying not just kingship but proven superiority over rivals.[53] Furthermore, although news of victory over his rival at Salamis provided the prestige crucial for Antigonus' declaration of royalty, it was the representational framing through the symbol of the diadem that gave external form to the status of *basileus*. In other words, the diadem visually communicated and confirmed the new and intangible royal title, and hence the diadem, from being a simple piece of cloth, became an extraordinary signifier of status, distinguishing Antigonus' transformation from dynast into king.

Demetrius was sent a diadem by his father in a letter addressing him as *basileus*, in reference to but also as a reward for the victory which Demetrius had engineered. Antigonus, while still vital, was already in his mid or late seventies.[54] Thus conferring diadem and kingship on Demetrius constituted Antigonus' attempt to create dynastic stability by identifying an heir.[55] Demetrius' receipt, not active take-up, of a diadem also showcases the differing agency of the heir, as is explored further in section 2, and it seems likely in that context that Antigonus' creation of his son's royal title was a performative act that showcased his own total and superior *basileia*. Further, within a few months of Salamis, Antigonus buried his recently deceased son Philip with royal honours at Antigonia on the Orontes:[56] as soon as he assumed royalty, Antigonus' family, and specifically his sons, became royal by extension. Antigonus' declaration of kingship was an immediate and total measure, transforming his entire family into royalty. Hence, while Antigonus took the diadem and title of *basileus* to illustrate the strength of his position and communicate the power that he possessed,[57] in the process it transformed him and the political reality around him.

This transformative effect, indeed, spread throughout the rest of the post-Alexander imperial system. Diodorus records:[58]

> And Ptolemy, not dispirited by the defeat, in equal measure took the diadem himself, and towards everyone signed himself as king (ἀνέλαβε τὸ διάδημα καὶ πρὸς ἅπαντας ἀνέγραφεν ἑαυτὸν βασιλέα). In rough equivalence with these, the remaining dynasts rivalrously proclaimed themselves as kings (οἱ λοιποὶ δυνάσται ζηλοτυπήσαντες ἀνηγόρευον ἑαυτοὺς βασιλεῖς): Seleucus, who had recently added the Upper Satrapies to his acquisitions, and also Lysimachus and Cassander, who were carefully maintaining the allotments they had been granted originally.
>
> Diodorus XX 53.3–4

This is a replication not just of the action of claiming kingship, but also its staging and representation. Antigonus' rivals imitated his example for framing for their own accessions, and in time it became a paradigmatic component of Hellenistic royal practice. It is, then, as a result of Antigonus' accession, and equally of his rivals' emulous replication of its staging, that the mechanism of assuming a diadem became cemented as a declaration of kingship. Taken together, this series of interdependent accessions entrenched the diadem itself as the definitive identifying symbol of royal status, the identifier par excellence of Hellenistic kingship, and established a lasting model for claiming kingly power and authority.

Although Diodorus and our other sources suggest that the remaining major dynasts declared their kingships in response to Antigonus so as not to lose face, scholars have also argued that other significant military events underpinned these declarations.[59] Military victory over a great rival was certainly the primary catalyst behind the sequence of accessions and assumptions of the diadem in the first instance, but military success was not the only thing that underscored the existence of the new Hellenistic kingships nor was it strictly needed prior to each accession in the sequence.[60] Here, we should remember, as we have established at length in Chapter 1, that the competitive nature of the early post-Alexander world created its own powerful reasons for imitation and parallelism, and that the evolving discourse of Hellenistic kingship was heavily premised on reciprocity and mutuality. In other words, once the title of *basileus* and the symbol of the diadem had been taken by Antigonus, as well as by Demetrius, to represent their superiority of power and status, they were subject to imitation in furtherance of the ideological conflicts of the *diadochoi*: the military victory that Antigonus and Demetrius had achieved prior to their innovation was not needed to support the imitation.

In terms of the sequence, Gruen has influentially argued that Ptolemy became *basileus* in early 304, after successfully aiding the Rhodians during Demetrius' siege of their city and in concert with the divine honours attributed to him by them as reward for his aid; Seleucus in 305/304, after reclaiming the Upper Satrapies; Lysimachus at some point in 304; and Cassander at some point around 303/302.[61] In my view, this elongates the chronology too far, contrary to the interconnected series of accessions that is clearly emphasized in all our extant literary sources. For Ptolemy's accession in particular, although there is a weight of scholarship that agrees with a date of 304, late 306 is potentially more plausible – after Demetrius' victory at Salamis yet before the onset of his famous siege of Rhodes in 305, thus in the context of having repulsed Antigonus' and Demetrius' invasion of Egypt by November 306.[62] There is conflicting evidence in all this, as with almost any key event in early Hellenistic history, but arguments for a date of 304, based primarily on Egyptian chronographic evidence,[63] neglect the fact that a declaration of *basileia* – kingship writ large on the international scene – was not necessarily coincidental with and synonymous with local recognition of pharaonic office in Egypt, with integration into local administrative systems and documentation after the appropriate rituals had been undertaken.[64] On this point, there is an analogy with the various recognitions of regal or quasi-regal authority from different local systems – for instance, in cuneiform documentary records from Babylonia – which predated 306 yet did not have substantive impact on international relationships and self-constructions.[65] *Basileia*, and its performance and symbolism, was the international brand of kingship in the early Hellenistic world.

The important issue to emphasize is the competitive rivalry that stimulated the sequence of accessions. In the case of diadem and *basileia*, we see the importance of these rivalrous interactions: the development of new imagery and ideology was based on competitive dynamics, and the persistence – indeed, intensification – of a competitive environment continued to stimulate new modes of representation and attempts to develop individualistic modes of performing power and status. In other words, the diadochan accessions illustrate how a competitive and mutually influential framework of ideology, imagery and symbolic action developed in this period and was central to the evolution of the Hellenistic model of kingship internationally. In all this, we have no reason to disbelieve the common imputation in the sources about Ptolemy and the other *diadochoi* declaring their kingships and taking the diadem so as not to lose face,[66] or in other words to remain competitive in the evolving international trends of royal power and status. These kinds of dynamics are instantiated in the Year of the Kings, but as has been explored in Chapter 1, they also explain the build-up to 306 and continue to characterize the developing ideological discourse of Hellenistic kingship well afterwards.

Diodorus' authorial input here is particularly helpful here, in his periphrastic use of the emotion ζηλοτυπία to explain the diadochan accessions subsequent to Antigonus' (οἱ λοιποὶ δυνάσται <u>ζηλοτυπήσαντες</u> ἀνηγόρευον ἑαυτοὺς βασιλεῖς, 'the remaining dynasts, *feeling rivalrous*, proclaimed themselves kings'). Here, ζηλοτυπία probably means a form of 'jealousy' targeted at others who have possession of a person or thing (whether a real or an abstract thing) which the person struck by ζηλοτυπία does not currently possess.[67] It conveys a form of emulative rivalry, as the derivation from ζῆλος would suggest,[68] or even invidious contention.[69] In this respect, it is a strikingly appropriate choice of word, exposing not just the competitive desire to possess something held by a rival but also the strategy of emulation that was used to obtain it subsequently.

Looking in the wider context of Diodorus' *Bibliotheke*, the imputation of ζηλοτυπία can be read as a negative interpretation of the actions of the Successors. In all of the other seven uses of the term (whether verbal or nominal) in the *Bibliotheke*, it conveys negative force. Thus five times it refers to romantic or sexual jealousy stimulating the intention or enactment of retribution against children.[70] Once, also in the period of the Successors, it leads to political betrayal, namely Telesphorus' betrayal of Antigonus on account of his jealousy of the latter's nephew Ptolemaeus.[71] The most telling articulation of this negativity, however, is in the praise of the Roman political culture in the fragmentary book XXXI:

> Hence it is that among the Romans the most distinguished men are to be seen vying with one another for glory (τοὺς ἐπιφανεστάτους ἄνδρας ὑπὲρ δόξης ἁμιλλωμένους), and it is by their efforts that virtually all matters of chief moment to the people are brought to a successful issue. In other states men are jealous of one another (ἐν μὲν γὰρ τοῖς ἄλλοις πολιτεύμασι ζηλοτυποῦσιν ἀλλήλους), but

the Romans praise their fellow citizens. The result is that the Romans, by rivalling one another in promotion of the common weal, achieve the most glorious successes, while other men, striving for an undeserved fame and thwarting one another's projects, inflict damage upon their countries.

Diodorus Siculus XXXI 6, trans. Walton

Diodorus creates an antithesis between ζηλοτυπία and ἅμιλλα ('competition' or 'strife' for superiority), both represented here in their verbal forms. The distinction operates on the differing respective outcomes of the emotions' manifestations: ζηλοτυπία leads to negative and destructive deterioration in all instances adduced above, while ἅμιλλα to positive and constructive improvement, as is also evident from use of ἅμιλλα in other areas of the *Bibliotheke*.[72] These are all instances of competition, and the negativity or positivity that results is reinforced by Diodorus' particular linguistic choices, linked to emotional states, which attempt to impose on the reader a value judgement. The *diadochoi*, in Diodorus' construction, were following a *zelotypic* model in emulating Antigonus' take-up of diadem and *basileia*, which we can divest of its negative connotations even while retaining the useful insight about the stimulative power of rivalry. In this case, Diodorus' analysis is complementary with our modern toolkits, and we are able to perceive a kind of isomorphism stemming from competitive rivalry.

2. The politics of (self-)coronation

Antigonus' action after Salamis was innovative, and the other Successsors' competitive imitation reified a new paradigm for taking *basileia*. This set the diadem's symbolism for the rest of the Hellenistic era: it became a metonym for kingship, and hence taking a diadem came to signify taking *basileia*. It is easy to forget that there was no such formula or reflex pre-existing the accession of Antigonus – not even for Alexander, as will be established in section 3, below. There was no coronational model that he could simply follow. This representational route was thus not a predetermined one, nor did it have a clear, discrete tradition, but was instead devised *for* Antigonus' moment of accession as a means of performing and representing his *basileia* that was symbolically explicable to its audiences. Moreover, as the diadem's use at the Lupercalia of 44 reminds us, context, usage and staging *matter*, and so it is worth scrutinizing dynamics of the coronational procedure.

Despite arguments to the contrary,[73] the Hellenistic royal diadem is functionally analogous to a crown, and hence taking a diadem is a form of coronation. Certainly, Antigonus' take-up of the diadem is a simple, time-limited coronation that lacks the more expansive formulary and ceremony present in coronation rituals in other societies and time periods.[74] But it is nonetheless an act of 'putting the crown on the king's head',[75] to define the act of coronation in its most basic terms, and with other coronations in world history it belongs to an essential common category of 'symbolic and ritual acts that served both to legitimate and to present monarchical rule'.[76] Technically, 'coronation' is terminologically obstructive, since it stresses the particular act of laying a crown,[77] when in fact accession scenes were more diverse than this single act, and indeed accessions themselves were merely 'parts of a whole world of symbolic action, gesture, and behavior' that sustained the construction of royalty;[78] yet it remains a helpful shorthand for describing the act of tying a diadem around a new king's head. We may even go further and suggest that tying the diadem is, like a coronation, a ritual act, in that it effects a transformation of the recipient into an elevated state.[79]

More specifically, since Diodorus' account of Antigonus' take-up of the diadem is preferable to Plutarch's, we are dealing with a case of *self*-coronation. In historical studies of Christian societies, often self-coronation has been considered a transgressive act for violating the theological prerogative of the priest, who mediates between divine power and secular authority.[80] Aurell's recent important study, however, demonstrates that there is a long history of self-coronation from antiquity into modernity, and even that Napoleon's famous self-coronation in 1804 was not as transgressive as has been popularly imagined.[81] In fact, there are many agents of enthronement and coronation in history, or more precisely there are different types of figures involved in the transforming a person into a king in different societies.[82] The determination of the figure who crowns the king – literally, who puts a crown on his head – is not an accidental or trivial decision,[83] but rather speaks to contingent dynamics of power and expresses implicit theorization on how absolute authority should be mediated. Self-coronations in particular are 'usually conceived by the kings and their advisors in order to expand their legitimacy and strengthen their power, so that kings controlled most a ceremony which was directed precisely to avoid other mediations'.[84] Further, self-coronation has a dramatic dimension inherent in the gesture, which increases its effectiveness in achieving its intended outcome.[85]

So, if in medieval European contexts self-coronations were intended 'to emphasise [royal rulers'] authority as well as their autonomy in temporal matters over the sacred hierarchy',[86] on what were they premised in the post-Alexander world? It is most plausible to think that Antigonus' act of tying a diadem around his head and taking the royal title were similarly intentioned in general terms, to emphasize unfettered authority and an independence of previous orders of authority,[87] but also as a specific declarative step to break the interregnum and make a universalistic claim to the entirety of the Macedonian empire.[88] It is no coincidence that this staged ritual of royal transformation occurred in a context of deep instability: the self-coronation served an important symbolic purpose in projecting a stabilization of and power over the fluctuating world around the new king.[89] In other words, the self-coronation emphasized and activated Antigonus' agency, and via this ritual of self-transformation he manipulated the reality around him:[90] *his* action and intention were decisive in unfolding a new social and political order.[91] Thus the form of the ritual (self-coronation, Antigonus tying the diadem around his own head) matched the content (the message of unrivalled superiority on the back of military victory) in a way that was perfectly aligned to context (interregnal deadlock, in a conflictual, competitive, intertwined interstate system).

The other striking detail about Antigonus' self-coronation is that immediately afterwards he sent Demetrius a diadem, making him *basileus* alongside him, partner in a single *basileia* but also designated successor to Antigonus' kingdom.[92] In Graeco-Macedonian history, there had never before been an example of a father–son diarchic rulership.[93] There were pragmatic concerns behind the step that have already been highlighted, but as to why the royal title was used to solve these is something of a puzzle. Partly, the solution must lie in acknowledging this as a performative act in its own right: Antigonus created the position of *basileus* for another, thus de facto he possessed his own *basileia*, and indeed a superior *basileia*. There is perhaps an analogy here with the Achaemenid understanding of the 'Great King' (in Greek, *basileus megas*; or even 'King of Kings', *basileus basileôn*), namely not the only king but the most powerful one and the world's imperial overlord.[94] Indeed, in terms of dynamics, creating another *basileus* is relatable to the agency of the self-coronation: both establish the unsurpassed, unmediated authority of Antigonus.

Equally, receiving a diadem – *being coronated* – was qualitatively different from taking a diadem – *self-coronating*. There is clearly a differential power dynamic here, with Demetrius subordinate to his father, receiving orders from him and carrying out military and political assignments, even if there was theoretically no qualification of lesser status in the grant of title.[95] There is also a distinction in agency, with the one who receives a diadem having their authority mediated by, and dependent on, the one who grants it. This difference in agency thus presupposes and in turn formalizes a functional disparity in power. This seems to remain the case throughout the Hellenistic period. There is a good example from the career of the Seleucid king Diodotus II Tryphon (r. 142–138), a general who seized power for himself yet nominally was regent for the boy-king Antiochus VI, whom Tryphon installed in opposition to Demetrius II. As Josephus tells us:

> On his return from Arabia to Syria with the child Antiochus, who was a young boy at this time, he [Diodotus] placed the diadem around his [Antiochus'] head (περιτίθησιν αὐτῷ τὸ διάδημα).
>
> Josephus *Jewish Antiquities* XIII 144

The dynamics of agency here in the take-up of the diadem align with the disparity in power relations: Diodotus, the power behind the throne, grants Antiochus, the puppet-king, the symbol of kingship and thus the kingship itself. Relatedly, when he eventually took the throne for himself in 141, Tryphon gave himself the appellation *Autokrator* in his numismatic self-presentation – thus was styled as a 'self-empowered' king – and even abandoned the century-and-a-half-old Seleucid era in public records in preference for his own individual regnal count.[96] The argument that has sometimes been made, that taking a diadem for oneself was a mark of the usurper, is not convincing, and it ignores the fact that *all* royal authority and status in the Hellenistic world was initially usurpatory.[97] Most importantly, this conflation with usurpation ignores the fact that self-coronation showcased individual agency, and hence was a fundamental political statement that had wide ramifications.

As well as ceremonially communicating differential power dynamics and agencies, the diadem played a key function in identifying the heir to the throne, thus marking out a successor. Demetrius was probably granted the royal title and diadem for the purpose of ensuring and presenting an image of stability for the future; as Wheatley and Dunn note, since Demetrius' own son Antigonus Gonatas was roughly thirteen years old in 306, this meant that there were three generations of Antigonids in place,[98] a veritable promise for a stable succession. More than this, the diadem was used to ritualize a distinction between accession and succession, between self-coronation and coronation, in that receipt of a diadem entailed incarnating an existing order of authority, mediated by the previous king, not establishing a new one. Thus, similarly, Ptolemy is described by Diodorus as taking a diadem for himself, self-coronating and thus establishing a new *basileia* in response to Antigonus, while his son Ptolemy II Philadelphus is described, in the context of being selected as heir to the kingship by his father, as receiving a diadem.[99] Like for Antigonus and Demetrius in 306, joint kingship was instituted for Ptolemy and Philadelphus for the years 285–282,[100] and so the diadem was probably likewise used to invest Philadelphus as (joint) *basileus*. Since Seleucus took up his own diadem, and since he, too, directly appointed his son, Antiochus, as joint king (by 294 at latest),[101] we may presume that assuming joint kingship and succession in the Seleucid royal house were ritualized via the diadem in the same fashion.

It is a reflection of its nature as the defining symbol of kingship that different orders of authority were typified through the diadem. Two further examples can be mentioned that support the model. In the first case, Ptolemy Ceraunus, eldest son of Ptolemy I who had been expelled from the succession in favour of his younger brother Ptolemy Philadelphus, assassinated Seleucus in August or September of 281 and attempted to create his own kingdom by carving out a power base centred in Thrace and Macedonia.[102] Our sources describe him as actively taking up the diadem,[103] thus creating a *basileia* without mediation by another's authority in a repetition of the dynamics of 306.[104] In fact, Ceraunus soon after granted his sibling-wife Arsinoe (II) a diadem, too, before an assembled army, thus performing his superior status and acknowledging her significance in his construction of royal stability.[105] In the second case, Diodorus tells us that Lysimachus took his own diadem in response to Antigonus, thus activating his agency. Yet later in time, Diodorus records that Lysimachus was captured by the Thracian warlord Dromichaetes, and in a constructed speech Lysimachus proclaims his regret to Dromichaetes for invading his territory and agrees to return any lands he has seized in the course of the invasion.[106] This is thus a military failure, bad enough for any Hellenistic *basileus*, but more damningly Dromichaetes gives Lysimachus a diadem on releasing him from capture.[107] The diadem, taken by the other *diadochoi* through active agency, is here is used to signify Lysimachus' functional inferiority to Dromichaetes, even dependence, in the aftermath of a military defeat.

3. A history of Alexander *diadumenos*

If this man is finer because his head had a diadem tied around it (εἰ δέ ἐστι καλλίων οὑτοσί, διότι διαδήματι τὴν κεφαλὴν διεδέδετο): perhaps these are majestic things for the Macedonians, but he should not for this reason be held up as better than a noble and strategic military man who utilized his judgement more than his fortune.

Lucian *Dialogues of the Dead* XII 3

So Hannibal, in Lucian's parodical afterlife of notable figures squabbling about perceptions of their eminence, argues to the judge Minos about Alexander the Great. Lucian is satirizing the post-Alexander tradition of debates around who is the best general (which often feature Hannibal),[108] as well as the wide industry of ancient works seeking to explain the reasons for Alexander's extraordinarily successful career. Yet he also captures the distinguishing power of the symbol of the diadem, and the extent to which it is attached to, perhaps even subsumed in, the figure of Alexander in his posthumous reception. The origin of this link between Alexander and the diadem is in the generation after his death, in the same time period as his Successors are creating their own independent positions and are increasingly using posthumous constructions of the figure of Alexander to develop their own legitimacy and ideological appeal. It is also, as we have seen above, the period in which the *diadochoi* themselves take up the symbol of the diadem and use it to distinguish their superiority and demarcate their royal authority and status.

There are accounts which suggest that Alexander wore a diadem in his own lifetime. These are imprecise and at times contradictory, but the available evidence places his take-up of the diadem at some point in 330, within a year of defeating Darius at the battle of Gaugamela and shortly after the latter's death in July 330.[109] However, there is no clear indication of what significance his wearing of the diadem had, as there are but few accounts which connect the diadem specifically to Alexander, and the majority of these are sensationalized tales with death omens and other harbingers of future events.[110] Other accounts are highly stylized, such as in speeches composed by the secondary authors, and so probably are invented or exaggerated in themselves and do not reflect the diadem's contemporary significance in Alexander's lifetime.[111] Furthermore, there is no material evidence to suggest that Alexander was ever depicted in his lifetime as wearing the diadem;[112] notably, the only two instances in which Alexander's image was potentially depicted on his own coinage do not include a diadem.[113] On the balance of the evidence, or the lack of it, I would argue that the diadem was not the principal signifier or symbol of Alexander's kingship. However, as Lucian intimates through his instantiation of a longer tradition, Alexander was in fact portrayed or constructed with a diadem after his death, in the development of a wide series of imagery and stories by the Successors,[114] and so it is likely that the deep connection between Alexander and the diadem symbol was forged posthumously by the *diadochoi* rather than by Alexander himself in his own lifetime.

Two figures in the era of the Successors evoked an image of Alexander and diadem by means of establishing his regalia on an empty throne before an audience of Macedonian soldiers, who were particularly sensitive to Alexander's memory and manipulable on that account.[115] Perdiccas used this stratagem at Babylon in June 323, in the aftermath of Alexander's death, and Eumenes used it in Cyinda in summer 318 and in Susiana in spring 317.[116] We have no convincing reason to dispute the historicity of these events.[117] It is also likely that Eumenes imitated his former master Perdiccas in this invocation. In both cases, an empty throne was unveiled, on which were placed items connected with Alexander: his arms, robes, ring and diadem in the Curtian account concerning Perdiccas;[118] his arms, sceptre and diadem in the Diodoran account concerning Eumenes.[119]

In each instance the regalia of Alexander were used to construct a symbolic connection between the diadoch (Perdiccas or Eumenes), on the one hand, and the dead Alexander, on the other. A sense of Alexander's posthumous, supernatural sponsorship is implied. In the Eumenes episode, in fact, Alexander's divinity is performatively accepted, in that the Macedonian soldiers, overawed by the invisible appearance of their late king, undertook *proskynesis* to Alexander,[120] which had been rejected in his lifetime.[121] A similar awe must be imagined for figures present at the Perdiccas episode in Babylon,[122] and in both cases there is an implicit theological link.[123] Both instances also arrogate a superior eminence to Perdiccas and Eumenes as intercessors, hinging on their ability to mediate between the late Alexander and the mass of officers and soldiers under their command. Indeed, each figure staging the scene was at that time struggling to assert his authority over other commanders and soldiers who wanted to follow different paths of action or even different leaders.[124]

The presence of the diadem as but one among many items on the throne indicates an as yet unfixed meaning for the diadem as the principal symbol of royal power, and we cannot use either case to suggest that Alexander had a specific conception of it. Perhaps the diadem's inclusion here with other regalia was for expedient purposes, to evoke a complete image of the late Alexander that included all potential regalia connected to him.[125] More extremely, one could speculate that our source traditions filled their stories with Alexander's reputed regalia, on the simple basis that a later writer habituated to the symbols of Hellenistic kingship or later depictions of Alexander might expect to see them these junctures. Nevertheless, these episodes probably played a role in the trend, started by the *diadochoi*, of creating an image of Alexander with a diadem and exploiting the power of this image for political purposes.

Arrian is silent about a diadem when he narrates the portent of an unknown figure, perhaps a slave, sitting on Alexander's throne, after which Alexander orders his torture to determine a possible conspiracy.[126] Diodorus and Plutarch, who tell variations of the same story, record that this man had assumed

Alexander's diadem and robes before ascending his throne and then was executed on the advice of Alexander's *manteis* ('seers', interpreters of omens).[127] All three sources place this account in the context of other omens boding imminent death for Alexander.[128] Particularly on the basis of the detail in Diodorus and Plutarch that Alexander had the man put to death, Bottéro concludes that Alexander was enacting here a Near Eastern 'substitute king' ritual, whereby Alexander attempted to deflect the omens of his death by putting somebody else in the position of king and then tricking fate into inflicting death on the substitute.[129] This is possible, but on balance there is no strong reason here to believe that the diadem was present at this scene, if indeed the account is historical at all; and we may note that the throne is again a magnetic *locus* of royal symbols that has attracted the diadem.

Two further anecdotes, which circulated in the Hellenistic world and were probably spread by their diadochan protagonists, hark back to Alexander's campaigns and describe other transferrals of his diadem, once to Seleucus and once to Lysimachus.[130] In terms of the narrative of Alexander's campaigns, the story involving Lysimachus is the earlier of the two, but it is very likely that both of these episodes were fabricated after their own accessions to kingship in 306–304.[131] The importance of the stories concerning Seleucus and Lysimachus was that the temporary wearing of Alexander's diadem portended future kingship:[132] the contact of the diadem with their head was not just premonitory but also transformative, hence ritualistic in nature.

In the Seleucus incident, Alexander's diadem is described as falling off his head, along with his *kausia*, and landing on a reed next to an Assyrian royal tomb while Alexander was sailing in the Babylonian marshes; Arrian then records that different reports say it was either an unknown sailor or Seleucus that swam to retrieve the diadem and carried it back on his head.[133] Clearly, we see Seleucus' insertion into the source tradition here,[134] and the meaning of that insertion is spelled out by Arrian: the retrieval of the diadem, temporarily wearing it on his head, signified (σημῆναι) that Seleucus would have a great *basileia*.[135] This is thus an omen, situated in broader sets of omens about Alexander's demise, signalling the transition of diadem and kingship from Alexander to Seleucus; it is also potentially part of a wider 'Seleucus legend', a complex of episodes within a discrete tradition telling the story of Seleucus' extraordinary rise to power.[136] This narrative speaks of a personal transferral of power to Seleucus and his rejuvenation of Alexander's *basileia*, so aligns with the universalistic implications of the accessions of 306–304. Further, as we have explored above with reference to the act of self-coronation, in this tale Seleucus is clearly activating his own agency, in that he takes the diadem and puts it on his own head, recalling the accessions of 306–304. At the same time the link to Alexander's kingship (and indeed Alexander's head) is suggestive, and Alexander is thus implicitly the mediator of Seleucus' coronation.

In the Lysimachus anecdote, Justin records that Alexander accidentally wounded Lysimachus' head with his spear while jumping from a horse, causing copious bleeding; in response, Alexander bound Lysimachus' head-wound with his own diadem.[137] Like for Seleucus, a portent of future kingship is explicitly indicated: indeed, it is merely the 'first sign' (*auspicium primum*) of Lysimachus' future kingship.[138] Indeed, in Appian's variant of the account, Alexander's own *mantis* Aristander predicts Lysimachus' future kingship on account of this incident.[139] Like the Seleucus tale, this story reinforces an image of a diademed Alexander for the purpose of strengthening a diadoch's image in the context of his kingship: Lysimachus' contemporary diadem would recall Alexander's symbolic transferral. In terms of agency, there is a distinction from the self-coronational model, in that Lysimachus is narrated as the recipient of Alexander's diadem. Alexander, in effect, coronates Lysimachus, and thus is the mediator of his investiture as king; Lysimachus, in light of the differing agency in accession and succession discussed above, is marked out as Alexander's direct successor by Alexander himself.

There was a wider trend of putting a diadem on Alexander's head in the numismatic iconography of the Successors.[140] This is particularly in new coin-types devised by Ptolemy and Lysimachus, where a portrait of Alexander includes a diadem alongside other symbols (Figures 6, 9). On the other hand, the other four *basileis* did not mint images of Alexander with a diadem: Antigonus retained Alexander's own imperial types, developing none of his own numismatic imagery;[141] Seleucus presided over a vast array of coin-types, but none featuring a diademed Alexander;[142] Cassander retained traditional Macedonian types common to Philip II and Alexander, except for some new bronze types, which did not feature Alexander with a diadem;[143] and Demetrius, after the death of Antigonus in 301, kept a few of Alexander's types but generally began to put his own diademed image on coins, in connection with highly specialized iconography linked to his own career.[144]

Alexander's appearance on coinage, even posthumous, was a departure from his own practices and from Graeco-Macedonian norms of numismatic iconography in general.[145] Alexander used the royal legend on some his coins from *c.* 324 onwards, beginning in the Babylon mint, though not all issues subsequently bore it.[146] With two possible exceptions,[147] Alexander never depicted himself on coins he issued, preferring standardized types empire-wide which bore his mythological sponsors: Athena, Heracles, Zeus and Nike.[148]

Similarly, while it became commonplace in the Hellenistic world, in previous Greek coinages placing an image of a ruler, or indeed any person, on a coin was almost without precedent; generally, images of persons on coinage were previously restricted to allegorized portraits or depictions of deities.[149] This is what makes the appearance of Alexander on diadochan coinages so striking.

As discussed in Chapter 3, the first series of coinage to depict an obverse Alexander portrait was issued by Ptolemy in Egypt after defeating Perdiccas' invasion of 320, three years after Alexander's death. In point of fact, Ptolemy was the only diadoch prior to the battle of Salamis to issue coins explicitly depicting Alexander at all. This new type, as we have discussed, bore a dramatic portrait of Alexander wearing an elephant-scalp headdress, in replacement of Heracles in his lion-scalp, alongside a ram's horn symbolizing the god Ammon, an *aegis* tied with snakes, and a headband that I would identify as a diadem (see Figure 6).[150] Modern arguments which maintain that it is not a diadem are based on the exact positioning of the headband: that it appears here without ties at the back and is bound across the hairline, as opposed to above, may indicate that it is not a diadem but a *mitra*, the cultic headband of Dionysus.[151] However, very simply we cannot see the ties at the back because the elephant-scalp obscures them. Indeed, bronze issues of early Ptolemaic coinage from *c.* 312 depict a portrait of Alexander (absent the elephant-scalp and *aegis*) with a diadem wrapped *across* Alexander's hairline, with ties clearly visible at the back (Figure 12),[152] as do Ptolemy's own later portrait-issues show a diadem *across* his hairline (Figure 8).[153]

In the development of a portrait of diademed Ptolemy alongside diademed Alexander, there is a iconographical narrative of royal succession that aligns with the diadem tales involving Seleucus and Lysimachus. Indeed, like in these stories, Ptolemy's portrait is introduced some time after the fact of his accession, and thus after the fact of his diadem.[154] Further, Ptolemy's new iconography was incredibly influential among the Successors. Seleucus introduced a gold series with an obverse type of Alexander wearing an elephant-scalp in *c.* 300–298,[155] which is clearly based on the Ptolemaic elephant-scalp types (Figure 13).[156]

However, Seleucus makes this coin issue his own, with a reverse-type of winged Nike *stephanophoros*, and the distinctive elements of Ptolemy's obverse-type – the diadem, ram's horn of Ammon and *aegis* – removed.[157] This selective appropriation of Ptolemaic imagery is consistent with Seleucus attempting to imitate Ptolemy's ideology but divest it of its particularity and transfer to his own ideological context, in which elephants played a significant role. Agathocles of Syracuse also adopted the elephant-scalp image, potentially in connection with his African expeditions of 310–307/306.[158]

Figure 12 Bronze hemiobol of Ptolemy, c. 312. Staatliche Museen zu Berlin, Münzkabinett 18214374 / Reinhard Saczewski. [CC PDM 1.0].

In another clear imitation of Ptolemy's types, Lysimachus introduced his famous portrait of Alexander bearing the horns of Ammon and diadem on a number of his obverse-types from c. 300–297 onwards (Figure 14).[159] This introduction corresponded with significant events: with the defeat of Antigonus and Demetrius at Ipsus in 301, Lysimachus now had claim to various lands in Asia Minor as part of a settlement between himself, Seleucus and Cassander.[160] Like Seleucus, Lysimachus personalized his imitation through new iconographical designs on the reverse-types. Most commonly, the reverses featured a seated Athena *nikephoros*, with the miniature figure of Nike in the process of wreathing the lambda of Lysimachos' name on the royal legend: an unmistakable and unsubtle symbolic message. In this image, Athena is also seated, with her spear resting idly at her side, almost communicating an Athena *promachos* at rest.

Demetrius adapted the horns of Ammon into the horns of Poseidon, a distinctive feature which he placed on his own obverse portrait along with a diadem and which is mirrored by the leaning Poseidon on the reverse (Figure 15).[161] The reverse-type of a leaning Poseidon is a development from Demetrius' reverse-types which commemorated his naval victory at Salamis, namely Poseidon in *promachos* pose.[162] This leaning Poseidon then metamorphoses into a seated Poseidon in subsequent reverse types.[163] We can see similarities with the Lysimachean image of a god at rest, but with Demetrius there is more of a marked progression: from Poseidon *promachos* at war, to Poseidon leaning on a rock, remaining ready for war, to seated Poseidon, in calm repose and ruling

Figure 13 Gold double-daric of Seleucus, *c.* 300–298. Staatliche Museen zu Berlin, Münzkabinett 18200205 / Lutz-Jürgen Lübke (Lübke und Wiedemann). [CC PDM 1.0].

Figure 14 Silver tetradrachm of Lysimachus, *c.* 297–282/281. Staatliche Museen zu Berlin, Münzkabinett / Lutz-Jürgen Lübke (Lübke und Wiedemann). [CC PDM 1.0].

after war. Notably, the diadem is present on the last two of these, thus clearly signifying a state of victory won and kingship achieved.

While Seleucus borrowed aspects of Ptolemaic numismatic iconography such as the elephant-scalp Alexander portrait, he never depicted himself with a diadem on his coinages. However, after his death, his son Antiochus did introduce obverse-types featuring a portrait of Seleucus with a diadem and horns (Figure 16).[164]

Figure 15 Silver tetradrachm of Demetrius, *c.* 290/289. Staatliche Museen zu Berlin, Münzkabinett 18203027 / Dirk Sonnenwald. [CC BY-SA 4.0].

Figure 16 Silver tetradrachm of Antiochus I, *c.* 276–274. Staatliche Museen zu Berlin, Münzkabinett 18228232 / Reinhard Saczewski. [CC PDM 1.0].

Philetairus, breakaway governor of Pergamum, also introduced a posthumous portrait of Seleucus with a diadem on Pergamene obverse-types, probably in a nod to his role in securing Seleucus' corpse from Ptolemy Ceraunus and delivering it to Antiochus.[165] Antiochus' circulation of an image of Seleucus as king in the early years of his own reign was a clear consolidating strategy,[166] as were the reverse-types of these issues, which continued Seleucus' distinctive horned horse images and then introduced Antiochus' new design of Apollo on the *omphalos*.[167] More significantly, the obverse-type of diademed Seleucus did

Figure 17 Silver tetradrachm of Antiochus I, 278–261. Staatliche Museen zu Berlin, Münzkabinett 18203079 / Dirk Sonnenwald. [CC PDM 1.0].

not endure for long, as Antiochus in relatively short order introduced his own portrait featuring a diadem (Figure 17). We thus see a similar transitional pattern to that evoked by the changes in Ptolemaic imagery, an image of one diademed king being replaced by another in a clear succession of power.

This signification of power transferral and royal succession through the symbol of the diadem, as introduced by Ptolemy in his coinage from the elephant-scalp Alexander to his own royal portrait, is employed by his son Philadelphus also, though differently. Philadelphus, more than any other sons of the *diadochoi* – perhaps with the exception of Antiochus, who decided to continue an unbroken Seleucid era based on his father's takeover of Babylon in 312/311[168] – emphasized the continuity of his kingship from his father Ptolemy, and thus continued to employ coin portraits depicting Ptolemy even in his own reign.[169] At certain points, however, he did emphasize his own position via numismatic iconography, as in the notable ΘΕΩΝ ΑΔΕΛΦΩΝ issue (Figure 18).[170] In this coin series, Philadelphus and his sister-wife Arsinoe appear on the obverse with the legend ΑΔΕΛΦΩΝ ('of [the] siblings'), with their parents Ptolemy and Berenice on the reverse ΘΕΩΝ ('of [the] gods'). Notably, each of the kings (and indeed queens), past and present, wears the diadem, and so the image projects continuity and succession through this symbol, as well as through the physiological similarities. The genitive legend on each side also blurs the lines of generational authority.

Ptolemy was the trendsetter in numismatic imagery, notably the elephant-scalp headdress and horn but most prominently the diadem. Just as Antigonus

Figure 18 Gold octodrachm of Ptolemy II Philadelphus, *c.* 260–240. Staatliche Museen zu Berlin, Münzkabinett 18203062 / Dirk Sonnenwald. [CC PDM 1.0].

established a model of accession and succession through the diadem in 306, so Ptolemy's early coin-types established the modes for symbolizing these in numismatic iconography. The imaging of succession in particular is clearly premised on the posthumous currency of a diademed Alexander. Thus, when the *diadochoi* and their sons depicted themselves wearing diadems, they were implicitly referring to Alexander's exemplar, which they themselves had developed. This was a mutually reinforcing relationship: images of the *diadochoi* with diadems strengthened the image of Alexander with a diadem, and this image of a diademed Alexander in turn underscored the diadem's use by the *diadochoi*. Thus where Smith argues that the diadem was 'originally empty of meaning, [and] could take on whatever significance *Alexander* gave it',[171] I would suggest instead that it was the *diadochoi* who filled the diadem with meaning and established it is the defining symbol of *basileia* in the Hellenistic world – and indeed beyond – in support of the creation of their new kingships.

5

Spear-won Land in Hellenistic Imperial Discourse

When Alexander crossed the Hellespont, it began a new Panhellenic campaign against the Persian empire, notwithstanding the fact that a smaller Macedonian expeditionary force appointed by Philip II had been operating there since 336.[1] There was ideological fanfare in the build-up: a nine-day festival in Dium in the winter of 335/334,[2] then a touring of cult sites en route to the Hellespoint in the spring of 334,[3] and finally a sacrifice of a bull to Poseidon and the Nereids, and a libation to the sea, in the middle of the strait itself during the crossing in May 334.[4] Diodorus tells us that, to stage the crossing, Alexander broke away from the main force, which was occupied with transferring the army at the shorter crossing point of Sestus to Abydus,[5] and landed a smaller force of his own in the Troad:

> Alexander marched with his army to Hellespont and transported it from Europe to Asia. And sailing with sixty long ships towards the Trojan land, first of the Macedonians, he cast his spear from his ship, planting it into the earth, and himself leapt from the ship, showing that he received Asia from the gods as a spear-won prize (παρὰ τῶν θεῶν ἀπεφαίνετο τὴν Ἀσίαν δέχεσθαι δορίκτητον).
>
> Diodorus Siculus XVII 17.2

Afterwards, Arrian tells us, Alexander ordered the building of altars to Athena, Heracles and Zeus, at both sides of the crossing.[6] This was probably a spatializing gesture,[7] a means of demarcating and unifying Alexandrian territory, and a move to memorialize the crossing itself with active sites of memory ritualizing worship of the gods that had enabled it.[8] A celebratory visit to the site of Ilium (Troy) followed, with more sacrifices, honours and lavish grants to temples and the community.[9] Then, Alexander and his armies went to war.

Nearly a century and a half later, in 196, on the other side of the Hellespont, the Seleucid king Antiochus III (r. 222–187) was holding a conference with Roman envoys at the city of Lysimachia. Relations between the two powers had deteriorated in light of Antiochus' expansionism in the Aegean and eastern Mediterranean. The Roman concern was to address Seleucid imperial encroachment into cities and regions previously held by the Ptolemaic ruler Ptolemy V Epiphanes (r. 210–180) and the Antigonid Philip V (r. 221–179) – the former under Roman protection, the latter recently defeated by a Roman army led by T. Quinctius Flamininus – plus incursions against autonomous *poleis*.[10] They were also worried about the large Seleucid army and navy that had newly arrived in Europe. The Seleucid response, however, claimed that ancestral right trumped more recent history. Polybius records:

> [Antiochos III] said that he had crossed over to Europe with his army to reacquire (ἀνακτησόμενος) the Chersonese and the cities in Thrace, since the rule over these places belonged to him more than anyone else: for while this was originally the *dynasteia* of Lysimachus, after Seleucus waged war on him and conquered him in this war the entirety of Lysimachos' *basileia* became a spear-won prize of Seleucus (εἶναι μὲν γὰρ ἐξ ἀρχῆς τὴν δυναστείαν ταύτην Λυσιμάχου, Σελεύκου δὲ πολεμήσαντος πρὸς αὐτὸν καὶ κρατήσαντος τῷ πολέμῳ πᾶσαν τὴν Λυσιμάχου βασιλείαν δορίκτητον γενέσθαι Σελεύκου). Owing to the distractions of his ancestors over successive periods, first Ptolemy wrested away these lands and made himself master of them, and second Philip. He was not acquiring (οὐ κτᾶσθαι) them now by taking advantage of Philip's circumstances, but *re*acquiring (ἀλλ' ἀνακτᾶσθαι) them by availing himself of his rights.
>
> Polybius XVIII 51.3–6

Each side made claims with arguments rooted in principles of legitimate ownership and transference of property, and there is a certain amount of casuistry, hinging on different conceptions which principles applied and when.[11] No agreement between the two positions was reached, and Polybius tells us that Antiochus broke off the conference, unwilling to commit even to the semblance of going before a Roman tribunal.[12] Antiochus continued funnelling troops into Greece and building his influence there, and within a few years war against Rome broke out.[13]

The premise that is seemingly central to these two episodes involving Alexander and Antiochus was that lands could be claimed as δορίκτητος (henceforth *doriktētos*), namely 'spear-won' – or, more precisely, 'acquired by the spear'. In other words, a ruler could assert a right to ownership of territory based on the principle of successful military conquest, and such rights were inheritable.[14] Predominantly, scholarly work on the concept of *doriktētos chōra*, 'spear-won land', has been about the role it played in international law, or in contemporary theories of legal legitimation.[15] The essential consensus has been that *doriktētos chōra* was a verbal formulation of the legal right of conquest, on which basis the ruler 'owned' the land and had total property rights over it.[16] By extension, *doriktētos chōra* is the legal framework for the existence and development of the Hellenistic kingdoms, which were founded on the acquisition of territory by usurpers. Further, *doriktētos chōra* has been seen as a form of 'entitling and glorifying propaganda',[17] linked to ideologies of martial valour and military conquest and represented symbolically in a variety of media.[18] In sum, *doriktētos chōra* is seen as an essential feature of the Hellenistic kingdoms, sustaining the existence of the dynasties and providing a basis for their inheritance by successors. It provides the ultimate foundation for major areas of royal activity at the state level.[19]

However, there is reason to be cautious about accepting this uncritically. For the period of Alexander's Successors in particular, Mehl concludes that the claim to *doriktētos chōra* was *not* used by the *diadochoi* to justify their claims to rule over Alexander's empire, or even part of it, essentially because they did not, in fact, conquer it.[20] Indeed, as we shall see in section 2, uses of *doriktētos chōra* in the period 323–276 are significantly more oblique and symbolic than simple assertions to ownership after successful conquest. More widely, apart from the dangers of seeing royal power in too formalistic terms,[21] the juridical argument is difficult to sustain for the early post-Alexander world, as there was no such thing as codified international law at this time.[22] In fact, while right by conquest might have a long history in Greece and the Near East,[23] it is only comparatively late in the Hellenistic period that we find explicit written records publicly documenting acceptance that these claims had legal force.[24] And, as Ma convincingly notes, focusing overly on legalities downplays the politics behind them, how legal postures mask and license aggression and impositions of control – most strikingly, how 'conquest is deproblematized by being grounded in the past'.[25] In short, legalities obscure political agenda and ideology.

Finally, even a quick glance at the two scenes above shows that there is a wide difference in the application and understanding of *doriktētos chōra* between Alexander at the Hellespont in 334 and Antiochus III at Lysimachia in 196. There was a historical evolution, which tells us that we are not dealing with a static, unchanging concept; and since each articulation involved an invocation of the past, manipulation was inherent in the practice, hence we are also not dealing with a neat, linear, uncontested tradition. The ideological aspect of *doriktētos chōra* needs to be unpacked, and accordingly this chapter examines its formative development in the period of Alexander and the Successors, discussing its relationship with the creation of Hellenistic kingship and then its longer-term legacy.

1. The myth-history of *doriktētos chōra*

Diodorus is the only one of our literary sources to record the detail that Alexander claimed Asia as *doriktētos* on his landing.[26] For those scholars who have accepted the account, the action conveyed Alexander's general intention, already in 334, to subdue the whole of Asia by imperial conquest.[27] On the other hand, some have concluded that the claim was fictional, invented by Diodorus' presumed source for this part of his narrative, Cleitarchus of Alexandria,[28] or fictionalized in light of Roman fetial priests' ritualistic process for declaring war.[29] More recently, it has been argued that Diodorus' narrative conflates three separate motifs – landing on Asian soil, acquisition by spear, and receipt of territory as a gift from the gods – and that the act of throwing a spear in particular is ideologically rooted in the Achaemenid traditions of rulership, a story which was then inserted *ex post facto* into the narrative of Alexander's exploits as part of a broader Persianization of his kingship after the death of Darius III.[30] In all of this, there has been little attention paid to earlier traditions of *doriktētos chōra*. In particular, there is a Greek myth-historical tradition that has not been fully scrutinized,[31] which is worth deconstructing as it contributes materially to our understanding of the phrase.

In addition to the fact that casting a spear has echoes in discourses linked to foundation and colonization,[32] the word *doriktētos* itself appears as early as the *Iliad*, in a famous segment where Achilles speaks of his affection for his prize-captive (δουρικτητή) Briseis, who has been taken away from him by Agamemnon.[33] The same word is next used in Euripides' *Andromache*, in the 420s, where the title character is called δορίκτητος (155–7). Respectively, then, Briseis and Andromache are described by the *Iliad* poet and Euripides as 'spear-captives' of Achilles and his son Neoptolemus, and indeed there is probably a direct intertext between the two uses of the word *doriktētos*.[34] Both passages allude to a right of conquest involving seizure of the spoils, in that Briseis and Andromache were taken as prizes after the successful military activity at Troy. There might also be a sense of inheritance in Euripides: Achilles was the one to slay Andromache's husband Hector, and so the right to her has passed to his son Neoptolemus. The only other Classical usage of *doriktētos* is also in Euripides, where the chorus in *Hecuba* bemoans that the land (*chthōn*) of Troy – here a metonym for Asia – is δορίκτητος Ἀργείων, a 'spear-captive of the Argives' (475–83). Trojan earth has suffered the same fate as Briseis and Andromache: Troy itself has become a spear-won woman, a feminine person subjugated by the Hellenic spear,[35] by right of spoils after conquest. The *Hecuba* thus expands the scope of the terminology *doriktētos*, from referring to women to referring to the land itself. It is important to note that the sack of Troy is the point of reference for this development.[36]

The Euripidean reference to land as 'spear-captured', as we have seen formulated in the *Hecuba*, is anticipated by Aeschylus, in a speech of Athena in the *Eumenides* (458 BC):[37]

> [*Athena:*] From afar I heard the shout of invocation, from the Scamander, where I was taking first possession of the land, which the leaders and foremost of the Achaeans had bound to me, a great portion from the spoils which were captured by the spear (τῶν αἰχμαλώτων χρημάτων λάχος μέγα), given to me as an absolute possession for all time, an apportioned gift to the sons of Theseus.
> Aeschylus *Eumenides* 397–402

Here Athena is describing γῆ ('land') in Asia that is αἰχμάλωτος ('spear-captured').[38] The reference seems to be to the lands adjacent to the river Scamander, where the major battles in the *Iliad* were fought, since the river linked the Trojan plains with the Hellespont.[39] Indeed, Mackie has suggested that the Scamander was linked inextricably with the city of Troy itself, and Achilles' defeat of it in book XXI a harbinger of its destruction.[40] As an extension of the defeat of the city, lands along the Scamander became part of the spoils of victory. Commentators since antiquity have recognized that this passage poetically references Athenian claims to Sigeum, a town in the Troad that had been Athens' first overseas possession but then repeatedly contested.[41] Most recently to Aeschylus' play, Sigeum had been fought over by Athens in Cimon's Hellespontine campaigns of the 460s, won from the Persians, and then enrolled as a tribute-paying member of the Delian League (likely by the end of the 450s).[42] Aeschylus' allusion to it is thus clear, specific and resonant in context. However, framed as Athena's λάχος μέγα, her unqualified 'great portion', Athens' claims may be much larger and reflect aspirations to hegemony over the Greek *poleis* of Asia Minor.[43] More pertinently, Athena's grant of the territory in perpetuity to the Athenians suggested not just the rooting of a contemporary territorial claim in the mythic past – as we know, in fact, the Athenians under Pisistratus claimed Sigeum in terms of participation in the Trojan War[44] – but rather an underpinning right based on the actualization of divine support.

With Troy and the Troad, in the context of the Trojan War and its aftermath, as a recurrent *locus*, we find in the earlier tradition of *doriktētos* and its cognates themes of (i) military victory generating rights of ownership; (ii) *post factum* settlement and distribution of property among co-combatants; (iii) inter-generational inheritance; and (iv) divine guarantee/mediation for rights and inheritances. It seems highly likely that this exercised a significant influence on Alexander's claim to Asia as *doriktētos* in May 334, which was premised on taking up a divine gift after successfully landing in the Troad and sinking a spear into the Trojan land itself. Further, this is coherently situated in a broader ideological scheme of crafting an analogy between the Achaean expedition to Troy and Alexander's own Panhellenic campaign. In being the 'first among the Macedonians' to leap ashore, Alexander repeated the actions of Protesilaus, the warrior who had been the first of the Achaeans to leap ashore at Troy but had died in doing so.[45] Alexander had publicly advertised this link, and thus pre-planned the action, through a propitiatory sacrifice at the hero's tomb at Elaeus prior to crossing the Hellespont, as part of the ideological build-up to the crossing.[46] There is precedent for this type of preparatory action, namely Agesilaus of Sparta's attempted sacrifice at Aulis in his build-up to invading Asia Minor in 396: a clear reference to the sacrifice of Iphigenia that launched the Achaean expedition to Troy, and a public propitiatory act to support Spartan attempts to build wider hegemony.[47] After Alexander's crossing, the king visited Troy itself, performing conspicuous remembrances of the Trojan War. In this broader ideological context, sinking a spear into Asia soil, a symbolic domination of a feminine entity,[48] and claiming that that gods had gifted it to him as *doriktētos*, cannot help but recall the Trojan War motif inherent in the terminology.

As an ideological performance primarily, this was no straight juridical claim to ownership. Indeed, unless the landing itself should be seen a symbolic conquest in its own right, perhaps a triumph in averting the 'trauma of the intercontinental crossing',[49] then Alexander had not yet conquered anything in Asia. There is a clear political rationale for this ideological performance at this point in time, namely the continued unification of his Panhellenic forces and the winning over of Greek populations in Asia Minor.[50] For this same reason, we see Alexander's production at this time of a new type of gold coinage, bearing symbols of Athena wearing a crested Corinthian helmet – doubtless a reference to the League of Corinth – plus Nike, victory personified, holding a *stylis*, a memorial of naval victory at Salamis in the Persian Wars.[51] Quite apart from whatever personal motivation there may have been for such a programme of allusions, using the legendary analogy of successful Greek conquest in Asia, namely the sack of Troy, framed Alexander's expedition of 334 as the replaying of an all-Greek struggle.

In addition to the myth-historical background in poetic retellings of the Trojan War and its aftermath, there were closer, more pragmatic historical models for Alexander regarding the concept of *doriktētos chōra*. One is the imperialistic rationales formally used by his father Philip II to justify his conquests of areas belonging to other Greek states, such as the city of Amphipolis, originally an Athenian colony.[52] This is one case where we see how conquest is de-problematized and justified by the reference to the past – a reference that was invoked to legitimise Philip's aggression and sanitize the act of warfare against the Athenian state. Another model is the administration of conquered territory and the Macedonian king's role in its distribution, often as an incentive for soldiers in the form of land grants, for which there is epigraphic evidence that pre-dates the beginning of the Persian campaign in 334.[53] This is to say nothing at all of the systems of governance and territorial administration in the Persian empire, Asia Minor in particular.[54]

In all likelihood, what we are left with at the Hellespont in 334 is an ideological model of the mythic conquest of Troy leading to divine-backed rulership in Asia as 'spear-won land', blended with a patrimonial legacy in the form of Philip II's expansionist rationales and a developed royal *praxis* for seizing conquered territories. Above all, claiming Asia as *doriktētos* was a public act of self-definition, rooted in the prototype of Greek victory in Asia, and it should be understood primarily as an ideological stance, a symbolic means of framing the significance of his actions that was designed to appeal to key stakeholders (armies, *poleis* in Asia Minor) but also interconnect with Alexander's wider royal self-fashioning. One reading of the myth-historical model of *doriktētos chōra* might be that Alexander is framed as the inheritor of a land already won by the spear in mythic times, with a *terminus a quo* for this right rooted deep in the past,[55] and that his successful landing was proof of his divine backing. Whatever the precise reading, themes of inheritance from and replication of earlier models are strongly redolent, and these are crucial, too, in the articulation of *doriktētos chōra* by the Successors after Alexander's death.

2. Spearman son of a spearman: narratives of conquest and inheritance

The striking image of a spear sinking into Asian soil after Alexander's crossing of the Hellespont seems to have had a strong artistic impact. Although the image of the spear-bearing ruler had been common from the Homeric age onwards,[56] under Alexander a statue-type developed which expressed this conventional image on a new and dynamic scale. The Alexander *Doryphoros* type created by

Lysippus,[57] drawing on Polycleitus' famous *Doryphoros* among other earlier models, had a distinctive Achillean quality, and surviving replicas in sculpture and painting depict Alexander (often heroically nude) with a raised arm holding a spear, with the point of the spear generally facing upwards – as per the Greek tradition of spear-bearing portrait statues – but sometimes facing the earth.[58] Stewart argues that this Alexander *Doryphoros* asserted his authority over his 'spear-won' empire through its empire-wide circulation.[59] Among the generation of Successors, particularly in the area of numismatic iconography, spears are widely in evidence, to the extent that one could call them omnipresent, and these probably symbolically translate the ideology of *doriktētos chōra* and allude to Alexander's means of framing the Asian conquests in particular.[60] Smith argues that *Doryphoros* statues contributed to the spear becoming a symbol of royal power in its own right.[61]

Most strikingly, it has been argued that a wall frieze – one of a sequence of five supposedly deriving from Hellenistic court art, perhaps Antigonid – found in the Villa Boscoreale is inspired by this scene.[62] In this frieze, a female personification of Asia looks on unhappily while personified Macedonia brings her spear over the Hellespont, a narrow blue rivulet in this image, to sink it into Asian soil.[63] Whatever else one may argue of these friezes (they have been

Figure 19 Fresco from the villa of P. Fannius Synistor, Boscoreale, *c.* 40–30 BC. Wikimedia Commons / ArchaiOptix. [CC BY-SA 4.0].

variously interpreted), there can be no doubt that the image of Asia as 'spear-won land' was memorable enough to be meaningful in Roman elite culture no less than in the Hellenistic world itself. Indeed, as we have seen, *doriktētos chōra* was fundamentally an inheritable construct, conceptualized in relation to the aftermath of conquest, not the act of conquest itself, and based on a distribution of spoils after that fact – hence was inherently transferrable.

This link with the division of spoils in the wake of successful military action partly explains the take-up of the terminology of *doriktētos chōra* in the period of the *diadochoi*, the generation getting to grips with the longer-term impact of conquest and presiding over systems of rule for diverse subjects. Moreover, it seems highly probable that their use of it was also premised on the developing trend of *imitatio Alexandri*, which was being deployed very early after Alexander's death by his erstwhile elite to garner higher status and win the loyalty of troops and commanders in different settings.[64] As with Alexander himself, I would suggest that we are not dealing with the articulation of a legalistic claim, but rather the forwarding of a political agenda that is translated into ideology via the use of a specialized language.

Diodorus' eighteenth book tells us twice in short succession that Ptolemy retained his satrapy of Egypt in Antipater's new satrapal distribution, at the Triparadeisus Settlement in 320, owing to his attitude after defeating Perdiccas' incursion. First, 'it was impossible to resituate him since it seemed that he held Egypt effectively as a spear-won prize (δορίκτητον) on account of his valour'.[65] Secondly, 'he now held Egypt as if it were a spear-won realm (βασιλείαν δορίκτητον)'.[66] It has been suggested that the terminology of *doriktētos* found in these cases was used in the historical work of Hieronymus of Cardia, Diodorus' putative source for his narrative of the Successors, which is possibly true given that a fragment of Arrian expresses Ptolemy's holdings ahead of Triparadeisus using a variant of the same terminology (δόρι ἐπικτήσηται, 'acquired by the spear').[67] Further, it has been argued that this was a real slogan used by the *diadochoi*,[68] especially given that it can be found multiple times in Diodorus XVIII–XX and the fragmentary books beyond. This seems likely, but it is difficult to confirm definitively given that this is an authorial judgement about Ptolemy's attitude and politics; indeed, the second example is a retrospective view of Ptolemy's royal accession, which would arrive only fourteen years later.

It seems most likely that if Ptolemy expressed, however formally or informally, a rightful claim to Egypt in the aftermath of defeating Perdiccas that was couched in terms of the land being *doriktētos*, this was political position, not a legalistic claim. More specifically, a manoeuvre that capitalized on Ptolemy's recent history of defeating Perdiccas, Antipater's rival, to retain maximal power and authority in his part of the post-Alexander system under Antipater's new *epimeleia*. This would not mean that Ptolemy was formally claiming ownership of the territory, nor entail that he was taking a stance as a secessionist, uninterested in the remainder of Alexander's former empire and the competitive international power games of the Successors.[69] Rather, it would mean that Ptolemy was exploiting recent history to solidify a personal power base soon after Alexander's death, using the language of spear-won rights that was evocative of Alexander's conquest and his own role in it, which symbolically entailed a division of the spoils to co-combatants, namely the *diadochoi*. Ideologically, this defined Ptolemy and his post-Alexander status through his connection to Alexander and his conquests. The development in 320/319 of a new coin series bearing a victorious Alexander wearing an elephant-scalp headdress, symbol of Ptolemy's recent triumph over Perdiccas, not to mention the successful retention of Alexander's body itself, is consistent with this self-definition.[70]

As Mehl notes, there was no act of conquest in the diadochan carving up of Alexander's empire,[71] so it would follow that asserting territory to be *doriktētos* in the early post-Alexander years was primarily a political stance by the *diadochoi* to maximize their accumulation of power and control in a system still nominally ruled over by a single royal dynasty. It spoke to their defining roles in acquiring the empire and their experience in upper echelons of Alexander's command, and it was not treasonable per se nor technically incompatible with governing regions of it on behalf of the Argead dynasty. Importantly, however, the basis for this assertion was collaborative engagement in Alexander's prior imperial conquests, not personal acquisition of territory through new conquest in the post-Alexander period. Diodorus' next record may bear out this point:

> For, they said, it was not about these things that they were at variance with Antigonus but because, although he and they had made war in common, first against Perdiccas and later again Eumenes, he had not turned over to his companions their share of the spear-won land (τὰ μέρη τῆς δορικτήτου χώρας).
> Diodorus XIX 85.3

This refers to the so-called Third Diadoch War, which had begun with exactly the demand from the other major diadochs reiterated here, that Antigonus should dilute his total control over the Asian domains of the Macedonian empire by sharing wealth won from defeating Eumenes and by handing over key satrapies to Cassander, Lysimachus and Ptolemy – as well as well as restoring Seleucus to the satrapy of Babylonia, from which he had been dispossessed by

Antigonus in 316.⁷² In other words, Antigonus was viewed as a threat by the other dynasts, and this was a hard-edged demand which sought to see that threat neutralized. As in the case of Ptolemy, this was not a legal argument. Rather, it was an opportunistic political demand intended to undermine Antigonus' superior accumulation of territory and wealth and continued upward trajectory while simultaneously enriching themselves. Further, the language of the demand is predicated on the existence of a unitary Macedonian realm, and the examples mentioned – Perdiccas and Eumenes – are the putting down of disruptors to system-wide stability in the form of a now-defunct viceregal faction. Hence, the request for a share in the *doriktētos chōra* was still ostensibly founded on the comradeship of a common inheritable enterprise, Alexander's conquests. As with Ptolemy after Triparadeisus, then, Antigonus' rivals were appealing to their equality of standing as co-creators and co-stewards of Alexander's empire in order to obtain a more favourable position from a figure more powerful than them. That this was all political sophistry was irrelevant, and the fact that all major players arrayed against Antigonus held the line was an attempt to give the demand some teeth. There is no logical inconsistency between separatist and unitarist ideologies here,⁷³ and indeed paradox is a general truth of the politics of Alexander's successors.

The next use of *doriktētos* in Diodorus' account of the Successors comes after the assassination of Alexander IV in 310/309, undertaken by Glaucias at the behest of Cassander:⁷⁴

> When [Glaucias] had done the ordered deed, Cassander, Lysimachus, Ptolemy and even Antigonus were relieved of their anticipated fears from the king: for there was no longer anyone left to succeed to the empire, and so each who was master over peoples or cities maintained his hopes for royalty and held the land appointed to him as if it were a spear-won kingdom (εἶχεν ὡσανεί τινα βασιλείαν δορίκτητον).
>
> Diodorus IX 105.3–4

This bears noticeable similarity with the second reference to Ptolemy's behaviour in Egypt in 320, and in fact the phrasing is precisely repeated: 'he held it as if it were a spear-won realm' (εἶχεν ὡσανεί τινα βασιλείαν δορίκτητον), used first for Ptolemy's attitude in retaining the satrapy of Egypt, now for the attitudes of each major Successor in keeping allotted territories after Alexander IV's death. Given this duplication, as well as the fact that the framing here is rhetorical as well as 'anticipatory and conjectural',⁷⁵ it is more difficult to argue that this represents an actual phrasing used by the *diadochoi* after Alexander IV's death – unless we suggest that it represents another short-termist political posture in response to the sudden interregnum, based on the model that joint authorship of Alexander's conquests entailed plural inheritable claims, ahead of the definitive resolution of the interregnum and formalization of new kingships that would eventually come with the Year of the Kings. Again, as above, this is not territory actively conquered by the dynasts, simply lands over which they exercised power on account of the various political settlements between 323 and 311.

What we have seen so far in potential articulations of *doriktētos chōra* by the Successors are not real legal claims, but they may be nonetheless meaningful ideological acts in that they establish the *diadochoi* as legatees for Alexander's empire independent of reference to royal authority, the kings Philip III Arrhidaeus (r. 323–317) and Alexander IV (r. 323–310/309). In other words, however much they are political postures designed to maximize opportunities for personal accumulation of wealth and territory under a single imperial system and defend against encroaching rivals, diadochan claims to *doriktētos* rights publicly extol their independent power and position and habituate the world to their potential as rulers, especially via foregrounding their link to Alexander's conquests. Invocations of *doriktētos chōra* thus create a narrative of inheritance from Alexander not entirely dissimilar to a narrative of succession, especially given Alexander's own preceding use of the term.

As in so many other respects, the real shift comes with the Year of the Kings, where we see the realization of this successional narrative. The context of Diodorus' next reference is after Ptolemy's successful defence of Egypt against Antigonus' and Demetrius' invasion:

> And after the deliverance from his enemies Ptolemy became exultant, sacrificed in thanksgiving to the gods, and entertained his friends at his hearth in brilliant fashion. He then wrote to Seleucus, Lysimachus and Cassander about his fortunate successes and about the crowd which had deserted to him; and, having contended over Egypt for a second time and considering that he held the land as spear-won (νομίσας δορίκτητον ἔχειν τὴν χώραν), he returned to Alexandria.
> Diodorus XX 76.6–7

The invasion was successfully repulsed by November 306,[76] which, as I have argued in Chapter 4.2, was the likely context of Ptolemy's accession, his take-up of the royal title and the diadem. Judging by Diodorus' language, this is a similar claim to the one made by Ptolemy fourteen years previously, after the defeat of Perdiccas in 320, and in fact Diodorus deliberately links the two events by saying that this was Ptolemy's 'second contest over Egypt' (τὸ δεύτερον ἠγωνισμένος ὑπὲρ τῆς Αἰγύπτου). This was a victory of even greater magnitude, however, given Ptolemy's recent defeat at Salamis and substantial loss of troops there,[77] and given that the Antigonid invading force reputedly numbered 80,000 infantry, 8,000 cavalry, 83 elephants, plus a substantial naval armament under Demetrius' command.[78]

In the form reported by Diodorus, Ptolemy's claim would follow a similar motif to the ostensible claim of 320, that of successfully defending and retaining a share of Alexander's conquests. The military victory was the performative proof of Ptolemy's suitability as inheritor, underpinning a claim designed to fend off rival attempts to dispossess him of his territory, which was framed as somehow rightful. In short, it was an expression that was concerned with why Ptolemy should keep Egypt and his other holdings. Indeed, the spectacular celebrations that Diodorus specifies in 306, plus the letters that Ptolemy sent to fellow members of the anti-Antigonid alliance, were perhaps the space and medium used for the re-articulation of these claims, and indeed for communicating his new royal accession.[79] The key differences in 306 were that Ptolemy was no longer answerable to a higher authority, whether a regent or supervisory general or nominal king, and that Antigonus had already projected his own new kingship to the world, no doubt now thinking that he could capitalize on this by finishing Ptolemy off in a swift *coup de grâce*.[80] Thus the ideological projection of holding *doriktētos chōra*, a re-performance of a similar claim fourteen years before, could now strengthen Ptolemy's own kingship with reference to an existing model of dynamic resilience, plus frame him more explicitly as successor to Alexander's *doriktētos chōra*, thus buttress his claim to universalistic dominion and reject Antigonus' own assertion of superiority.[81] This was an opportune counter-reaction to the exceptionalism invoked in the new Antigonid *basileia*.

This still aligns with the widely dominant scheme in diadochan self-fashioning and legitimation, namely a link to Alexander – real or symbolic – generating prestige and status that rationalized the take-up of territory and authority after his death.[82] The shift to individual inheritance in 306, from a political stance intended to maximize wealth and territory under an imperial system to a revised ideological claim of independent power and control of Alexander's legacy, was swiftly followed by an envisioning of *doriktētos chōra* as referent to the domains controlled by the new Hellenistic kings. The formalization of the new kingships, and their mutual inter-state recognition across the international Hellenistic world, obviated the need to present claims to *doriktētos chōra* in terms of

Alexander's kingdom, however much Alexander's spear-cast remaining a recurrent ideological touchstone. This evolution from an inheritance claim based on determinative contribution to Alexander's conquests, to an assertion of rightful control in the present day founded on self-justifying terms, becomes particularly clear when we encounter Seleucid and Ptolemaic conflict over Syria and the surrounding regions. As Diodorus records, in the fragmentary book XXI, in reference to the situation after the defeat of Antigonus at Ipsus in 301:

> And Seleucus, after the division of Antigonus' kingdom, took his army and went down to Phoenicia and attempted, in accordance with the agreement which had been made, to make Coele Syria his own. But Ptolemy had already taken possession of the cities in this place and was denouncing Seleucus on the basis that, although he was his friend, he had accepted, in his own share from the agreement, land that was held by Ptolemy; in addition to these things, that he had been a common partner in the war against Antigonus and yet the kings had given him no share of the spear-won land (ὅτι τοῦ πολέμου τοῦ πρὸς Ἀντίγονον κεκοινωνηκότος οὐδὲν αὐτῷ μετέδωκαν οἱ βασιλεῖς τῆς δορικτήτου χώρας).
>
> Diodorus XXI 1.5

There was a chequered, fractious history building to this point. Ptolemy had annexed Syria and Phoenicia first in 319 but left garrisons in only a few key cities,[83] which he lost when he withdrew in 314, after which Antigonus took the territory.[84] Ptolemy and his ally Seleucus, who had been dispossessed of Babylonia by Antigonus in summer 316,[85] then sent an expedition to reconquer the areas in 312 and defeated Demetrius at Gaza in the early winter of that year.[86] However, he was forced to withdraw once again in 311. Ptolemy then reasserted control over Syria and Phoenicia in 302/301 as part of a new phase of anti-Antigonid action, even though Sidon and Tyre remained in Antigonid hands.[87] Meanwhile, armies led by Lysimachus, Cassander and Seleucus converged on Antigonus and Demetrius near the town of Ipsus in Phrygia, resulting in the death and defeat of Antigonus and the flight of Demetrius.[88]

The behemoth of Antigonid power was broken at Ipsus in 301, with Demetrius merely retaining a powerful navy and a form of thalassocratic rule over a string of islands and port-cities in the Aegean and eastern Mediterranean, rather than the wide expanse of rule of before.[89] The agreement referred to in Diodorus XXI is a pact between Cassander, Lysimachus and Seleucus made after victory at Ipsus in which they agreed to partition Antigonus' former domain between them. As part of this common agreement, Coele Syria and Phoenicia were to go to Seleucus, while Cassander and Lysimachus would take parts of Asia Minor.[90]

However, since Ptolemy had already taken Coele Syria and Phoenicia in the build-up to Ipsus, without actually taking part in the battle, he disputed their allotment to Seleucus; moreover, he criticized the other three kings for not giving him any share at all from Antigonus' former domain. In this claim, even though he had not personally been present at Ipsus, Ptolemy had nonetheless made war on Antigonus in common with the other kings, had been part of a mutual enterprise, and thus deserved a share of the spoils. Notably, this passage does not designate the Syrian lands held by Ptolemy as *doriktētos*. Instead, this term is used in reference to lands of the now defeated and deceased Antigonus: hence, the entirety of Antigonus' domain is framed as *doriktētos chōra* to be distributed among his victors.

Here, for the first time, the terminology of *doriktētos chōra* is used in reference to one of the dominions of the *diadochoi*, and the claim to it now refers to the take-up of that dominion after total defeat has been inflicted.[91] Clearly, Cassander, Lysimachus and Seleucus were party to this new application of the term, even while Ptolemy had been excluded from the joint agreement. There are two further striking features worth noting in this vein. First, Ptolemy's complaint is a repetition of the strategy that the same four dynasts had employed when demanding that Antigonus share the wealth and territory that he had accumulated after defeating Eumenes in 316. Now, the shoe was on the other foot, since Ptolemy could no longer claim a common role in territorial acquisition – unlike when the single imperial state conquered by Alexander was at issue in 316, when it was asserted as being overly concentrated in a single pair of hands. Secondly, even though the *doriktētos chōra* in question was now understood as the territories of Antigonus, the model invoked by Alexander remained, in that it was premised on a plural sharing of the spoils after successful military activity – a sense that Alexander had himself translocated from the mythic scheme of division of spoils in the aftermath of the Trojan War.

Inheritance remained a major key of the discourse around spear-won spoils, as did, by extension, a retrospective frame of reference which advertised a prior military victory. The evolved concept seen in 301 – *doriktētos chōra* constituting the territory of a defeated ruler – became the normative understanding of the term. Indeed, Seleucus' reported response to Ptolemy's complaint was premised on this understanding:

> To these charges Seleucus replied that it was only just that those who were victorious on the battlefield should dispose of the spoils (δίκαιον εἶναι τοὺς τῇ παρατάξει κρατήσαντας κυρίους ὑπάρχειν τῶν δορικτήτων); but in the matter

of Coele Syria, for friendship's sake he would not for the present interfere, but would consider later how best to deal with friends who chose to encroach.

Diodorus XXI 1.5

Seleucus frames Ptolemy as not being an active party in the allied conquest of Antigonus, thus not entitled to a share of what was *doriktētos*. There is an implied contrast here with the articulations of *doriktētos chōra* prior to this point, which hinged upon the construct of collaborative achievement of Alexander's empire. Now, so Seleucus' stance makes clear, Ptolemy was no longer a joint author of victory, merely an opportunistic over-reacher on the fringes of the actual conquest. Moreover, Seleucus asserts that, although for the present he was tolerating Ptolemy's over-reach in Syria, he was retaining a rightful claim to the lands as *doriktētos chōra* for the future. This is a clear assertion that mere occupation could not trump an earlier rightful conquest, no matter how long the occupation lasted or how long ago the conquest was. There are again echoes of Alexander's own claim in 334, which rested upon an earlier successful conquest, in his case a mythical one.

We do not see the explicit articulation of *doriktētos chōra* again in the period of the Successors, though it is evident that the conceptualization of the term arrived at after Ipsus continued to exercise some force in later generations. In the context of the so-called Sixth Syrian War (171–168), for instance, Ptolemy VI (r. 180–164, 163–145) tried to refute Antiochus IV's (r. 175–164) claims to territory in Syria, which rested on the post-Ipsus accord that allotted them to Seleucus I, by positing a pre-Ipsus agreement between Ptolemy and Seleucus that granted them to Ptolemy in exchange for Seleucus' dominion over the rest of Asia.[92] The terminology of *doriktētos chōra* is not used by our source Polybius here, so it seems likely that we are dealing with dynastic manoeuvring of a more general type, employing a different form of ancestral precedent to forward a strategic agenda, but one which seeks to undercut the discourse of *doriktētos chōra* which remained popular in Seleucid self-fashioning.[93] The attempt to undermine, however, would indicate that the conception of *doriktētos chōra* established after Ipsus achieved some permanence.

It is this same understanding that was employed in Antiochus III's ancestral claims to the Romans at Lysimachia in 196, discussed at the opening of this chapter. In this case, Seleucus I's total victory over Lysimachus at Corupedium in 281 would entail the transference of Lysimachus' kingdom to Seleucus as *doriktētos chōra*. Just as Seleucus expressed in response to Ptolemy's encroachment into Syria, Antiochus III argued to the Romans that an act of conquest was not superseded by subsequent occupation: Seleucus' defeat of Lysimachus gave the Seleucids a right to Lysimachus' kingdom that was unaffected by later occupation by the Antigonids, Ptolemies, and indeed the Romans, who had never conquered the land from its rightful owners, the Seleucids.[94] This was not a one-off claim, as we have records that Seleucus' heir Antiochus I (r. 294–261) sold lands from Lysimachus' former domain to the city of Pitane after Seleucus' death, a sale that was upheld as legitimate by the early Attalids, acting as arbitrators in a dispute over the land between Mytilene and Pitane.[95]

The construct of *doriktētos chōra* remained concerned with inheritance and the valorization of prior victory. These themes can be traced in a poetical expression of spear-won rights in Theocritus' encomium of Ptolemy's son and heir, Ptolemy II Philadelphus (r. 285–246),[96] which was produced in the 270s:[97]

> And no-one has leapt to these shores from a swift ship,
> armoured, an enemy to cattle of Egypt;
> such a man has settled in these broad plains:
> yellow-haired Ptolemy, proficient in wielding a spear (ἐπιστάμενος δόρυ πάλλειν),
> who cares wholly for preserving his whole patrimony,
> like a good king, and acts to acquire things for himself (τὰ δὲ κτεατίζεται αὐτός).
>
> Theocritus *Idylls* 17.100–5

This is a clear reference to the word *doriktētos*, comparable to a similar tmesis found in *Iliad* XVI.[98] Here we see an image of Philadelphus being able to defend his land – his πατρώια, his 'inheritance' from Ptolemy – through his proficiency with the spear (δόρυ), and can also acquire (κτεατίζεται) new domains in his own right, too.[99] In other words, Philadelphus ruled over Egypt as though it were his spear-won land and also conquers new territories by the spear. Thus while it may well be true that the Ptolemies did not employ the concept of *doriktētos chōra* in forwarding of external territorial claims as regularly as the Seleucids,[100] it would seem that it remained an important component of dynastic ideology nevertheless, one which very specifically conveyed the projection that the Ptolemies were the secure, rightful rulers of Egypt and left open that expectation that future lands would be acquired, part and parcel of the universalistic dominion claimed by all the Successor dynasties.[101]

Moreover, we see the discourse of *doriktētos chōra* naturalized into a Ptolemaic ideological framework, one which stresses – more so than any other Hellenistic dynastic ideologies – inter-generational replication and continuation from father to son. Indeed, Philadelphus is elsewhere in the poem called 'spearman son of a spearman' (αἰχμητὰ Πτολεμαῖε / αἰχμητᾷ Πτολεμαίῳ), part of a constellation of constructed father–son parallels that is a major theme of the poem.[102] It also captures the peculiarly Ptolemaic emphasis on defence of territory and the rightful nature of inheritance, which was the central theme in all of Ptolemy I's invocations of *doriktētos chōra*. In this, Theocritus' expression is evocative of Ptolemy I's attitude after defending against Perdiccas' invasion in 320 and his claim after the Antigonid invasion in 306. There is even perhaps a nod to Alexander's landing in the Troad with the assertion in lines 100–1 that 'no-one has leapt armoured to these shores from a swift ship' (οὐδέ τις αἰγιαλόνδε θοᾶς ἐξήλατο ναός / θωρηχθεὶς), hence that Egypt formed a discrete part of what had been Alexander's empire.

On the balance of evidence, *doriktētos chōra* is primarily concerned with inheritable claims based on a prior conquest, not about the designation of a new or contemporary conquest. It involves invoking the past and appealing to ostensible rights on that basis, in an attempt to assert the prerogative of the past over the present in pursuit of a contemporary agenda. This is true right the way from Alexander's crossing of the Hellespont in 334, where the model is inheritance from the spoils of the Trojan War; through the period of the Successors, where political claims are made around participation in Alexander's conquests and concomitant demands to involvement in the wealth and territory that came with his imperial legacy; then made anew in the translation of that cooperative enterprise into a narrative of succession, and with the evolved deployment in reference to the domains held by a defeated king; all the way down to Antiochus III's invocation of patrilineal right in conference with Roman delegates at Lysimachia in 196, where Seleucid expansionism is rationalized and defended on the basis of ancestral conquest by the dynastic founder. While it may have had a more legalistic discourse later on, in concert with the codification of law via publication of arbitration agreements, *doriktētos chōra* in the early Hellenistic period centred more around ideology than legality, and more around politics than the law. It was deployed in the pursuit of a range of strategic objectives, both symbolic and pragmatic.

Most importantly, there is no evidence to suggest that any and all conquered territory constituted 'spear-won land', which belies the common scholarly shorthand discussed at the opening of this chapter; there is no evidence that the king owned all land in his kingdom as a result of the designation of his domain as *doriktētos chōra*; and there is no evidence to suggest that the conceptualization of *doriktētos chōra* was static and unchanging. The importance of *doriktētos chōra*, in terms of the creation of Hellenistic kingship in the generation of the Successors, was that it represented a common ideological thread from Alexander's arrival in Asia and the collaborative conquest of the Macedonian empire to the diadochan inheritance of that empire and the construction of their own new kingships, and thus featured in the development of narratives of succession and the development of new authority after Alexander's death.

Conclusions

As Alexander lay dying in Babylon in June 323 he supposedly pronounced, when prompted about the succession, that he wished his empire to devolve upon 'the strongest', and that he foresaw a 'great funeral games' coming to pass after his death.[1] Like many such stories of suspiciously pithy last words, the authenticity is dubious and the traceability of authentication impossible, even though the words themselves possess *a* truth that meets the expectations of the moment and the mythologization that underpins them is itself revealing.[2] But, as the later writers who incorporated different variations of the story surely knew, their fabrication makes these words no less accurate a reflection of the struggle for superiority that was instigated after Alexander's death among his friends, generals and companions – the *diadochoi*, Alexander's Successors. In literary terms, putting these words in Alexander's mouth gives him a prophetic power, and the events in question a predestination, making the decades-long conflict of the Successors the inevitable, programmatic unfolding of a narrative already signposted.[3] In real political terms, it probably also suited the ambitious Macedonian elite to have their rivalry rooted in Alexander's precognitive vision, just as they themselves implicated Alexander's image and model in their diverse pursuits of power and status in the years that followed.

This study has been concerned with the history of the struggle signalled in Alexander's apocryphal words: the search for superiority in the generation of Alexander's Successors, 323–276 BC, the major product of which was the creation of Hellenistic kingship. Focusing primarily on kingship's ideological performance and how that develops rather than on its structural evolution, a series of key aspects have been investigated that have contributed to a fuller knowledge and understanding of the creation of *basileia* after Alexander's death. The premise of the book, as outlined in Chapter 1, has been that early Hellenistic kingship can (and should) be approached as an international phenomenon, not simply as a series of regional, biographical and dynastic studies. In spite of the post-colonialist view that Hellenistic kingship cannot be unified as an analytical category – aphoristically, 'no single model accounts for Hellenistic kingship'[4] – the chapters of this book have shown that it is in fact viable and productive to do so. This is not least because the *diadochoi* operated in the same context of imperial dissolution, originated from comparable backgrounds in Greece and Macedon, and generated highly similar outputs in the pursuit of independent power, namely *basileiai* of roughly similar forms and appearances in spite of situational diversities. This does not deny that local levels saw different specific means for the interpenetration of royal power, nor that regional histories present their own distinctive complexities and hence require interpretative specialization. Rather, it simply recognizes that the developers of early Hellenistic kingship were international actors, too, and that the supra-regional stage was a centrally important *locus* for ongoing competitive projections of power and status.

As well as locating this work in the history of scholarship and articulating a rationalized approach for an international-focused study of early Hellenistic kingship, Chapter 1 offered an extended examination of certain foundational theoretical and methodological issues. Drawing on comparative works on kingship in world history as well as specialist Hellenistic studies, it examined the nature of royal ideology and performance. After outlining some of the contexts and functions of royal ideology – in short, the where, how and why of ideology – it emphasized its performative nature, the fact that it contributes to creating the reality of kingship, and its engagement of audiences on the basis of cultural intelligibility and alignment in traditions. The four primary genealogies of Hellenistic kingship were also treated – Achaemenid, pre-Achaemenid Near Eastern, Argead Macedonian, and Greek cultural – alongside the potential function of *imitatio Alexandri* as a kind of genealogical 'bricolage'. All of these genealogies have their place in the creation of Hellenistic kingship, but at the international level we see more diffusion of royal ideology derived from Graeco-Macedonian models on account of the differing audiences found at local and supra-local levels. Finally, it offered a competitive model for conceptualizing the evolution of a common ideological discourse of kingship in the early Hellenistic period, which demonstrated the impact of rivalry in four key areas: the field in which ideology developed, the dynamics resulting in continued innovation in ideology, the causes of parallelism and 'sameness' between the royal ideologies, and the reasons for their longevity.

Building on the models and theorizing laid down in Chapter 1, the remaining four chapters offered individual studies of key features in the creation of early Hellenistic kingship. Chapter 2 used Craterus' monument at Delphi, vowed *c.* 322/321, as a heuristic for the performative politics of status in the very earliest years after Alexander's death. The monument's verse inscription engages archaistic discourses of commemoration and valuation to project Craterus' superiority, while the content invokes ancestral Heraclean paradigms attached to the Argead dynasty, all likely manifested as part of Craterus' royal aspirations that were cut short due to his untimely death. Chapter 3 followed with a study of how heroic paradigms were used by the *diadochoi* as a model for projecting their eminence and royal suitability. After offering some theoretical reflections on the complex and associative rather than simple and unitary nature of *imitatio*, it discussed three primary case studies: Ptolemy's use of the *aegis* symbol to link Alexander with his heroic model Achilles and in turn symbolize his own succession from him in an invented iconographic narrative; Lysimachus' use of lions to symbolize his kingship, linking both to Heracles and more closely to Alexander as an intermediary model; and Pyrrhus' alternating use of both Achilles and Heracles to project his royal image and further specific aspirations of rulership.

If Chapters 2 and 3 form a natural pair in their focus on how the *diadochoi* imported archaising and heroic imagery of leadership and authority to underpin royal aspirations, then Chapters 4 and 5 are unified in tackling features widely recognized as foundational in the creation of Hellenistic kingship. Chapter 4 shows how 'diadem plus royal title' emerged as the lasting Hellenistic formula for royal accession after the 'Year of the Kings'. Antigonus established this new paradigm after Salamis, and the remaining Successors competitively emulated the details and framing. This was a self-coronation, a ritualized showcase of the new kings' active agency and unfettered authority, in contrast to the passive agency that was developed for signifying succession. Further, the Successors solidified an image of a diadem-wearing Alexander through various means and media to generate a retrospective model for their own symbolism and to visualize narratives of succession. Chapter 5 focuses on the concept of 'spear-won land' (*doriktētos chōra*), uttered by Alexander on his arrival in Asia Minor, which was not a juridical precept to legalize takeover of territory but more likely an ideological claim founded on the myth-historical model of spoils from the Trojan War. The *diadochoi* invoked the concept, too, initially as an opportunistic political stance to maximize power and authority under a manipulable imperial system by appealing to co-authorship of Alexander's empire, then, after Ipsus in 301, to refer to a diadochan dominion after total defeat. In all cases, *doriktētos chōra* was primarily concerned with asserting the prerogative of the past over the present in pursuit of contemporary agendas.

Among other insights, what emerges from these studies is the competitive formulation and reciprocal embedding of the ideologies that set the *diadochoi* on the path to kingship and, after accession, sought to sustain and further augment their power. For all the reasons set down in Chapter 1, the ongoing search for distinction in self-presentation was matched by significant imitation and parallelism. Apart from the fact that the *diadochoi* were former colleagues, continuing ideological contact and counter-contact was in all likelihood due to interstate proximity. Plutarch neatly captures this in a censorious judgement of early Hellenistic political ambitions in his biography of Pyrrhus:

> They have not sea, not mountain, not inhospitable desert as the boundary of their ravenous greed (πλεονεξίας), nor do the terminal points separating Europe and Asia delimit their hot desire: how they could possibly be unaffected, maintaining their hold and not transgressing against one another even when they are adjacent and in neighbouring existence, one cannot say.
>
> Plutarch *Pyrrhus* 12.2–3

Plutarch is obviously crafting a negative, 'pleonectic' characterization, and he is hinting at a somatic, medical model of kingship – as elsewhere in the *Pyrrhus*, when he calls *pleonexia* a *nosos* ('disease') that is congenital in the Hellenistic dynasties.[5] Nevertheless, his rhetorical question is well-put: how can states of roughly equal standing and structural set-ups co-exist with shared boundaries in a competitive inter-state system without frequent challenges to one another? This pertains not just to outbreaks of military conflict and other international relations issues, but also to the ideological competition we have seen in this study. It bears out one of my core contentions, that rivalrous international contact led to a shared vocabulary and syntax of royal ideology in the early Hellenistic world, and that these ideological entanglements were a formative and distinctive constituent feature in the emergent *koine* of Hellenistic kingship.

Indeed, the period of the *diadochoi*, as well as being the period of Alexander's Successors, and thus the continuation of his story, is also the foundational period for the much longer-term institution of Hellenistic kingship. It is worth emphasizing and remembering that what was laid down by the Successors was picked up, and continued to be picked up, right until the end of the Hellenistic dynasties but even beyond them. Whether we see this through the contiguous and co-extensive state cult of Ptolemies that stretched an unbroken chain of worship from the founding figures of the dynasty to contemporary incarnates;[6] or the sudden keenness of Antiochus III to remember ancestral *doriktetos chora* ('spear-won land') inherited from Seleucus while in conference with Rome in 196;[7] or the call-back to the triumphalist naval iconography of Demetrius Poliorcetes in Octavian's victory issues after defeating Antony at Actium in 31;[8]

or even the renascence of the Hellenistic royal diadem in late antique Rome, Byzantium and Sasanian Persia:[9] there are widespread examples offering essential proof of the fact that the period of the *diadochoi* was foundational for Hellenistic kingship, whose ideologies became a distinctive brand for creating and structuring political realities even centuries after the fact.

The work here has largely been concerned with lumping rather than splitting, and indeed there remains a lot more such work to be done, chronologically and thematically. This book is not, of necessity, a complete account of the creation of early Hellenistic kingship, something which would run to several volumes given the scale and scope of the world in question. But it has (hopefully) shown a robust starting point that could ramify widely, both methodologically and in terms of the individual studies. In my opinion, there are outstanding questions to be answered around the political shift from personal authority-building to longer-term consolidation and dynastic embedding. Additionally, another feature not covered here but extremely important in any study of kingship in world history is the religious basis for royal power and how this was both theorized and instrumentalized.[10] Father–son joint kingship also, which has seen some recent scholarly inroads for later periods, needs to be taken right back to its foundational moment in 306 and deconstructed for the peculiarity that it is, influential though it became.[11] A companion volume, *Royal Traditions and the Consolidation of Power by Alexander's Successors*, covers precisely these topics – so this is not the end of the story by any means.

Notes

1 Approaching the World of Early Hellenistic Kingship, 323–276 BC

1. For accounts of the battle, Diod. XX 49–52; Plut. *Demetr.* 15–17; App. *Syr.* 54; Paus. I 6.6; Polyaen. *Strat.* IV 7.7; Just. *Epit.* XV 2.6–7. All dates are hereafter BC except where specified as AD.
2. On the defensive strategy and Cyprus, Diod. XIX 79.4–7. The same essential strategy is recorded for Ptolemy's other overseas expansions, e.g. Coele Syria and Phoenicia (Diod. XVIII 43; App. *Syr.* 52), Cilicia (Diod. XIX 79.6–7). Cf. Hölbl 2001: 28. These expansions were not entirely motivated by defensive concerns (Worthington 2016: 7–8, 85, 155, 195), as they were aggressive imperial conquests in their own right, but 'fortress Egypt' was probably a real aspiration, especially given the invasion of Egypt by Perdiccas and the royal army in 320 (see Chapter 3.2) and then again in 306/305 by Antigonus and Demetrius (Diod. XX 73.2, launched from Syria and Phoenicia no less). Cf. Meeus 2014: 263–306.
3. Diodorus records total Ptolemaic forces suborned of 16,000 foot and 600 horse (XX 53.1), Plutarch 12,000 foot and 1,200 horse (*Demetr.* 16.4).
4. See e.g. Errington 1970: 49–58; Bosworth 2002: 29–63; Meeus 2008: 39–82.
5. On the assassinations, Diod. XIX 11, 105; Paus. I 25.6, IX 7.2.
6. Boiy 2000: 115–21; 2007: 84–92; 2011: 1–12. Antigonus had attempted to use his Asian *strategia* in place of Alexander IV's regnal years in Babylonia – perhaps building towards lasting institutionalization of his own rule, but the unwillingness (or inability) to use the royal title is telling.
7. Strootman 2014a: 228.
8. See Chapter 4.1.
9. Bilde et al. 1996: 10–11; Oakley 2006: 8.
10. Further explored in Chapter 4.
11. Argued by Ogden 2002: 10, accepted by Lane Fox 2011: 4. Earlier statements to similar effect: e.g. Gehrke 1982: 247; Hammond 1993: 12; Gruen 1993: 4; Bilde et al. 1996: 9.
12. Bilde et al. 1996: 11; Gruen 1996: 116.
13. E.g. Martin 2000: 153; Stephens 2003: 32; Erciyas 2005: 121; Pfeiffer 2008: 14–15; Anson 2014: 7; Masséglia 2015: 21. Cf. Shipley 2000: 92, on Hellenistic palaces; Gradel 2002: 60, on kingship in Julius Caesar's era. Critiques: Martin 2000: 151–60; Eckstein 2009: 248–53; Strootman 2014a; Anagnostou-Laoutides 2017: 150.

14 E.g. Ma 2013: 329; Kosmin 2014a: 3. Cf. Ober 2015: 301–2. Eckstein 2006; 2008 laid the foundation for this model.
15 Cf. Ma 2013: 329. For the 'balance of power' paradigm, Rostovtzeff 1941: 1.189–602, with further historiography at Strootman 2014b: 308 n.4. Critiques: Austin 1986: 454–7; Ager 2003: 49–50; Strootman 2014b: 307–10.
16 On universalism, Bang 2012: 60–75, esp. 64–9; Strootman 2010: 139–57; 2014b: 307–22.
17 See the oft-cited *Suda* s.v. βασιλεία [2] (β147).
18 Chrubasik 2016: esp. 2–10.
19 Cf. Mitchell and Melville 2013: 3.
20 E.g. Bosworth 2002: v.
21 E.g. Walbank 1984: 62–100; 1996: 119–30; Billows 1995; Eckstein 2009: 247–65; Strootman 2014a. Preaux 1978: 181–294 stands alone as a brilliant typological sketch.
22 Bilde et al. 1996: 11; Gruen 1996: 116.
23 For reactions to Droysen's *Hellenismus*, Tarn 1933: 123–66; Préaux 1965: 129–39; Bichler 1983; Momigliano 1994: 147–61; Demandt 1996: 17–27; Bosworth 2009: 1–27; Lane Fox 2011: 1–30; Moyer 2011a: 1–41.
24 Cf. Bichler 1983; Momigliano 1994: 147–61; Gehrke 2007: 355–79; Prag and Quinn 2013: 1–13.
25 E.g. Amitay 2010, arguing, as did Droysen, for the figure of Alexander as a 'unique forerunner of Christ' (7).
26 See Samuel 1989: 1–12. Moves away from Droysen: Will 1979: 79–95; Briant 1990: 40; Cartledge 1997: 5.
27 E.g. Momigliano 1975; Préaux 1989; Samuel 1983; 1989; Will 1985; N. Lewis 1986; Green 1989: 165–92; 1990. On violence and social unrest among ethnic groups, Fischer-Bovet 2015: 3–45.
28 Samuel 1989; Ma 2008: 371–85.
29 Ma 2008: 371–85; Fischer-Bovet 2014a: 4–6.
30 Ma 2008: 371–86.
31 Fischer-Bovet 2014a: 7; Kosmin 2014b: 173–98.
32 E.g. Ma 2003: 187; 2013: 333–4, 349; Vlassoupoulos 2013: 284. 'Dominant ethnoclass' derives from Briant's analysis of the Achaemenid empire's Persian elite: Briant 1988: 137–73.
33 Cf. Ma 2008: 371–86; Strootman 2014a: 7–13.
34 Notably, Sherwin-White and Kuhrt 1993. Cf. Strootman 2014a: 7–13. Mitchell and Melville 2013: 2 exemplifies the trend more recently: 'Alexander's and indeed the Greeks' formative encounter with kingship was with the Iranian kingship of the Achaemenids and their founding figure, Cyrus the Great.'
35 Note, especially, the industry of biographies: Antigonus (Briant 1973; Billows 1990), Seleucus (Mehl 1986; Grainger 1991), Ptolemy (Ellis 1994; Worthington 2016), Eumenes of Cardia (Schäfer 2002; Anson 2004, 2nd edn. 2015), Cassander (Landucci

Gattinoni 2003a), Lysimachus (Landucci Gattinoni 1992; Lund 1992), Antigonus Gonatas (Tarn 1913; Gabbert 1997), Pyrrhus (Lévêque 1957), Demetrius Poliorcetes (Manni 1951; Wheatley and Dunn 2020) and Agathocles (De Lisle 2021).

36 E.g. Hauben and Meeus 2014: 1–6, warning against generalization. Reversing this trend, more recently Fischer-Bovet and von Reden 2021.
37 E.g. Kosmin 2014b: 173–98, esp. 175.
38 Peremans 1987: 327–43. Further developed by Clarysse 1991: 21–38; Koenen 1993: 25–115; Selden 1998: 289–412.
39 Moyer 2011b: 115–45.
40 Stephens 2003. Cf. Kosmin 2014b: 173–98.
41 Ma 2003: 177–95. Kosmin 2014b: 173–98 applies, with modifications, the 'seeing double' paradigm to Seleucid Babylonia.
42 Stephens 2003: 32, indeed, quotes the 'no single formula' axiom.
43 Strootman 2014a: 2. On Hellenistic kings and cities (an enormous scholarly area), e.g. Ma 1999; Strootman 2011: 141–54; 2020: 137–78.
44 Cf. Strootman 2014b: 307–22; Canepa 2015: 68.
45 E.g. Cannadine and S. Price 1987; Woodacre et al. 2019.
46 Quigley 2005: 4. Cf. Aurell 2020: 37–8, on ritual (as opposed to ceremony) as hinging on its transformative capacity.
47 Cf. Woodacre 2019: 9–10.
48 Hekster and Fowler 2005: 16. Cf. Ristvet 2015: 32.
49 Cf. Hekster and Fowler 2005: 10.
50 On the greater need for stable symbolism and ritual in unstable political contexts, e.g. Kuhrt 1987: 20–55. Cf. Mitchell and Melville 2013: 18.
51 See 'The Sociology of Charismatic Authority', reproduced at Gerth and Mills 2009: 245–52. On some applications to kingship, e.g. Thornton 1963: 1–11; Emerson 1983: 413–44; Mann 2013: 35–48, esp. 42–5. On Weber and Hellenistic kingship, Gehrke's fundamental article: 1982: 247–77 (= 2013: 73–98).
52 Emerson 1983: 432 suggests that maintaining charismatic leadership through war could necessitate campaigns against increasingly large enemies, as the number of followers attracted to a leader's banner increases.
53 Cf. Emerson 1983: 430; Bang 2012: 66–7; Chrubasik 2016: 8–9. Ma 2003: 179 satirizes (over-)uses of sociological/anthropological models.
54 Cf. Ando 2000: 30, on the emperorship and Augustus' charismatic legacy.
55 Oakley 2006: 4; Graeber and Sahlins 2017: 1; Woodacre 2019: 1.
56 Walzer 1967: 194. Cf. Cannadine 1987: 1–7.
57 Woodacre 2019: 9–10.
58 Quigley 2005: 4
59 E.g. Bloch 1987: 271–97; general discussion at Graeber 2017: 378. Cf. Ristvet 2015. Geertz 1980 shows the opposite, a society where '[p]ower served pomp, not pomp power' (13).

60 Geertz 1980. Cf. Cannadine 1983: 161, on the efflorescence of royal ceremonial in modern Britain corresponding with the increasing weakness of the royal institution itself. Also Al-Azmeh 1997: xiv: 'The hallucinatory narcissism of royal iconography and other forms of enunciation, including theories of authority and the sacralisation of power, often coexists with the humbler realities of a very much diminished royalty, which tends to take on ever more sublime forms and prerogatives in periods of decline.'
61 Cf. von Hesberg 1999: 64–75; Mitchell and Melville 2013: 12.
62 Mitchell and Melville 2013: 17.
63 See e.g. Cannadine 1987: 2–7; Graeber 2017: 378–9. Cf. Ristvet 2015: 2.
64 Canepa 2009: 1. Cf. Cameron 1987: 106–36, esp. 122–9.
65 See e.g. Valeri 1985: 145–8; Quigley 2004: 21.
66 Cf. Mitchell and Melville 2013: 3.
67 Cf. Al-Azmeh 1997: xiv.
68 Woodacre 2019: 9.
69 Kantorowicz 1957.
70 Franko 2003: 71–87.
71 Parker 2011: 358–9, 367–74.
72 Mitchell and Melville 2013: 12.
73 Hekster 2015: 1, on Millar 1992: 6. Cf. Mitchell and Melville 2013: 16.
74 Elsner 1998: 58. Cf. Dahmen 2007: 1–5.
75 Machiavelli *Discourses* 3.38, 1.34. (trans. Thomson).
76 Hekster and Fowler 2005: 10. Cf. Gehrke 2013: 73 (= 1982: 247): '[T]he king was not merely head and centre of the State, but also precisely its constituent. The very principle of statehood subsisted in the person of the king.'
77 Cf. Bell 2004: 1–2; Hekster and Fowler 2005: 10.
78 Cf. Bell 2004: 1–4.
79 Hekster and Fowler 2005: 11.
80 See the analogy of modern British royal ceremonial and the use of television: Cannadine 1983: 101–64. Cf. Woodacre 2019: 9, on the amplification of the ceremonial aspect of monarchy by modern media.
81 Cf. Dean 2019: 183.
82 Price 1991: 1.65–6; Meadows 2014: 169–95.
83 The basic figure of 20,000 coins per obverse die is drawn from de Callataÿ's usage in reference to Alexander and the Hellenistic rulers: 2012: 178. Morkholm 1991: 16 gives a very low 'safe' minimum of 10,000 but notes that this number may have to be doubled; Kinns 1983: 1–22 argues for a minimum of 23,000 on the basis of a study of Amphicyonic issues, where his maximum estimate goes as high as 47,000; and Bland 2012: 521 operates on an average of 30,000 in a study of third-century AD Roman imperial coinage.

84 See de Callataÿ 2012: 175–90.
85 Scholz-Cionca 2017: 186–207 (quotation from 187).
86 For the Hellenistic period in particular, see Chaniotis 1997: 219–59; von Hesberg 1999: 64–75; Kuttner 1999: 96–123. Cf. Bartsch 1994: 10–12 on Roman emperors.
87 E.g. Kastan 1986: 459–75; Sharpe 2006: 99–116.
88 On theatricality/tragedy in Plutarch, see e.g. De Lacy 1952: 159–71; Mossman 1988: 83–93; 1992: 90–108; Braund 1997: 113–17; Duff 2004: 271–91.
89 See e.g. Chaniotis 1997: 223–4.
90 See e.g. Carney 2015: 61–90, esp. 62.
91 Bentley 1964: 150: 'A impersonates B while C looks on.'
92 Sharpe 2006: 100; Chrubasik 2016: 8; Dean 2019: 185.
93 Bilde et al. 1996: 11. Cf. Davies 2002: 1–22 on the horizontal and vertical relationships of the Hellenistic dynasties.
94 Woodacre 2019: 8, 13; Dean 2019: 186.
95 On coins, Millar 1993: 230, 237; Dahmen 2007: 3.
96 Cf. Lloyd 1989: 50, on tradition and innovation in the context of ancient science: 'At one extreme, we may say, tradition with no innovation at all equals stagnation. At the other, innovation with no tradition at all would produce unintelligibility.'
97 See e.g. Chapter 2.3.
98 Cf. Cannadine 1984: 105–6, 162. See also Geertz 1973: 3–30, on 'thick' description.
99 Ma 2013: 330–5. Cf. Briant 1994: 283–310. On the Ptolemaic economy, the point had already been made about a multiplicity of models by Préaux 1939: 570; more recently, Manning 2010: 3 explicitly speaks of the 'hybridity' of the Ptolemaic state in terms of 'combined elements of pharaonic, Persian, Macedonian, and Greek practice'. Cf. Shipley 1993: 282; Chaniotis 2005a: 62; Canepa 2015: 68.
100 Cf. Strootman 2014a: 8–9.
101 Ma 2013: 335.
102 Cf. Canepa 2010: 6. Lane Fox 2007: 267–311 is a good summary of the different models.
103 Ma 2013: 333–4. See also Ma 2003: 191.
104 Ma 2013: 334; 2003: 179–83. Cf. Stewart 1993: 171–81.
105 Ma 2003: 188; Manning 2010: 86–7.
106 See e.g. Briant 1990: 40–65; 2002: 2. However, cf. Canepa 2015: 70, on the overlaying of Seleucid royal tradition in post-Achaemenid Iran. Kosmin 2014a: 257 also suggests that the Seleucid blueprint for post-Hellenistic kingship and Roman imperialism might be comparable with the precedential nature of the Achaemenid model for the Hellenistic.
107 Briant 1990: 40–65; Ma 2003: 179; 2013: 333–4; Strootman 2014a.
108 See e.g. the accounts at cf. Ael. *VH* 9.3; *Suda* s.v. Λεοννάτος. Paspalas 2005: 72–101 is an interesting account of the limits of Persianization in the age of the Successors.

109 Briant 1979: 1375–414. Cf. Tuplin 2014: 245–76; Ma 2003: 191.
110 See Lane Fox 2007: 267–311; Wiemer 2007: 283–309. Note also Briant's own later clarifications of the phrase at 2002: 2, 876.
111 Bang 2012: 62.
112 Cf. Canepa 2015: 67–8.
113 On the colonial question, Moyer 2011a: 33.
114 Ma 2013: 334. Also e.g. Kuhrt 1987: 20–55.
115 For the former, e.g. Hölbl 2001; Manning 2010; Lloyd 2011: 83–106; Fischer-Bovet 2014a; for the latter, Kuhrt 1987: 20–55; Boiy 2004; Kosmin 2014b: 173–98. Cf. Kosmin 2018: 6–7 for cautionary words about Seleucid performance of ancient local traditions, which may have been 'infrequent, temporary, unpredictable, visibly costumed, and fractured by misunderstanding, ritual failure, condescension, and resentment'.
116 Diod. I 84.8.
117 Ma 2013: 330. Cf. Ruzicka 2012: 210–13, on the reappearance after Alexander of east–west tensions classic to earlier Near Eastern history.
118 Manning 2010; Hölbl 2001.
119 Cf. Strootman 2014a: 8–9.
120 Strootman 2010: 145–51.
121 Strootman 2010: 139–57.
122 Hall 2012: 304–9.
123 Hall 2012: 304–9.
124 Diod. XVIII 3.
125 See e.g. the distribution of Babylon in 331, the first time a Persian (Mazaeus) was appointed to a satrapy by Alexander, but with power circumscribed by a military commander (Apollodorus) and a financial overseer (Asclepiodorus): Arr. *Anab.* III 16.
126 As a case in point, see Roisman 2012 for a study of the shifting loyalties of the 'silver shields'.
127 See Boehm 2021 for a recent study.
128 Strootman 2011b: 141–55 provides a strong summary, esp. 145: 'It is easy to overestimate the power of Hellenistic kings, or to take for granted the subordination of cities. In fact, kings were as dependent on cities as cities were on them.'
129 Lund 1992: 156; Ma 2013: 336–7; Strootman 2014a.
130 See de Callataÿ 2012: 175–90; Thonemann 2015: esp. 1–42.
131 Mørkholm 1991: 63–7.
132 Cf. Millar 1993: 230, 237; Dahmen 2007: 3.
133 See e.g. Ma 2013: 324–5; Kosmin 2014a: 100–3; 2018.
134 Collins 1997: 436–76; Lianou 2010: 123–34; Kosmin 2014a.

135 Diod. XX 37.1–6. On the importance of such attempts at capturing a blood-link to the Argead line in this period, see e.g. Carney 2000: 114–52; Meeus 2009a: 63–92; 2009c: 235–50.
136 Carney 2006; 2015: 1–26, esp. 8–9, 15–17.
137 See e.g. Carney 2000; 2006; 2015: 1–26, 61–90.
138 Drews 1983; Carlier 1984; Ogden 1997; Mitchell 2013.
139 Mitchell 2013: 57–90.
140 See Drews 1983; Carlier 1984; Mitchell 2013; Atack 2020.
141 Bilde et al. 1996: 9–10.
142 See Carney 2015: 191–206 (quotation from 199).
143 Cf. cultural appropriation in the so-called Second Sophistic, including where 'a process of acculturation took shape through a selective borrowing of cultural traits, particularly of those that harmonize most with earlier practices' (van Nijf 2001: 317).
144 See e.g. Cohen 1995: 483–506; Carlier 2000: 259–68.
145 See the balanced treatment of Borza 1990: 77–97; and more recently Carney 2015: xiv–xv.
146 Spawforth 2007: 90–1. Cf. Carney 2010: 44.
147 On Philip's coinage, see Chapter 2.3. On his arguable attempt at self-divinization, Diod. XVI 92.5. Plut. *Alex.* 4.9 records that Philip II had his chariot victory at Olympia engraved as a coin-type.
148 On Alexander and the Trojan War schema, see Chapter 5.1; and Achilles, Chapter 3.2. On Alexander's coinages, Mørkholm 1991: 41–54; M. Price 1991.
149 On *imitatio Alexandri* and Alexander's reception, the bibliography is huge but see e.g. Green 1978: 1–26; Trofimova 2012; Moore, ed., 2018. Wallace 2018a: 162–3 n.2 lists other major works.
150 See e.g. Wallace 2018a: 164–75.
151 On Persianization, see the evidence summary at Mullen 2018: 234 n.3. On Egypt and Babylon, see recently Naiden 2019: 91–138.
152 See further Chapter 3.1.
153 Briant 1994: 283–310. Cf. Ma 2013: 326.
154 Versluys 2017: 206, with helpful wider discussion at 201–7.
155 See e.g. Stewart 1993; Ogden 2011; Palagia 2018: 140–61.
156 For the Realist interpretation of Hellenistic inter-state relations, see Eckstein 2006: 79–117. Cf. Fischer-Bovet 2014a: 9.
157 Diod. XVII 117.3, with a slightly modified version at XVIII 1.1–3; Curt. X 5.5; Arr. *Anab.* VII 26.3; Just. *Epit.* XII 15.8–11.
158 Just. *Epit.* XI 15.11. Cf. Alexander's utterance τῷ κρατίστῳ ('to the strongest'), already perhaps modelled on the τῇ καλλίστῃ ('to the most beautiful') engraved on the Apple of Discord: Yardley and Heckel 1997: 292.

159 On the *agōn* in ancient Greek culture, e.g. Barker 2009, esp. the summary and literature reviews at 2–3 nn.6–10; Reid et al. 2020. See also Cornell 2002: 44 (post-Homer, 'the competitive spirit was extended to all areas of life').

160 This idea of a distinctive Greek agonism, or agonal mentality, essentially stems from Jacob Burckhardt's lectures, published in 1898–1902 as *Griechische Kulturgeschichte* (translated into English in 1998 as *The Greeks and Greek Civilization*). Nietzsche is also credited with developing this idea in *Homer's Wettkampf* (1872). For more recent discussion, Murray 2006: 247–61; Joho 2020: 267–88.

161 Lungstrum and Sauer 1997: 7; Ulf 2011: 85–111; Kyle 2015: 16, 24.

162 See e.g. Fitzgerald 1987: 1–18; Lloyd 1989: 50–108; Barker 2009. A classic study of 'agonistic exchange' in Homeric society is Beidelman 1989: 227–59. See Alwine 2015 on enmity in the competitive, honour-driven Classical Athenian society.

163 Duplouy 2006. On capital, Bourdieu 1986: 241–58.

164 Eckstein 2006: 93.

165 Carney 2015: 265–81.

166 Macedonian expansionism as a Hellenistic genealogy: Ma 2013: 327–9.

167 See e.g. Diod. XXXI 6.

168 See e.g. Lloyd 1989: 50–108; Ober 2008; 2015.

169 Cf. Zanker 1988: 17, on the architectural effects of the competitive environment of late Republican Rome: 'The compelling need to outdo the competition led to the use of every imaginable form of pretension or novelty of design.'

170 Cf. Klooster 2011: 115–46.

171 *Suda* s.v. βασιλεία [2] (β147). On birth vs behaviour: Mitchell and Melville 2013: 12.

172 Cf. Cannadine 1984: 133, on ritual innovations of competing world powers in the late 1800s.

173 Cf. Canepa 2015: 68.

174 Cf. Cannadine 1987: 15–16; Lloyd 1989: 50.

175 Cf. van Wees 2011: 2–6.

176 Cf. Beidelman 1989: 249, on the necessity of agonism in the Homeric world.

177 Cf. Eckstein 2006: 94, on military emulation; Fischer-Bovet 2014a: 7, on external pressures as drivers of change. See also Canepa 2009: 2–3, on competitive interaction between the late Roman and Sasanian empires, from both friendly exchange and hostile contact; Bertelli 2001: 3–4, the spread of ritual practice in Medieval Europe.

178 Cf. Fuchs 2001, on (early modern) mimesis as a strategy of resistance to homogenization as much as a strategy of homogenization per se.

179 Ober 2008: 80.

2 The Performance of Status in the Early Hellenistic World: Craterus at Delphi

1 The idea of a single Year of the Kings (Jahr der Könige), stemming ultimately from Droysen (1952 edn. 2.302), although contradictory, usefully captures the interdependent nature of the accessions, akin to a 'domino effect'. See Müller 1973 (also cf. Mileta 2012: 315–34). See Chapter 4.1 for a full study.
2 Strootman 2014: 5–7. On the long influence of Seleucid kingship in particular, Kosmin 2014a: 256–8.
3 Cf. Meeus 2013: 113–48, on the dangers of hindsight.
4 See Chapter 5.2 on ideologies of cooperation in relation to co-authorship of empire.
5 The best summaries of their careers is Heckel 2006, supplemented by Heckel 1992. A few highlights, noted telegraphically: Peithon attempted to carve out a power base in the Upper Satrapies as early as 323 (Diod. XVIII 7, suggesting that Peithon explicitly aimed at τῶν ἄνω σατραπειῶν δυναστεύειν, 'lordship over the Upper Satrapies'), and in fact temporarily became *epimelētēs* (alongside Arrhidaeus) after Perdiccas' assassination in 320 (Diod. XVIII 36.6); Leonnatus affected Alexander's hairstyle and modes of luxurious display, and sought to marry Alexander's sister Cleopatra (*Suda* s.v. Λεοννάτος; Plut. *Eum*. 3); Cleitus bore a trident and was acclaimed as Poseidon after a naval victory in the Lamian War in 322 (Plut. *Mor*. 338a); Asander was honoured with a *phyle* named Asandris in the Latmus/Pidasa *sympoliteia* of *c*. 323–321, a union which he probably presided over (*SEG* 47.1563); Archon established a monument at Delphi in *c*. 321 which aimed at projecting his (and his family's) fame (*GHI* 92; see section 2, below); Peucestas adopted Persian style and language from late in Alexander's lifetime and, in a Persian-derived, Alexander-like fashion, magnificently sacrificed and feasted Eumenes' coalition armies in Persepolis in 317 in an attempt to become their leader (Diod. XIX 14, 22–3).
6 Cf. Seyer 2006: 184.
7 Ashton 1993: 125–31. More recently Anson 2012: 49–58; Ashton 2015: 107–16.
8 Arr. *Anab*. VII 4.5, 12.4.
9 See Plutarch *Alexander* 47.9–10, but more emphatically stressed at *Eumenes* 6.1–2 in a post-Alexander context. Although rooted in his service under Alexander, perhaps Craterus' traditionalism was his attempt to show uniqueness, and individuality, in a representational landscape at that point dominated by Alexander-associated Persianisms (cf. Ael. *VH* 9.3; *Suda* s.v. Λεοννάτος). Note here Arr. *Succ*. 1.27, indicating that Craterus conspicuously wore the Macedonian *kausia* in battle against Eumenes. Craterus also repudiated his Persian wife Amastris soon after Alexander's death (Memnon *BNJ* 434 F4.4). See also section 4, below.
10 See now primarily Meeus 2009b: 287–310.
11 E.g. Ashton's proposition (1993: 125–31; 2015: 107–16) that Craterus was constructing the ships needed for carrying out Alexander's supposed 'last plans' (Diod. XVIII 4).

12 On the Lamian War, Ashton 1984: 152–7.
13 Diod. XVIII 18.7, also recording that this was a prelude to helping Craterus return to Asia. Why at this early stage? Was it an early appearance for Craterus' larger ambitions (*pace* Dunn and Wheatley 2012: 43 n.33), perhaps stimulated by Perdiccas' recent successes against Ariarathes in Cappadocia and his strengthened grip on the regency of both kings (see Bosworth 1993: 427)? Cf. Anson 2012: 55–6, that Craterus would approach Perdiccas in order to obtain for himself some kind of supervisory *strategia* over Asia Minor (in my view unlikely). An outright military assault on Perdiccas (Laqueur 1919: 219) is highly unlikely.
14 Diod. XVIII 23.3–4, 25.3–4; Arr. *Succ.*. 1.20, 24.
15 On Perdiccas vs Ptolemy, see Diod. XVIII 25.6, 29.1, 33–6, with Roisman 2012: 92–110.
16 Diod. XVIII 25.6, 29.1–3.
17 Diod. XVIII 29.4–32; Plut. *Eum.* 5–7.
18 Diod. XIX 59.3. *Pace* Nep. *Eum.* 4.4, a condensed account.
19 Anson 2012: 57 suggests that Craterus would probably have become royal *strategos* in Asia after the Perdiccan war, subordinate to Antipater. I read the power dynamics differently (see also *Suda* s.v. Κρατερός on the relative positions of the two).
20 For a survey of possibilities, Dunn and Wheatley 2012: 39–48.
21 Plut. *Alex.* 40.5. Plin. *NH* XXXIV 64 calls it a *venatio Alexandri*.
22 Beginning with Perdrizet 1899: 273–9 and Willrich 1899: 231–50, many attempts have been made to link the statue group with (i) a lion hunt mosaic from the House of Dionysus at Pella (*c.* 320–300); (ii) a lion hunt marble relief from Messene (late 4th–early 3rd century); and (iii) the Alexander Sarcophagus from Sidon (*c.* 320–300) – as well as various other artefacts, major and minor. For a recent review on this point, Cohen 2010: 76–8 (with 313 nn.38–48), also rightly stressing the paradigmatic nature of these scenes, which do not necessitate (indeed, perhaps render counterintuitive) strict figural identification.
23 Perdrizet 1899: 273–4. Cf. Stewart 1993: 270; Dunn and Wheatley 2012: 40.
24 Bosworth 2002: 277 plausibly suggests during Polyperchon's *epimeleia* of 319–316 based on the fact that Craterus II is named a 'child' (παῖς) in line 3 of the inscription, which he takes as meaning at the time of dedication. Although we should not interpret this word too prescriptively, as the archaistic language of this couplet in particular militates against a literal reading, Bosworth's supposition is certainly to be preferred to the date suggested by others, namely 300 or even later (see again Dunn and Wheatley 2012: 39–48); as both Bosworth himself and also Stewart 1993: 271 rightly note, the sculptors of the project, Leochares and Lysippus, began their trades in the 360s and would be octogenarians by 300 (the last recorded activity of Lysippus, at any rate, is in 316, coinciding with the foundation of the city of Cassandria: Athen. 784c–d). On archaeological and art-historical grounds, many scholars (e.g. T. H(lscher 1973: 182–3; Willers 1979: 21–6; Voutiras 1984: 57–62)

also prefer an early date. The argument that the comparative palaeography of the inscribed letters implies a date between 300 and 270 began with Perdrizet (1899: 274–5, with n.3) and has been accepted by a number of scholars since (NB Moretti *ISE* II 73; Hansen *CEG* II 878); however, at more than 125 years old, I am hesitant to regard a conclusion of this kind, already chronologically subjective, as insuperable. More speculatively, a date of 319–316 could be strengthened if we chose to agree with Palagia's argument (2000: 203–6, *pace* Stewart 1993: 281–2) that a Messenian marble relief depicting a lion hunt scene was commissioned by Polyperchon, who controlled the city of Messene from *c.* 316 onwards; on this basis, we could posit a progression from Craterus' initial dedicatory activity, *c.* 322–321, through Craterus junior's completion of the dedication under Polyperchon's aegis (or, indeed, Polyperchon's completion under Craterus junior's name), *c.* 319–316, finally to Polyperchon's commissioning of the Messene imitation, *c.* 316 onwards.
25 Second-in-command: Arr. *Anab.* VII 12.4. European deputy: Just. *Epit.* XIII 6.9.
26 See esp. Pollitt 1986: 38; Paspalas 2000: 211–19.
27 Cf. Pollitt 1986: 38; Stewart 1993: 273; Seyer 2006: 184.
28 Voutiras 1984: 62.
29 The problematic nature of *imitatio* as a conceptual monolith has been well-discussed by Green 1978: 1–26. Cf. Cohen 1995: 483–506, accepting Green's typology of *imitatio*, *aemulatio* and *comparatio* and applying it to Alexander and Achilles. For more reflection on this problem, see Chapter 3.1.
30 Homolle 1897: 598–600.
31 Fearn 2013: 232.
32 Cf. Christian 2015: 236.
33 See Voutiras 1984: 57–62; Stewart 1993: 271; Bosworth 2002: 277 n.118; Dunn and Wheatley 2012: 43.
34 Voutiras 1984: 58.
35 See Cummins 2009: 317–34; Scott 2010: 134; Aston 2012: 41–60.
36 Scott 2010: 133.
37 See e.g. Sider 2006: 327–46.
38 Currie 2005: 136.
39 E.g. Peek 1961: 297–8.
40 See Barbantani 2012: 37–55.
41 Viz. 'greatly renowned', as opposed to 'holding various opinions' (cf. Diog. Laert. 9.3[23]).
42 Most obviously, Odysseus πολύτροπος (an ambiguous word, aptly meaning many things) in the opening line of the *Odyssey*: Strauss Clay 1983: 25–34, esp. 31–2.
43 *Il.* IX 673, X 544, XI 430; *Od.* XII 184.
44 Cf. Strauss Clay 1983: 26–7, on Odysseus' shadowy anonymity in the opening lines of the *Odyssey*: 'He is far better characterized by the multiplicity of his experience … and his sufferings … and his intelligence.'

45 Discussed in Chapter 1.
46 E.g. *Homeric Hymn to Aphrodite* 6.9 (earrings from the Horae to Aphrodite); *Od.* I 312 (gift from Telemachus to *incognito* Athena); *Od.* IV 614 and XV 114 (gift from Menelaus to Telemachus – here, Menelaus gives the worthiest gift possible in response to Telemachus' performative demonstration of his noble); *Od.* VIII 385 (Alcinous proposes that twelve *basileis* give cloak, tunic and a talent of gold to Odysseus).
47 E.g. *Od.* I 393, linking *basileia* to state of honour. At *Odyssey* XVIII 158–62, Penelope can become 'more greatly ... honoured' (τιμήεσσα ... μᾶλλον) by her husband and son than before: already she has an embedded, hierarchical 'honour', yet it can be enhanced via extraordinary action.
48 On some of these complexities of 'honour', Scodel 2008; Cairns 2011: 23–41.
49 Pindar *Isthmian* IV 7.
50 On this poem, Boeke 2007: 111–30, 164–6.
51 See Fearn 2013: 231–53.
52 Pindar *Nemean* V 1–5.
53 Fearn 2013: 231–53.
54 Boeke 2007: 165.
55 Again Boeke 2007: 165.
56 Goldhill 1991: 166 (original parentheses).
57 Paspalas 2000: 212 for a discussion of some cognate terms, e.g. ταυροκτόνος at Soph. *Phil.* 400–2, referring to the lions harnessed to Cybele's chariot.
58 Kurke 1991: 8.
59 See Chapters 1 and 4.1.
60 Nagy 1974: 231–55; 1999: 16–17.
61 Svenbro 1993: 14–15.
62 Svenbro 1993: 55. 1. On the other hand, *kleos* itself is extremely rare in dedicatory inscriptions and, to my knowledge, refers to contexts of athletic victory (e.g. *IvO* 174, for the boxer Pelasgus, at Olympia, in the late 4th/early 3rd century, using καλόν *kleos*; see also Archon's monument, discussed further below).
63 See Nagy 1974: 231–55.
64 See Nagy 1974: 231–55; Svenbro 1993: 23, 54–5.
65 Cf. the μνημεῖα ἀΐδια ('eternal memorials') at Thuc. II.41.4, within Pericles' funeral speech, where Pericles asserts that Athens does not need a Homer to be its ἐπαινέτης ('praise-poet'), because it creates its own 'eternal memorials' through its actions. See also Meyer 2005: 53–6 on the close association of μνήμη and *kleos*. This may be a very close parallel to the performance-derived *kleos* ἀΐδιον of Craterus' monument. See also Plut. *Per.* 12.4, where ἀΐδιος δόξα will stem from Athens' Periclean building programme.
66 Bacchyl. *Dith.* 17; *Ep.* 9.40.
67 *P.Oxy.* 1790 fr. 1.47.

68 Heraclitus DK B29. *Pace* Kahn 1979: 329–30 nn.313–14, sceptical of Heraclitean influence on Simonides. Cf. the ἀέναος τίμα of Pindar's *Olympian* XIV 12.
69 Fearn 2013: 236–7.
70 Cf. R. Thomas 1995: 104–29. Cameron 1995: 272–3, referring to essentially the same model in Simonides' Plataea elegy: 'It is a device that elevates both poet and subject'; he also refers to the process by which Homer was made into a panegyrical model by later elaborators of that genre.
71 cf. R. Thomas 2007: 163: '[V]ictory celebration and funerary monuments share one thing, which is the preoccupation with memory and fame (*mnēma, kleos*): both were, in a way, trying to avoid oblivion.'
72 Svenbro 1993: 164; Day 2010: 44.
73 Svenbro 1993: 26–43.
74 On this centrality of the *oikos* in Pindar, Kurke 1991: 13–82.
75 *Il.* IX 410–16.
76 On 'Homeric' Macedonia, Cohen 1995: 483–506; Carlier 2000: 259–68.
77 More on this in Chapters 3.2, 5.1.
78 Cf. Peek 1961: 297–8.
79 *Il.* I 320–48, III 118–20, IV 192ff., VII 276ff., XIX 184, 196–7, 250ff., XXIII 883.
80 See Dyson and Lee 2000: 141–73.
81 E.g. Carney 2015: 265–81.
82 See Chapter 5.1.
83 *Il.* I 129, IV 33–40, V 642, VIII 241, 288, XIII 813–14 (see next note), XIV 251, XX 30; *Od.* III 85, IV 176, VIII 495; Hes. *Op.* 189; Xen. *Anab.* VII 1.29
84 The only outlying Iliadic usage is XIII 813–14, where Ajax declares that he recognizes Hector's intention 'to sack' (ἐξαλαπάξειν) the Achaeans' ships. The verb still probably has a city as its frame of objective reference, since the ships effectively function as the Achaeans' home community during their long siege of Troy. On the other hand, the only outlying usage in the *Odyssey* (IV 176) has no concrete objective reference beyond a hypothetical *polis*.
85 On this metonymy, Paspalas 2000: 211–19.
86 Borza 1990: 5.
87 Hdt. V 22.
88 For general discussion of this issue, see the balanced treatment of Borza 1990: 77–97. Also useful are the recent comments of Carney 2015: xiv–xv.
89 See Whitmarsh 2002: 174–5. Cf. J. M. Hall 1997: 63–4.
90 On the lasting symbolic of the Heraclid family, see Sahlins 2011: 63–101.
91 Currie 2005: 134. It is noteworthy that later Philip II and then Alexander the Great are said (Plut. *Alex.* 4.10–11) to have disdained the foot race; perhaps they did not want to undermine their ancestor's efforts in the potential event of a defeat.
92 See e.g. ANS 1944.100.12153-12155 (wolf), 1963.268.52 (lion).

93 See e.g. Hatzopoulos 1996: no.73. Cf. Hammond 1972: 155–6; Cohen 2010: 73; Christesen and S. C. Murray 2010: 430–1.
94 Carney 2015: 265–81.
95 Franks 2015: 35–46.
96 ANS 1944.100.12171. See also Yale University Art Gallery 2007.182.307: didrachm, bearded Heracles / horse.
97 On the *topos*, see Rodríguez Pérez 2011: 1–18.
98 Greenwalt 1993: 509–19.
99 E.g. the Eurymedon vase: MKG, Hamburg, 1981.173. Cf. Llewellyn-Jones 2017: 97–115.
100 For a similar discussion see Franks 2015: 35–46.
101 Yale University Art Gallery, 2004.6.1480.
102 Yale University Art Gallery 2001.87.9717-9718. These *hopla* are famously borne by Alexander the Great and Ptolemy in an Olympian vignette early in Theocritus *Idyll* XVII 30–1.
103 Diod. XVI 8.7. cf. Plut. *Alex.* 4.9.
104 On the latter, see Markle 1976: 80–99.
105 Isocrates *To Philip* (5.)105–6.
106 Markle 1976: 80–99.
107 Ma 1999 remains a superb study.
108 E.g. ANS 1944.100.12295.
109 Cf. the ithyphallic hymn for Demetrius, delivered in 291/290, in which the Athenians mirror in song the importance of Poseidon that had featured in Demetrius' own self-representation: Holton 2014: 370–90.
110 Meadows 2014: 169–95; Thonemann 2015: 3–23.
111 Among other scholars, the date of 336 is particularly favoured by Price (1991: 1.27–30), and a date of c. 333 by de Callataÿ (2012: 178–9). Troxell 1997: 86–9 convincingly gives a date of 333/332 on the basis of comparison with prior Tarsian satrapal coinage; accepted and further reinforced by Le Rider 2007: 8–14, 113–23.
112 On the subsequent dominance of Phidian Zeus, Barringer 2010: 155–77.
113 See Troxell 1997: pl. 18A–B. Cf. Le Rider 2007: 118–19.
114 E.g. ANS 1944.100.31023.
115 Thonemann 2015: 3–23.
116 Cf. Franks 2015: 35–46.
117 For a thorough (though at times perhaps unrealistic) overview of the extent to which Alexander modelled himself on Heracles, see Amitay 2010.
118 Noting the reservation expressed in the previous note, for the extent to which Alexander modelled himself on Heracles, see Amitay 2010.
119 Palagia 1986: 137–51.
120 Cf. Stewart 1993: 273.

121 Marini 2007: 4–16 discusses the possibilities of date and authorship.
122 Cf. the characterizations of the Ptolemaic court at Polybius XV 25.23 (full of ὕβρις, ὑπερηφανία and ῥᾳθυμία), as well as the ὑπερηφανία of the Pontic king Pharnaces at XXIV 1.2. Interestingly, it is the overbearing Roman behaviour towards Perseid Macedonia that constitutes ὑπερηφανία at Polybius XXVII 8.12 and XIX 4.9.
123 See section 1, above.
124 Strootman 2014: 156–60, on purple especially.
125 Given the contrast with Antipater's smallness, it seems that ὄγκος here does not mean 'pride' or 'haughtiness': cf. Plut. *Eum.* 6.2, on the spread of Persian ὄγκος and τρυφή, to the detriment of Macedonian national customs.
126 Aelian *VH* 9.3; *Suda* s.v. Λεοννάτος (λ249).
127 E.g. Demetrius at Gaza. Diod. XIX 81.4; Pyrrhus in Macedonia: Plut. *Pyrrh.* 11.5.
128 Arr. *Succ.* 1.27. Cf. Plut. *Eum.* 6.1.
129 For performance, cf. the poet Arion's σκευή at Hdt. I 24.4, σκευή for comic dramatic production at Lys. 21.4 For religious office in particular, Andocides 1.112 (ceremonial, priestly σκευή) and Eur. *Bacch.* 178–80 (equipment for worshipping Dionysus).
130 See Spawforth 2007: 82–120.
131 Spawforth 2007: 84.
132 Diod. XVIII 33. Cf. XI 53, 67 (Sicilian tyrants).
133 See n.10 above.
134 Plut. *Eum.* 7.2.
135 See the reconstruction of section 1, above, esp. n.24.
136 See Alonso Troncoso 2009: 276–98.
137 Voutiras 1984: 58.
138 Day 2010: 39, 183–7.
139 Athenaeus 696e–697a [15.52]. On Hermippus and the *ithyphallos*, Markovich 1988: 8–19.
140 Plut. *Lys.* 18.2–4.
141 Cameron 1995: 263–302.

3 Heroic Paradigms of Rulership and the Politics of *imitatio*

1 On the location of the Aspasians and the Macedonian campaigns against them, Bosworth 1988: 119–21; Heckel 2020: 223–8. For the Indian campaigns in general, Bosworth 1988: 118–39; Rapin 2017: 37–121; Heckel 2020: 221–64.
2 On Arrian's use of Ptolemy, e.g. Bosworth 1980: 17–34; Squillace 2018: 119–39, esp. 121–4; Leon 2021: esp. 24–32.
3 Cf. Howe 2009: 215, arguing that Ptolemy is sometimes presented as superior to Alexander in Arrian's account of the Indian campaigns.

4   On spoliation, Ready 2007: 13–17.
5   Bosworth 1996: 45–6, with nn.44–7.
6   See Friedrich 2003: 133.
7   Most obviously, Sarpedon's thigh injury at Tlepolemus' hands at *Il.* V 660–2. Cf. Felton 2017: 246: Areïlycus' wounds 'probably reflect reality rather than metaphor'; and Brügger 2018: ad loc. 309, that '[w]hen a weapon pierces the body in its entirety, this usually results in death for the warrior concerned'. Also note that Areïlycus was perhaps mid-flight, hence the thigh-wound: Janko 1994: ad loc. 307–10.
8   Even if Ptolemy had provided simply the 'facts' that Arrian would later embellish in his own heightened show of Homerizing (cf. Bosworth 1996: 46), it is telling that they could speak for themselves, and in a sense anticipate or dictate the nature of their own reception because of their original arrangement (cf. Bing 2009: 1–2, on reception of particular strings of words). For a wider look at Arrian's Homeric language, Liotsakis 2019: 205–24.
9   On *Il.* XVI and Patroclus' central role in it, see Janko 1994: 309–14; Brügger 2018: 9–13.
10 Cf. Howe 2009: 224.
11 See also Howe 2009: 215–33, on similarity with pharaonic traditions of royal accomplishment, aimed at an Egyptian elite.
12 On Alexander as Achilles *redivivus*, see the summary of past scholarship at Liotsakis 2019: 12 n.33. Portraits of Achilles seem to have taken on aspects of Alexander's imagery in the Hellenistic period, in a kind of circular mimesis: Trofimova 2012: 33–58. On Hephaestion as Patroclus, e.g. Palagia 2000: 167–206; Liotsakis 2019: 201–5.
13 Bosworth 1996: 47.
14 For monomachy in the *Iliad*, see Glück 1964: 25–31; van Wees 1988: 1–24. Pritchett 1984: 15–21 enumerates no fewer than seventeen discrete examples of monomachy from the literary record, in both mythical and historical events, and puts this in an ancient Mediterranean context. On the individual, cf. Zanker 2004: 104: 'The foregrounding of the individual is ... cardinal in the imaging of the heroic mythical past.'
15 Diod. XVIII 31.1.
16 Some of the more prominent examples include: Alexander and Spithridates at Granicus (Diod. XVII 20.3–5); Alexander's general Erigyius and Satibarzanes at Issus (Arr. *Anab.* II 8.9; Curt. III 9.8) and Gaugamela (Arr. *Anab.* III 11.10; Diod. XVII 57.3); Ariston and Satropates (Curt. IV 9.25; Plut. *Alex.* 39.2); Neoptolemus and Eumenes (Diod. XVIII 31; Just. XIII 8.8; Nep. *Eum.* 4.2; Plut. *Eum.* 7.7–13); Seleucus and Nicanor (App. *Syr.* 55); Craterus' personal killing of many enemies (Plut. *Eum.* 7.3); Pyrrhus and Pantauchus (Plut. *Pyrrh.* 7.4); Pyrrhus and a Carthaginian champion (Plut. *Pyrrh.* 24.2–3); Demetrius at Salamis (Diod. XX 52.1–2). Without a

good reason for scepticism, we should accept their historicity, even while allowing for significant literary stylization. For comparative evidence of monomachy, Pritchett 1984: 15–21. See also Eckstein 2006: 197–200, comparing Hellenistic monomachy with the Roman *spolia opima*; Oakley 1985: 392–410, on single combat in Regal Rome but also in the Roman Republic, with more recent comments by Armstrong 2016: 118, 268–9.

17 Van Wees 1988: 23.
18 Cf. Mitchell 2013: 57–90 on the link between *aretē* and the right to rule in Archaic and Classical Greece, esp. the idea (67) that the Hellenistic ideological emphasis on warfare and imperialism is to be linked to earlier traditions of proving *aretē*. Cf. Gehrke 1982: 247–77.
19 See Ready 2007: 3–43; Scodel 2008.
20 On Hellenistic individualism, see Pollitt 1986, where it is identified as one of the five big themes distinctive of Hellenistic art; see also Chaniotis 2005: 194. Cf. the qualifications of Masséglia 2015: 5, 312 on social grouping.
21 On individualistic scenes in Archaic art, see T. Hölscher 2003: 1–17.
22 See Krentz 2002: 23–39; T. Hölscher 2003: 1–17; Tejada 2004: 129–46. Cf. Brown Ferrario 2014, on 'Great Man' tradition.
23 See the important studies of Goukowsky 1978–81; Ogden 2011.
24 See e.g. Burkert 1979: 1–34, esp. 5–10.
25 Important studies include Green 1978: 1–26; Bohm 1989; Trofimova 2012; Wallace 2018a: 162–96.
26 Fowler 2000: 119.
27 Cf. Potolsky 2006: 51.
28 Cf. Potolsky 2006: 52: 'Imitation is the effective origin of tradition itself.'
29 See e.g. Fantuzzi and Hunter 2004; Acosta–Hughes 2010.
30 See e.g. Fantuzzi and Hunter 2004: 376–7; Sens 2004: 65–83; Hunter 2005: 187–206; Gutzwiller 2014: 75–96.
31 Cf. Klooster 2011: 120–1.
32 Cf. Harrell 2002: 440, 441–8; Morgan 2015: 9, 225.
33 See Millar 1993: 230, 257; Dahmen 2007: 3.
34 Sammons 2017: 157.
35 See Roisman 2012: 97 (Diodorus shows 'almost shameless bias'), with earlier references at n.30.
36 Cf. Holton 2018a: 106–8.
37 On this striking coin series, e.g. Lane Fox 1996: 87–108; Holt 2003; Bhandare 2007: 208–56.
38 For the initial series coin, see: *PCO* I 1.26. Scholars place the coin anywhere between 322 and 319 BC. 322: Zervos 1967: 1–16; Kuschel 1961: 16–17 (dates to 322/321). 321: Mørkholm 1991: 63; Stewart 1993: 233; Hazzard 1995a: 72. 320: Le Rider de

Callataÿ 2006: 100, 131; von Reden 2007: 35 (dates to 321/320). 319: Lorber 2005: 62; Dahmen 2012: 286. Lorber has now proven that the series post-dated Perdiccas' invasion. The suggestion by Emmons 1954: 69-84, esp. 73-4, that it was connected to Ptolemy's annexation of Syria in 319 is unlikely.

39 Dahmen 2007: 112-14. See also Chapter 4.3.
40 Holton 2018b: 107-8. That the elephant-scalp refers to Ptolemy's defeat of Perdiccas is argued by Kuschel 1961: 16-17, her date of 322/321 for the issue is inconsistent with the chronology of Perdiccas' invasion (Boiy 2007: 148; Meeus 2012: 77-8). Rosen 1979: 467 and n.30 believes the viewer would not link it to Ptolemy.
41 Prior symbolism argued for the elephant-scalp include: Ammon; Heracles; Dionysus; Alexander's conquest of India; Africa; an implication of 'power far extended'. For convenient summary, see Stewart 1993: 233, with bibliography at 233-4 nn.13-14. Important studies since include Köhler 1996: 111-12 (the Dionysian conquest of India); von Reden 2007: 37 (Alexander's Indian conquests plus Heracles); Lorber 2011: 293-356 (a positional parallel for Egyptian headwear, the trunk matching the *uraeus*).
42 On Cleomenes of Naucratis, Burstein 2009: 107-44; Baynham 2015: 127-34.
43 Diod. XVIII 28.1-2. For the carriage, see Diod. XVIII 26.1-28.4; Stewart 1993: 216-21. Erskine 2002a: 169, 174 calls it a 'temple on wheels'.
44 See Ready 2007: 3-43; Scodel 2008.
45 Cf. Deacy 2008: 55.
46 Cf. Athena's enhancement of Diomedes' arms at *Iliad* V 1-8.
47 Edwards 1991: 169-70.
48 See e.g. Aphrodite's protection of Aeneas (enfolding him in her robe) at *Il.* V 310-17. On the scheme, with references, Marks 2010: 300-22.
49 However, cf. *Il.* XXIV 20-1: Apollo uses the *aegis* (loaned from Zeus) to protect the dead Hector from Achilles' desecration.
50 In the *Iliad*, the *aegis* connected to Athena is held and shaken in order to inspire fear or courage (II 445-50, V 735-40) but can also be worn to protect (XXI 400-5). Conversely, the *aegis* connected to Zeus can be held and shaken (IV 165-70, XVII 590-5; shaken by Apollo: XV 225-30, 305-10, 315-20, 360-5), but it is *not* worn and carries no connotations of protection.
51 Cf. Deacy 2008: 59.
52 *Il.* I 194-218.
53 Athenian black-figure amphora, *c.* 525-475, Leagros Group. Beazley 351214 (Essen, Folkwang Museum A176)
54 XVII 555-75.
55 Rutherford 2019: 135.
56 Rutherford 2019: 135-6.
57 Plut. *Alex.* 2-3; Diod. XVII 1.5.

58 Thonemann 2015: 11–12.
59 See Stewart 1993: 243–52; Ogden 2015: 129–50.
60 See e.g. *PCO* I 1.108–27.
61 See Lorber 2005: 45–64; Dahmen 2012: 281–92.
62 See Fleischer 1996: 30–1.
63 On Alexander's remains as a hero's bones, Erskine 2002a: 174–5; Amitay 2010: 90–3. Examples of translocating mythical heroes' bones: Pelops (Paus. V 13.4–6), Oedipus (Paus. I 28.7; cf. Soph. *OC* 1518ff.), Hector (Paus. IX 18.5; Lycophr. *Alex.* 1189–213; *Schol. in Hom. Il.* 13.1 (= Aristodemos *FGrH* 383 F7)), Orpheus (Paus. IX 30.9–11), Orestes (Hdt. I 66–8; Paus. III 3.5–6, III 11.10), Tisamenus (Paus. VII 1.8), Minos (Diod. IV 79.3–4), Theseus (Plut. *Thes.* 36; Plut. *Cim.* 8), Rhesus (Polyaen. *Strat.* VI 53), Arcas (Paus. VIII 9.3–4), Hippodamia (Paus. VI 20.7), Alcmene (Plut. *Mor.* 557e–578a), Aristomenes (Paus. IV 32.3) and Melanippus (Hdt. V 67–8). In general see McCauley 1998: 225–39. Cf. more 'historical' heroes, too, e.g. Leonidas of Sparta: Paus. III 14.1, with McCauley 1998: 288–9 n.15.
64 Erskine 2002a: 163–79; Holton 2018a: 103–4.
65 Parker 2011: 120–1.
66 Cf. Lund 1992: 53–4, on Lysimachus' influence in controlling the land link between Europe and Asia.
67 See Heckel 1982: 373–81.
68 Was this as satrap or *strategos*? See Delev 2000: 384, with n.5. A broad *strategia* over Balkan and Euxine areas east of Macedon seems likeliest, rather than the transposition of a Persian governing title to a European area adjacent to Macedon itself.
69 See the treatment of Lund 1992: 22–32. Early accounts of Seuthes' actions may be found at Diod. XVIII 14.2–4; Arr. *Succ.* 10 (Roos).
70 Though he did, seemingly, take Antipater's side and allowed crossings through his territory: Lund 1992: 54–5.
71 Arr. *Succ.* 1.38; Lund 1992: 54. On the post-Alexander *sōmatophylakia*, see Heckel 1980: 249–50; Holton 2018b: 125–6 n.4.
72 Lund 1992: 55–7.
73 See Diod. XIX 105. The official date for Alexander IV's death is given by the *Marmor Parium* (*FGrH* 239 B18), which places it within the archonship of Hieromnemon, i.e. late June 310–late June 309.
74 Diod. XX 37.1–6. On the importance of such attempts at capturing a blood-link to the Argead line in this period, see e.g. Carney 2000: 114–52; Meeus 2009a: 63–92; 2009c: 235–50.
75 Just. *Epit.* XV 3.15.
76 *Pace* Heckel 1992: 247 n.75, that this was the same lion hunt in which Craterus saved Alexander's life.

77 Heckel 1992: 247; 2006: 153–4, connecting this to Lysimachus' role as *somatophylax*.
78 Curt. VIII 1.14–16. *Pace* Bosworth 2002: 275 and n.110.
79 See Lund 1992: 6–7, with sources for story variations at 210 n.18.
80 Lund 1992: 6–7. Most other scholars agree that the story of the cage is either a *topos* or outright fiction, e.g. Bosworth 2002: 276 n.112; Yardley and Atkinson 2009: 164, 227. Heckel 1992: 247–8 suggests that Trogus was the source of the story's circulation in Latin texts, but that its original promulgation in the Greek source tradition was by a contemporary or near-contemporary of Lysimachus.
81 Lund 1992: 6–8, 160–1. cf. Baldus 1978: 196–8; Huttner 1997: 146–51.
82 Baldus 1978: 191, 196–8, followed by Lund 1992: 160.
83 Lund 1992: 160; Billows 1995: 102; Meadows 2012: 129 and n.38.
84 de Callataÿ and Kan 2009: 111 n.3, *pace* Callataÿ 2012: 181. Cf. M. Thompson 1968: 163–82, with pl. 16–22.
85 Plut. *Alex* 2.2. Largely the same story at Ephorus *FGrH* 70 F217. On the mythologization here, Ogden 2011: 8–12.
86 *Pace* Baldus 1987: 402–6.
87 See Pollitt 1986: 289–90.
88 Diod. XVIII 27.1–3. Cf. Stewart 1993: 216–18.
89 On lion symbolism in ancient Macedon, see Cohen 2010: 64–118.
90 Memnon *BNJ* 434 F1.7.5–6. On the *Leontophoros*, Murray 2012: 171–8.
91 Cf. Tarn 1913: 131.
92 On Demetrius and Lamia, Wheatley 2003: 30–6.
93 Bosworth 2002: 277.
94 E.g. Patroklos at *Il.* XVI 467; Menelaos at *Il.* XVII 61–9, 109–12.
95 Cf. Briant 1991: 242–4 (royal hunt); Palagia 2000: 181; Paspalas 2000: 111–19.
96 Hdt. VII 125–6; Paus. VI 5.4.
97 Paus. VI 5.4–5.
98 For summary, Cohen 2010: 68–71, with bibliography at 313 nn.10–13.
99 See also e.g. Xen. *Cyn.* 11.1; Arist. *HA* 579b, 606b; Plin. *HN* VIII 17; Dio Chry. 21.
100 Cohen 2010: 70–1.
101 As a single treatment of Pyrrhus, Lévêque 1957 has yet to be surpassed.
102 Chapinal-Heras 2021: 95.
103 Cf. Masséglia 2015: 38–40.
104 On the history of Dodona, see Dieterle 2007; Chapinal-Heras 2021. On the coin, Pötscher 1966: 113–47; Breitenberger 2007: 17.
105 See Dieterle 2007: 225 and 380, F603; Chapinal-Heras 2021: 82.
106 Paus. I 13.3. See Dieterle 2007: 225–6 and 375, F425; Chapinal-Heras 2021: 82. For the link to Gonatas' dedication of 274, Dakaris 1971: 43–6.
107 On Hellenistic royal benefaction and gifting, especially to temples, recently Eyal 2013: 134–5; Strootman 2020: 137–78. Bringmann 2000 remains an important study.

108 BMC Greek (Thessaly) 111.8; ANS 1979.151.2; MFA 1985.235.
109 Fleischer 1996: 29–30 for general overview.
110 On the signification of beardedness and beardlessness, Alonso Troncoso 2010: 13–24.
111 Stewart 1993: 158–9; Trofimova 2021: 66–7.
112 Plut. *Pyrrh.* 1. For earlier stress on this lineage, Pind. *N.* 4.51–3, 7.37–8; *Paian* 6.109.
113 See e.g. ANS 1944.100.57085. Rutter 1997: 177 allows the possibility that this may be a personification of the Phthia region in Thessaly, from which Pyrrhus hailed. It seems more likely that the 'mother' image of Phthia aligns with (i) Dione and (ii) the Sicilian context of widespread worship for Demeter, who is also represented on Pyrrhus' coins there in maternal guise, opposite her daughter Kore (see e.g. ANS 1944.100.57086-57088).
114 *Iliad* XVIII 478–608. On reception, Hardie 1985: 11–31.
115 Cf. Callen King 1991: 12.
116 Gehrke 1982: 247–77; Austin 1986: 450–66.
117 Just. *Epit.* XVII 3.
118 See e.g. Brosius 2021: 150–1 (near eastern and eastern Mediterranean context) and Ogden 1999 (Hellenistic royal polygamy and international diplomacy).
119 Diod. XXII 8.2.
120 Erskine 2002b: 97–115.
121 For examples, ANS 1906.26.13, 1944.100.57090-57095. Some face right rather than left, e.g. ANS 1944.100.57096-57097.
122 Patterson 2010: 76–9.
123 Plutarch *Pyrrhus* 22.4–6.
124 Patterson 2010: 76.
125 Plut. *Pyrrh.* 6.4–5.
126 Plut. *Pyrrh.* 6.5.
127 In point of fact, Plut. *Pyrrh.* 6.2 explicitly states that Demetrius was delayed 'by matters that he had in hand', but that Pyrrhus was able to come to Antipater.
128 E.g. *Od.* XI 8–168 (Tiresias instructs Odysseus to sacrifice these three animals).
129 Diod. IV 39.1.
130 For examples, BM 2002,0101.1732, 2002,0101.1734.
131 See e.g. the 'baleful birth' in the *Liber de Morte*, foretelling Alexander's death: Baynham 2000: 242–62; Djurslev 2021: 29–55.

4 Diadem and *basileia*: A Zelotypic Model

1 On the theocratic Hasmonean state, including its Hellenistic character, Kropp 2013: 31–5. Cf. Regev 2011: 48, who prefers Strabo's account (XVI 2.40) that Alexander

Jannaeus was the first Hasmonean to call himself *basileus* instead of *hiereus* (i.e. the *Kohen Gadol*, the Judaean high priest).

2 Cf. Regev 2011: 46 n.1.
3 Cf. Babota 2020.
4 See also the condensed account at 1 Maccabees 1.7–9: 'So Alexander reigned for twelve years and then died. And his followers then ruled in his place, each in his own land. And after his death they all put diadems upon themselves; so did their sons after them for many years.'
5 On Seleucid rule in Judaea, Eckhardt 2016a: 57–87; 2016b: 55–70.
6 Cf. Trampedach 2013: 249–50, also speculating on audiences for 'Hellenistic self-presentation'.
7 Cf. Meyers and Chancey 2012: 45, on the numismatic iconography of the Hasmoneans, indicating borrowing from and participation in Hellenistic royal culture.
8 First extant usage is Xen. *Cyr.* VIII 3.13, and it is in fact the only pre-Alexander usage of the word. Smith 1988: 34 and n.27 argues that, from the beginning, διάδημα had the limited sense of 'royal headband'.
9 Attempts to argue for a Macedonian metal 'diadem' are based primarily on excavations from pre-Hellenistic Argead Macedonian tombs at Vergina and result from results confusion in modern parlance for 'diadem'. There is no evidence, especially in the period of the *diadochoi*, for metal 'diadems' in the principal regalia of the Hellenistic kings. See Lehmann 1980: 527–31; Calder 1981: 334–5; Fredricksmeyer 1981: 330–4; Calder 1983: 102–3; Fredricksmeyer 1983: 99–102; Andronikos 1984: 171–5; Ritter 1984: 105–11; Smith 1988: 34–5; Fredricksmeyer 1997: 97–109; *OCD*[4] s.v. 'diadem'; Strootman 2014a: 217 n.21.
10 White: Plin. *NH* XI 16; Luc. *Dial. Mort.* XIII 4; Ael. *NA.* XV 2. White with blue: Curt. III 3.19. White with purple: Curt. III 6.4–5.
11 Smith 1988: 34 and n.26, 111 adduces compelling reasons for considering it white.
12 Bevan 1902: 1.57 and Lattey 1917: 329 suggest that it was linen.
13 See e.g. the debate about whether the headband on Ptolemy's first issue of his coinage depicting Alexander with an elephant-scalp is a diadem or a *mitra*, based on positional issues: Ritter 1987: 298; Stewart 1993: 233; Collins 2012: 382; Dahmen 2012: 291. Cf. Grimm 1978: 103; Von Reden 2007: 37, with n.29.
14 Strootman 2014a: 216.
15 Smith 1988: 36 and n.45 notes the possibility but considers it unlikely. Cf. Novák 2012: 9–34.
16 Ritter 1965, esp. 6–31, 31–41, 49–55, 125–7; 1984: 105–11; 1987: 290–301; Musgrave et al. 1984: 71, 72 and n.32 (cloth diadem is Persian, the metal Macedonian); Fredricksmeyer 1986: 216, 227; Collins 2001: 200–1 and n.10; 2012: 371–402, esp. 377–85; Elliott 2008: 180. Cf. Nieswandt 2012: 63–159; Wiesehöfer 2012: 55–62.

17 Droysen ed. 1952: 2.6; Hoffmann 1906: 55–6; Mamroth 1949–52: 13; Franke 1952–3: 108; 1956: 110; Taeger 1957: 32, 460; Fredricksmeyer 1981: 332–3; 1983: 99–100; Hammond 1989: 24; 1991: 81. Cf. Lichtenberger 2012: 163–79.
18 Smith 1988: 36–8, 111 (along with victory symbolism); Stewart 1993: 233; Fredricksmeyer 1997: 97–109; 2000: 142, 155, 161. Cf. Meyer 2012: 209–31.
19 Bevan 1902: 2.274; Alf(ldi 1985: 105–32; Smith 1988: 34–8; Chamoux 2002: 228; von Reden 2007: 37 and n.29 (on Ptolemaic coinages, both victory band and Dionysian attribute). Cf. S. Lehmann 2012: 181–208; Mileta 2012: 315–34.
20 Von Lieven 2012: 35–54. Cf. Smith 1988: 36. On the Egyptian headband, Stanwick 2002: 35.
21 Martin 2012: 249–78.
22 Cf. Lichtenberger et al. eds 2012.
23 On the reconstruction, North 2008: 144–60.
24 Cic. *Phil.* 2.85; Livy *Per.* 116; Quint. *Inst.* 9.3.61.
25 Capponi 2021: 67.
26 North 2008: 146.
27 Cf. Gradel 2002: 136.
28 Capponi 2021: 65–6.
29 The dating is controversial, with some believing the accessions rolled on until 302. In addition to the discussion below, see Meeus 2014: 294, with nn.114–16 for general overview of the debate and earlier references.
30 The date for Alexander IV's death is unclear, but there are factors which suggest that it occurred during 310 or 309, not later: Wheatley 1998: 12–23, esp. 17–18; Yardley, Wheatley and Heckel 2011: 233–7; Wheatley and Dunn 2020: 162, with n.12.
31 Cf. Mileta 2012: 316 on the paradigmatic impact.
32 Gruen 1985: 254.
33 See the overview at Mikalson 1988: 75–85; Wheatley and Dunn 2020: 203–36. For the wider context, Shipley 2018: 46–54.
34 Overview and sources at Wheatley 2002: 39–47; van der Spek 2014: 323–44.
35 Recent treatment at Wheatley 2014: 501–15; van der Spek 2014: 323–44; Kosmin 2014a: 32–4; Ogden 2017: 15–16.
36 Kosmin 2014a.
37 See reconstruction and sources at Wheatley and Dunn 2020: 113–26.
38 Mikalson 1988: 83; Paschidis 2013: 121–41.
39 Wheatley 1998: 12–23 believes that news was withheld; Landucci Gattinoni 2003a: 113–21 suggests (perhaps more convincingly) that Cassander did *not* withhold the news.
40 Landucci Gattinoni 2003a: 129.
41 Just. *Epit.* XV 2.10 records that Antigonus ordered that he and Demetrius be styled kings after Salamis, while App. *Syr.* 54 simply writes that the army began to call Antigonus and Demetrius kings afterwards. Neither mentions the diadem. The

anonymous Heidelberg Epitome writes that Antigonus called himself king and took up the diadem: ὠνόμασεν ἑαυτὸν βασιλέα καὶ ἐφόρεσε διάδημα (*BNJ* 155, F1.7).

42 See Gruen 1985: 255–7; Billows 1990: 157–8; Wheatley and Dunn 2020: 160–3.
43 Wheatley and Dunn 2020: 160 n.5.
44 Cf. Müller 1973: 80–1. On the theatrical/tragic messenger trope, it is significant that Aristodemus is called Demetrius' αὐτάγγελον ('messenger of his own words', i.e. an eyewitness). But it is rare that a messenger brings good news in a tragedy (cf. Barrett 2002: xv), hence Plutarch's construction of Antigonus' anxiety and the special formulation of Aristodemus' message as a εὐαγγέλιον ('good news-item') after delivery. Plutarch's theatrical/tragic modelling is well-established (esp. in the Hellenistic *Lives*): De Lacy 1952: 159–71; Mossman 1988: 83–93; 1992: 90–108; Duff 2004: 271–91.
45 Cf. O'Neil 2000: 125.
46 E.g. Granier 1931: 98–101; Ritter 1965: 79–89, 89–91; O. Müller 1973: 81–7; Hammond 2000: 144–5. It is based largely on Appian's statement (*Syr.* 54) that army acclaimed Antigonus and Demetrius. Gruen 1985: 256 provides the right assessment here, as does O'Neil 2000: 125. On the wider debate about the existence of a Macedonian *Staatsrecht*, Errington 1983: 89–101 is an effective summary and rebuttal.
47 E.g. Billows 1990: 158.
48 Strootman 2014a: 230 contends that Plutarch's account 'does not mention the binding on of a diadem', meaning that Antigonus was 'probably already wearing a diadem when he came out of the palace to confront the crowd'. However, Plutarch is extremely clear that the *philoi* of Antigonus *crowned* him immediately after the public acclamation (Ἀντίγονον μὲν οὖν εὐθὺς ἀνέδησαν οἱ φίλοι). The verb ἀνέδησαν literally means 'bound [up]' in the sense of 'crowned' with a headband, hence must here mean a diadem.
49 Plut. *Demetr.* 18.4.
50 Roskam 2009: 124–7; Asirvatham 2017: 262–74, esp. 271–2.
51 E.g. Plut. *Mor.* 778b–f. Cf. *Mor.* 49b–c.
52 Cf. e.g. Gehrke 1982: 247–77; Gruen 1985: 253–71; Austin 1986: 450–66; Billows 1990: 156–7; Bosworth 2002: 247; Wheatley 2009: 61.
53 For the argued link to athletic *tainiai*, cf. Alföldi 1985: 105–25; Chamoux 2002: 228. More recently, Mileta 2012: 315–34 also suggests that the diadem has agonistic symbolism; but he pushes the parallelism with athletic *tainiai* too far.
54 Born *c.* 382: [Luc.] *Macrob.* 11 (= Hieronymos, *FGrH* 154 F8); App. *Syr.* 55; Plut. *Demetr.* 19.4. Cf. Heckel 2006a: 32.
55 Tatum 1996: 142; Mileta 2012: 316.
56 Philip is wrongly called Phoenix by Diod. XX 73.1, who is otherwise explicit that he was 'buried with royal honours' (βασιλικῶς ἔθαψε).

57 Billows 1990: 158.
58 Plutarch's account of the remaining diadochan accessions (*Demetr.* 18.1–2) is demonstrably mistaken in several important details (see the thorough critique at Gruen 1985: 253–71), not least in claiming that Cassander did not take the royal title.
59 Overview at Meeus 2014: 295–7.
60 Meeus 2014: 297. Cf. O'Neil 2000: 118–37.
61 Gruen 1985: 253–71. See also O. Müller 1973; Billows 1990: 155–60; O'Neil 2000: 118–37.
62 On this point, I find the following discussions most convincing: Lehmann 1988: 1–17, esp. 2–8; Worthington 2016: 160–2. Cf. Hölbl 2001: 20. For a convenient list of possibilities, Meeus 2014: 295 n.120. For the Antigonid invasion of Egypt, Wheatley and Dunn 2020: 171–7.
63 Gruen 1985: 257–8 places it between January and July 304. The evidence: the *Marmor Parium* (*FGrH* 239 B23) places the accession between July 305 and July 304; the chronography of Claudius Ptolemaeus (cf. Skeat 1969: 2–4, 28) records Ptolemy's first regnal year in his account of November 305–November 304; and two Egyptian papyrus documents (*P. Dem. Louvre* 2427, 2440) record Alexander IV as still being king in January 304. We know (cf. von Reden 2007: 21) that Ptolemy was not called pharaoh until 28 Daisios (= 12 January) 304, at the memorial day for Alexander the Great's death, but this does not tell us that Ptolemy became *basileus* at the same time (cf. Mileta 2012: 315 n.2). Cf. the Seleucid era which, according to the Macedonian calendar, began in October 312, but only began in April 311 in native Babylonian documentation (cf. Bosworth 2002: 219–20).
64 Cf. Worthington 2016: 161–2.
65 See e.g. Boiy 2000: 115–21.
66 Meeus 2014: 295–6; Worthington 2016: 161–2.
67 See Sanders 2014: 165 for this type of ζηλοτυπία, with a discussion of other types at 163–5; importantly, this does not necessarily convey 'sexual' jealousy (49, 164–5). It would seem that we are not dealing here with the Stoic conception of ζηλοτυπία, which according to Konstan 2006: 223 'occurs because another person has what we ourselves already possess: we want to be the only one who has it'.
68 Sanders 2014: 4, 46–7. Cf. Konstan 2006: 223 on the Stoic sense of *zelos*, as meaning 'pain at someone else getting what one wanted, when one does not get it oneself'.
69 See Konstan 2006: 225, on Polybius IV 87.1–5, concerning the ζηλοτυπία of Hellenistic royal courtiers.
70 III 64.3, 68.4, IV 9.4, 9.6, 54.7.
71 XIX 87.3.
72 E.g. XI 2.1 (Xerxes emulates Carthaginians), 8.3 (Greek combatants at Thermopylae), 32.4 (Spartans and Athenians *versus* the Persians), 42.2 (Aristides,

Xanthippus and Themistocles build up Athenian naval power); 84.2 (Tolmides vies with the fame of Myronides, leading to naval successes), XIII 47.4 (causeway to Euboea built quickly), 70.4 (aid for Lysander), XIX 33.4 (Indian women vie for honour, leading to greater adherence to justice and familial bonds), 83.5 (Ptolemy's and Seleucus' troops at Gaza), XX 6.1 (Greek and Carthaginian rowers compete).
73 Smith 1988: 37.
74 See e.g. Bak 1990.
75 Aurell 2020: 11.
76 Bak 1990: 1. For work on (medieval) coronations, Aurell 2020: 5.
77 Aurell 2020: 10.
78 Bak 1990: 9.
79 Aurell 2020: 38–9. This is also evident in the temporary wearings of a diadem in the invented stories of Lysimachus and Seleucus, discussed in section 3: the contact of the diadem with their head was not just premonitory but transformative, and in Lysimachus' case it is significant that Alexander installs him as king, thus is mediator of his authority.
80 Aurell 2020: 3, 10.
81 Aurell 2020.
82 Aurell 2020: 11–12; also Weiler 2010: 57–88.
83 Aurell 2020: 11.
84 Aurell 2020: 47.
85 Aurell 2020: 45.
86 Aurell 2020: 12.
87 Cf. Fredricksmeyer 2000: 143, on Alexander.
88 On diadochan universalistic ambitions, Strootman 2014b: 307–22.
89 Cf. Cannadine 1983: 160; 1987: 3, 8; Aurell 2020: 31.
90 Cf. Aurell 2020: 29, with 29–31 for wider discussion about agency (esp. 30: self-coronation 'responds to the action of individual agency rather than to social structures').
91 Aurell 2020: 49.
92 On Hellenistic joint kingship, Strootman 2014a: 104–5; Holton 2018b: 101–28. On Antigonid succession, Le Bohec-Bouhet 2005: 57–70.
93 Holton 2018b: 104.
94 Cf. Strootman 2014b: 311.
95 Cf. Holton 2018b: 101–28.
96 Kosmin 2018: 93.
97 Aurell 2020: 76.
98 Wheatley and Dunn 2020: 163 n.19.
99 Diod. XX 53.3: ἀνέλαβε τὸ διάδημα καὶ πρὸς ἅπαντας ἀνέγραφεν ἑαυτὸν βασιλέα. D.L. 5.78 (= Hermippos, *FGrH* 1026 F75): παραδόντος τὸ διάδημα τῷ ἐκ Βερενίκης.

100 Buraselis 2005: 92.
101 Cf. Plut. *Demetr.* 38.8. The cuneiform tablet first attesting to the joint reign of Seleucus and Antiochus dates to 1 Araḫsammu 18 SE = 18 November 294 (Boiy 2004: 138–9). However, this is simply a *terminus ante quem*: Antiochus I's joint kingship may have come even earlier.
102 On Ceraunus, see *EAH* s.v. 'Ptolemy Keraunos'.
103 Memnon of Heracleia *BNJ* 434 F8.3.
104 *Pace* Ritter 1965: 108–13, that Ceraunus gave the diadem to himself because he was a usurper. This is true only insofar as *all* the first Hellenistic kings were usurpers.
105 Just. *Epit.* XXIV 3.1–3; Memnon of Heracleia, *BNJ* 434, F8.3.
106 Diod. XXI 12.6.
107 Diod. XX 12.6.
108 See e.g. Livy XXXV 14.5–12; App. *Syr.* 2.10; Luc. *Dial.* I 12–13, II 25; *True History* II 6–9.
109 Diod. XVII 77; Curt. VI 6; Just. *Epit.* XII 3.
110 I would include here the tradition about Macedonian kings, including Alexander, wearing a diadem wrapped around the *kausia*. Cf. Kingsley 1984: 66–8; Lichtenberger 2012: 163–79.
111 E.g. Arr. *Anab.* VII 9.9 (Opis mutiny). Cf. Bosworth 1988: 103–5; Nagle 1996: 151–72.
112 Smith 1988: 37 n.49, 58–62; Strootman 2007: 371 and n.53; Dahmen 2012: 281–92.
113 A Memphite bronze coin and the so-called 'Porus medallions': M. Price 1991: 1.33, 452–3, 496, with pls. CXLIX g–h. Cf. Dahmen 2012: 281–92.
114 Cf. Palagia 2000: 188, 196, that images of Alexander the Great and Philip III on the Alexander Sarcophagus originally featured diadems. This is far from certain: von Graeve 1970: 138–42; Stewart 1993: 301–2.
115 Cf. Roisman 2012: 73, 82–3.
116 Cf. Anson 2015: 150–1 n.16. For the date of Susiana, Meeus 2012: 91.
117 So Ritter 1965: 62–8; Atkinson and Yardley 2009: 176. *Pace* Anson 2004: 150–1 n.16, that the Susiana account is reduplicating Cyinda.
118 Curt. X 6.4.
119 Diod. XVIII 60.4–61.1; XIX 15.3. cf. Nep. *Eum.* 7.2–3; Plut. *Eum.* 13.4–8; Polyaen. IV 8.2.
120 Diod. XVIII 61.1: 'they performed *proskynesis* to Alexander, as to a god (προσεκύνουν ὡς θεὸν)'.
121 For a recent summary on *proskynesis*, O'Sullivan 2020: 260 n.1.
122 Cf. Curt. X 6.4, detailing tears at the sight.
123 Cf. thrones with regalia in the 'Grand Procession' of Ptolemy II: Athenaeus V 202a–b. Strootman 2014a: 259–60 suggests that these thrones had 'diadems' laid on

them too, but this is unconfirmed: the language used is *stephanê* and *stephanos* ('wreath').
124 Cf. Diod. XVIII 61.3.
125 On Hellenistic regalia, Strootman 2014a: 214–20.
126 Arr. *Anab.* VII 24.
127 Diod. XVII 116.2–4; Plut. *Alex.* 73.3–74.1. On the *mantis*, Flower 2009: esp. 178–81 in connection with Alexander.
128 Cf. McKechnie 2009: 206–26, a full typological reconstruction of the omens.
129 Bottéro 1992: 138–55; accepted by Heckel 2006a: 114. Cf. McKechnie 2009: 210–11; Ogden 2017: 37–8.
130 There is a similar anecdote involving Ptolemy, in the *Alexander Romance*, on which Ogden 2017: 39.
131 Lund 1992: 3.
132 Lund 1992: 157.
133 Arr. *Anab.* VII 22 (= Aristoboulos, *FGrH* 139 F55). Also present at App. *Syr.* 56. Cf. Baynham 2000: 255. Ogden 2011: 99; 2017: 40; Kosmin 2014a: 99.
134 On these traditions, Ogden 2017: 33–8.
135 Arr. *Anab.* VII 22.5.
136 See Fraser 1996: 37–46; Kosmin 2014a: 94–100; Ogden 2017 (diadem at 33–40).
137 Just. *Epit.* XV 3.13.
138 Cf. Yardley, Wheatley and Heckel 2011: 262.
139 App. *Syr.* 64.
140 On Hellenistic royal coinages, Mørkholm 1991; Fleischer 1996: 28–40; de Callataÿ 2012: 175–90.
141 De Callataÿ 2012: 180.
142 Cf. Erickson 2013: 110–11.
143 Mørkholm 1991: 59–60.
144 Newell 1927.
145 Fleischer 1996: 29.
146 M. Price 1991: 1.32–3.
147 See n.113, above.
148 For up-to-date summary, Thonemann 2015: 10–17.
149 Mørkholm 1991: 27; Fleischer 1996: 29; von Reden 2007: 36 and n.26; Kroll 2007: 113–22.
150 For the first coin-type, *PCO* I 1.26. On the dispute regarding type of headband: Köhler 1996: 112 and n.394. Cf. Rosen 1979: 466–7 and n.30.
151 Ritter 1987: 298; Stewart 1993: 233; A. W. Collins 2012: 382; Dahmen 2012: 291. For similar arguments, Grimm 1978: 103; Smith 1988: 56–7, 61. Cf. Von Reden 2007: 37 and n.29.
152 See also *PCO* I 2.B5, B12. *Pace* von Reden 2007: 37 n.29; Dahmen 2012: 287.

153 *PCO* I 1.91. Cf. Lorber 2012: 213.
154 See the chronology of Lorber 2005: 45–64 (298/297 introduction).
155 *SCO* I 101. Cf. Erickson 2013: 110.
156 Hadley 1974: 53; Stewart 1993: 315; Dahmen 2007: 15; 2013: 111.
157 Dahmen 2007: 15; Erickson 2013: 111.
158 De Lisle 2021: 128–30.
159 e.g. ANS 1908.115.6. Cf. De Callataÿ 2012: 181, dating it to 297/296.
160 Polyb. V 67.8. Hadley 1974: 63 also adds that this would have resonated with contemporary Alexander cults in Asia Minor.
161 Cf. Holton 2014: 377–8.
162 E.g. ANS 1944.100.13639. Cf. Newell 1927: 24, 31, 58, 103–8.
163 E.g. ANS 1944.100.13759. Cf. Holton 2014: 377–8.
164 E.g. *SCO* I 323.
165 E.g. *SCO* I 309. On the corpse, App. *Syr.* 62–3. Cf. Holton 2018b: 123–4.
166 Cf. Holton 2018b: 101–28.
167 *SCO* I 322–3. Cf. Erickson 2019: 45.
168 See Sherwin-White and Kuhrt 1993: 27; Boiy 2004: 144; Kosmin 2018.
169 E.g. *PCO* I 1.177.
170 E.g. *PCO* I 1.307.
171 Smith 1988: 36 (emphasis mine).

5 Spear-won Land in Hellenistic Imperial Discourse

1 Diod. XVI 91.2; Just. *Epit.* IX 5.8; Polyaen. *Strat.* V 44.4. Cf. Kholod 2018: 406–46.
2 Diod. XVII 16.3–4; Arr. *Anab.* I 11.1. Cf. Spawforth 2007: 92–3.
3 Arr. *Anab.* I 11.5.
4 Arr. *Anab.* I 11.6. Cf. Just. *Epit.* XI 5.4, implying that Alexander erected twelve altars while on the ship.
5 Arr. *Anab.* I 11.6. This is the same route, in reverse, by which Xerxes had crossed to Europe in 480: Bosworth 1988: 38.
6 Arr. *Anab.* I 11.7.
7 Cf. Kosmin 2014a: 200, on altars on the Jaxartes, plus Visscher 2020: 43–5.
8 Cf. Winter 2010: 312–24. NB These are the same gods on Alexander's coinages after 333/332, whom Stewart 1993: 158–61 argues are his three primary pillars of divine support.
9 Diod. XVII 17.17.3; Strabo XIII 1.26; Plut. *Alex.* 15.7–9; Arr. *Anab.* I 11.7–12.1; Just. *Epit.* XI 5.12. Cf. Erskine 2001: 227–31; Courtieu 2004: 123–58.
10 Cf. Gruen 1984: 620–4; Grainger 2002: 76–97; Eckstein 2008: 311–16.
11 Cf. Ma 1999: 29–31; Chaniotis 2005a: 182–3; 2005b: 458–60.

12 Polyb. XVIII 52.3-5.
13 See Grainger 2002 for detailed study.
14 See the discussion of the four different rights to property (donation, inheritance, purchase, conquest) at Chaniotis 2004: 185-213.
15 The fullest discussion remains Mehl 1980/1: 173-212, which tests whether it represented 'Rechtstitel schlechthin für territoriales Eigentum' (177) in the Hellenistic period, but see also Schmitthenner 1968: 32-9; Billows 1995: 24-33; Virgilio 2003: 75-85. Cf. Boffo 2001: 233-55.
16 This view was developed early, e.g. Tarn 1913: 191; 1921: 19; Rostovtzeff 1941: 1.267. But it also represents the consensus of the last few decades, e.g. Davies 1984: 296; Hammond 1988: 389; Billows 1990: 244-5; Fredricksmeyer 1991: 203; Mørkholm 1991: 26; Smith 1993: 110-11; Stewart 1993: 167; Mileta 2002: 158; Austin 2003: 125; Virgilio 2003: 75-6; Eckstein 2006: 85, 87; Barbantani 2007: 70; Capdetrey 2007: 136; Grainger 2007: 119; Green 2007: 135; A.W. Collins 2012: 372. Holt 2016: 50. For more measured views, cf. Turner 1984: 122 n.5, 148; Foraboschi 2000: 37-43; Manning 2003: 158, 177; Aperghis 2006: 88; Manning 2010: 124-5.
17 Billows 1995: 25.
18 E.g. Walbank 1984: 66; Stewart 1993: 158-71; Billows 1989: 173-206; 1995a: 24-33; Landucci 2003b: 199-224; Virgilio 2003: 75-85; Barbantani 2007: 69; D'Agostini 2018: 64-5. Cf. J. Hornblower 1981: 53, that the term derives from Hieronymus as a real slogan from the period.
19 Davies 1984: 296.
20 Mehl 1980/1: 195-6. Cf. Billows 1995: 26 n.3, strongly disagreeing on this point.
21 Cf. Aperghis 2006: 88. Royal absolutism was merely theoretical – rarely was it practicable, owing to the need to maintain relations with powerful social groups: see e.g. Elias 1983 on the court in mediating these relations.
22 Cf. Bosworth 1988: 38 n.35; Ma 1999: 32.
23 Mehl 1980/1: 180; Davies 1984: 296-7; Chaniotis 2005b: 457-8.
24 See the study of the inscription *SEG* 46.1225 (= Ager 1996 no. 158), dating to 112 BC, at Chaniotis 2004: 185-231; 2005b: 455-64.
25 Ma 1999: 32.
26 Cf. Just. *Epit.* XI 5.10: 'first Alexander cast a javelin (*iaculum*) into the enemy earth'. He and Arrian (*Anab.* I 11.7) also mention that Alexander landed fully armed.
27 Instinsky 1949; Hammond 1986: 75, 78; 1988: 389; Billows 1995: 25.
28 Zahrnt 1996: 144; Lehmann 2015: 77.
29 Walbank 1950: 80; Badian 1965: 166 n.1.
30 Degen 2019: 53-95. Cf. Schmitthenner 1968: 32.
31 Schmitthenner 1968: 32-4 covers this earlier usage, arguing in particular that Alexander and the successors actualized a heroic paradigm, and that the claim to *doriktētos chōra* was 'aus homerischem Geist entwickelt'; but the argument is not

extensively developed, nor has it been much picked up subsequently. Briefly mentioned in J. Hornblower 1981: 51; Austin 1993: 207. Cf. S. Hornblower 1996: 314, who takes Thuc. IV 98.8 as a reference to 'the *Homeric* concept of "spear-won territory"' (emphasis mine).

32 Schmitthenner 1968: 34–5.

33 *Il.* IX 342–3. Cf. XVI 56–9, where the keyword is split by tmesis: 'I acquired [her] with my spear (δουρὶ δ' ἐμῷ κτεάτισσα).'

34 Kyriakou 1995: 145–6. It is also used as a term for female prize-captives in Hellenistic poetry, e.g. Apollonius' *Argonautica* (806) and Lycophron's *Alexandra* (933, 1116, 1359, 1450).

35 Cf. Hall 1993: 108–33 on the Greek feminization of Asia.

36 Cf. the schematic intensification in hostilities between Greece and Asia in the opening chapters of Herodotus' *Histories* (I 1–5), where various acts of retaliatory 'seizure' (ἁρπάζειν) of women lead ultimately to the 'capture' (ἅλωσις) of Troy.

37 Sommerstein 1989: 17–18.

38 A functional synonym of *doriktētos*: *Schol in Hom. Il.* 9.343 (D scholia); *Schol in Eur. Andr.* 155; *Schol in Eur. Hec.* 478. Cf. Schmitthenner 1968: 32.

39 Kraft, Kayan and Erol 1980: 776–82.

40 Mackie 1999: 485–501, esp. 493. Achilles battles Scamander: *Il.* 21.1–380.

41 Sommerstein 1989: 151; Futo Kennedy 2006: 41–3.

42 Meiggs 1943: 21–34.

43 Sommerstein 1989: 152. Cf. Futo Kennedy 2006: 41–50.

44 Hdt. V 94.2.

45 *Il.* 2.701–2.

46 Motive explicitly outlined at Arr. *Anab.* I 11.5. See Bosworth 1980: 100; Stewart 1993: 78; Erskine 2001: 229 n.21; Amitay 2010: 13. On Protesilaus' disembarkation, Paus. IV 2.7. Roisman 2008: 106 rightly sees Alexander's sacrifice at Protesilaus' shrine as propitiatory, linking more to the Trojan War than the story of desecration by Xerxes' satrap (*pace* Instinsky 1949: 18–26).

47 Xen. *Hell.* III 4.3–4, with 5.5, V 1.33, VII 1.34–35; Plut. *Ages.* 6.4–6; Paus. III 9.1–5. Cf. Roisman 2008: 103–5.

48 Cf. Cartledge 1998: 56.

49 Cf. Kosmin 2014a: 96–7.

50 On Panhellenism, see e.g. Flower 2000: 96–135; Lehmann 2015: 39–78. On the Greeks of Asia Minor, e.g. Nawotka 2003: 15–41; Thonemann 2012: 23–36; Lehmann 2015: 79–114; Wallace 2018b: 45–72.

51 Price 1991: 1.29–30; Stewart 1993: 159–60; Thonemann 2015: 11–12.

52 See Dem. 12.21–3, a section of an ostensible letter by Philip to the Athenians outlining his right to Amphipolis based on three principles: occupation by his ancestors, military conquest, diplomatic recognition in a treaty. Cf. Chaniotis 2004: 191–2.

53 Hammond 1988: 382–91; 1993: 19–21. Cf. Ober 2015: 269.
54 See e.g. Dusinberre 2013: 33–49.
55 On the importance of the *terminus a quo* in determining legitimate ownership of territory, Chaniotis 2015b: 458–60.
56 See e.g. Hector at *Il.* VIII 492–6. Cf. Barker 2009: 71 and n.118. In general, Barbantani 2007 [2010]: 67–138, esp. 70–2.
57 Not necessarily a single statue, but a type which inspired many replicas: Smith 1988: 62; Stewart 1993: 161.
58 Stewart 1993: 160, 163–4, 167.
59 Stewart 1993: 161–71, esp. 167.
60 See e.g. Billows 1989: 173–206; 1995a: 27–8.
61 Smith 1988: 154; 1993: 207.
62 See widely different interpretations at Smith 1994: 100–28; Billows 1995: 45–55; Virgilio 2003: 76–85; Stephens 2005: 239–40; Palagia 2014: 207–31.
63 Palagia 2014: 221–2 for further images.
64 See Chapter 2 and also Chapter 3.1.
65 XVIII 39.5.
66 XVIII 43.1.
67 J. Hornblower 1981: 51–3; Arr. *FGrH* 156 F9.34. Cf. Mehl 1980/1: 187–95.
68 J. Hornblower 1981: 53.
69 Meeus 2014: 263–306.
70 See Chapters 3.2 and 4.3.
71 Mehl 1980/1: 195–6.
72 Diod. XIX 57.1. The diadochs requested Cappadocia and Lycia for Cassander, Hellespontine Phrygia for Lysimachus, the whole of Syria for Ptolemy, and Babylonia returned to Seleucus.
73 On the unitarism/separatism debate, Wheatley 2009: 53–68, esp. 55–60; Meeus 2014: 263–306.
74 Diod. XIX 105.2.
75 Gruen 1985: 254.
76 For the Antigonid invasion of Egypt, see Wheatley and Dunn 2020: 171–7, with 173 for a suggested date of Antigonus' departure from Egypt as December 306.
77 Diod. XX 53.1; Plut. *Demetr.* 16.4.
78 Diod. XX 73.1–2.
79 The letters potentially link back to Diod. XX 53.3, where after Ptolemy's accession 'he thereafter signed himself as king' (πρὸς ἅπαντας ἀνέγραφεν ἑαυτὸν βασιλέα).
80 Cf. Wheatley and Dunn 2020: 171.
81 See Chapter 4.1. On the universalistic nature of the Hellenistic kingships, see Bang 2012: 60–75, esp. 64–9; Strootman 2010: 139–57; 2014b: 307–22.
82 See a fair summary at Billows 1995: 33–44.

83 Diod. 18.43; *Marmor Parium, FGrH* 239, B12.
84 Diod. XIX 57–9.
85 Diod. XIX 55–6.
86 Diod. XIX 79–80.
87 Diod. XX 113.
88 For a full account of Ipsus, with sources and scholarship, see Wheatley and Dunn 2020: 237–51.
89 Wheatley and Dunn 2020: 263.
90 Cf. Polyb. V 67.8, XXVIII 20.6.
91 Originally suggested by Bickerman 1932: 51–2. Cf. discussion by Ma 1999: 31.
92 Polyb. 5.67.10. See another account at Diod. XXX 2. Cf. Walbank 1957: 592–3.
93 See the conclusions of Mehl 1980/1: 207–11.
94 See Ma 1999: 29–33; Chaniotis 2005b: 458–60.
95 Ager 1996: no. 146, ll. 130–50. See also Boffo 2001: 239–40; Chaniotis 2005a: 183; 2005b: 459–60.
96 Cf. Roy 1998: 113.
97 On the date, Hunter 2003: 3–7.
98 See n.33 above.
99 Cf. the Adulis inscription (*OGIS* 54) of Ptolemy III, similarly emphasizing new conquests *in addition to* maintaining patrimonial inheritance. Cf. Chaniotis 2005a: 58; Barbantani 2007 [2010]: 67.
100 Mehl 1980/1: 207–11; Koenen 1993: 29.
101 Cf. Holton 2018a: 108–11.
102 Theoc. *Id.* 17.56–7. See Barbantani 2007: 69–70; Holton 2018a: 101–13.

Conclusions

1 Diod. XVII 117.3 and Arr. *Anab.* VII 26.3 report τῷ κρατίστῳ ('to the strongest'), though Diod. XVIII 1.4 changes this to τῷ ἀρίστῳ ('to the best'). Curt. X 5.5 also uses *optimus* ('best'). Just. *Epit.* XII 15.8 features *dignissimus* ('the most deserving': so rendered by Yardley and Heckel 1997: 290), but also speaks of a *uir fortis* ('strong man'). Cf. Antela-Bernárdez 2011: 118–26.
2 See Guthke 1992 for an illuminating (post-antique) cultural history of 'last words', esp. 67–97 for the issues touched on here. It is interesting to note a classic feature of the genre in Alexander's case: conflicting accounts about exactly what was said.
3 Diod. XVIII 1 outright suggests the story's prophetic implications through an analogy with Hector's dying precognition of Achilles' demise, claiming it is a Pythagorean doctrine for 'immortal' souls to know the future at the point of death.
4 Bilde et al. 1996: 11; Gruen 1996: 116.

5 Plut. *Pyrr.* 7.2. Cf. Braund 1997: 113–27. Strootman 2014b: 307–22 takes a phrase from this passage as emblematic of the universalistic aims of the diadochs as a whole.
6 Holton 2018a: 113–14.
7 Polyb. XVIII 51.3–6. See Chapter 5.
8 Bosworth 1999: 1.
9 Canepa 2009: 196–9.
10 Cf. Oakley 2006; Graeber and Sahlins 2017: 1–22.
11 Holton 2018b: 101–28.

Bibliography

Acosta-Hughes, B. (2010), *Arion's Lyre: Archaic Lyric into Hellenistic Poetry*, Princeton.
Ager, S. (1996), *Interstate Arbitrations in the Greek World, 337–90 B.C.*, Berkeley.
Ager, S. (2003), 'An Uneasy Balance: from the Death of Seleukos to the Battle of Raphia', in A. Erskine (ed.), *A Companion to the Hellenistic World*, Oxford, 35–50.
Al-Azmeh, A. (1997), *Muslim Kingship: Power and the Sacred in Muslim, Christian and Pagan Polities*, London.
Alföldi, A. (1985), *Caesar in 44 v.Chr, Band I: Studien zu Caesars Monarchie und ihren urzeln*, Bonn.
Alonso Troncoso, V. (2009), 'Some Remarks on the Funerals of the Kings: from Philip II to the Diadochi', in P. Wheatley and R. Hannah (eds), *Alexander & His Successors: Essays from the Antipodes*, Claremont, CA, 276–98.
Alonso Troncoso, V. (2010), 'The Bearded King and the Beardless Hero: From Philip II to Alexander the Great', in E. Carney and D. Ogden (eds), *Philip II and Alexander the Great: Father and Son, Lives and Afterlives*, Oxford, 13–24.
Alwine, A. (2015), *Enmity and Feuding in Classical Athens*, Austin.
Amitay, O. (2010), *From Alexander to Jesus*, Berkeley.
Anagnostou-Laoutides, E. (2017), *In the Garden of the Gods: Models of Kingship from the Sumerians to the Seleucids*, London.
Ando, C. (2000), *Imperial Ideology and Provincial Loyalty in the Roman Empire*, Berkeley.
Andronikos, M. (1984), *Vergina: The Royal Tombs*, Athens.
Anson, E. M. (2012), 'The Macedonian Patriot: The Diadoch Craterus', *AHB* 26, 49–58.
Anson, E. M. (2014), *Alexander's Heirs: The Age of the Successors*, Oxford.
Anson, E. M. (2015), *Eumenes of Cardia: A Greek among Macedonians*, 2nd edn, Leiden.
Antela-Bernárdez, B. (2011), 'Simply the Best: Alexander's Last Words, and the Macedonian Kingship', *Eirene* 47, 118–26.
Aperghis, G. G. (2004), *The Seleukid Royal Economy: The Finances and Financial Administration of the Seleukid Empire*, Cambridge.
Armstrong, J. (2016), *War and Society in Early Rome: From Warlords to Generals*, Cambridge.
Ashton, N. G. (1984), 'The Lamian war – *stat magni nominis umbra*', *JHS* 104, 152–7.
Ashton, N. G. (1993), 'Craterus from 324 to 321 B.C.', *Ancient Macedonia* V, Thessalonica, 125–31.
Ashton, N. G. (2015), 'Craterus Revisited', in P. Wheatley and E. Baynham (eds), *East and West in the World Empire of Alexander: Essays in Honour of Brian Bosworth*, Oxford, 107–16.

Asirvatham, S. (2017), 'Flattery, history, and the Πεπαιδευμένος', in T. Howe, S. Müller and R. Stoneman (eds), *Ancient Historiography on War and Empire*, Oxford, 262–74.
Aston, E. M. M. (2012), 'Thessaly and Macedon at Delphi', *Electrum* 19, 41–60.
Atack, C. (2020), *The Discourse of Kingship in Classical Greece*, London.
Aurell, J. (2020), *Medieval Self-Coronations: The History and Symbolism of a Ritual*, Cambridge.
Austin, M. M. (1986), 'Hellenistic Kings, War and the Economy', *CQ* n.s. 36, 450–66.
Austin, M. M. (1993), 'Alexander and the Macedonian Invasion of Asia: Aspects of the Historiography of War and Empire in Antiquity', in J. Rich and G. Shipley (eds), *War and Society in the Greek World*, London, 197–223.
Austin, M. M. (2003), 'The Seleukids and Asia', in A. Erskine (ed.), *A Companion to the Hellenistic World*, Oxford, 121–33.
Babota, V. (2020), 'Alexander Janneus as High Priest and King: Struggling between Jewish and Hellenistic Concepts of Rule', *Religions* 11, 40.
Badian, E. (1965), 'The administration of the empire', *G&R* 12, 166–82.
Bak, J. M. (1990), 'Coronation Studies – Past, Present, and Future', in J. M. Bak (ed.), *Coronations: Medieval and Early Modern Monarchic Ritual*, Berkeley, 1–15.
Baldus, H. R. (1978), 'Zum Siegel des Königs Lysimachos von Thrakien', *Chiron* 8, 195–201.
Baldus, H. R. (1987), 'Die Siegel Alexanders des Grossen: Versuch einer Rekonstruction auf literarischer und numismatischer Grundlage', *Chiron* 17, 395–448.
Bang, P. F. (2012), 'Between Asoka and Antiochus: An essay in world history on universal kingship and cosmopolitan culture in the Hellenistic ecumene', in P. F. Bang and D. Kolodziejczyk (eds), *Universal Empire: A Comparative Approach to Imperial Culture and Representation in Eurasian History*, Cambridge, 60–75.
Barbantani, S. (2007 [2010]), 'The Glory of the Spear – a powerful symbol in Hellenistic poetry and art: The case of Neoptolemus «of Tlos» (and other Ptolemaic epigrams)', *SCO* 53, 67–138.
Barbantani, S. (2012), 'Hellenistic Epinician', *BICS Supplement* 112, 37–55.
Barker, E. T. E. (2009), *Entering the Agon: Dissent and Authority in Homer, Historiography and Tragedy*, Oxford.
Barringer, J. M. (2010), 'Zeus at Olympia', in J. N. Bremmer and A. Erskine (eds), *The Gods of Ancient Greece: Identities and Transformations*, Edinburgh, 155–77.
Bartsch, S. (1994), *Actors in the Audience: Theatricality and Doublespeak from Nero to Hadrian*, Cambridge, MA.
Baynham, E. J. (2000), 'A Baleful Birth in Babylon: The Significance of the Prodigy in the *Liber de Morte* – an Investigation of Genre', in A. B. Bosworth and E. J. Baynham (eds), *Alexander the Great in Fact and Fiction*, Oxford, 242–62.
Baynham, E. J. (2015), 'Cleomenes of Naucratis: Villain or Victim?', in T. Howe, E. E. Garvin and G. Wrightson (eds), *Greece, Macedon and Persia: Studies in Social, Political and Military History in Honour of Waldemar Heckel*, Oxford, 127–34.
Bell, A. (2004), *Spectacular Power in the Greek and Roman City*, Oxford.

Beidelman, T. O. (1989), 'Agonistic exchange: Homeric reciprocity and the heritage of Simmel and Mauss', *Cultural Anthropology* 4, 227–59.

Bentley, E. (1964), *The Life of the Drama*, New York.

Bertelli, S. (2001), trans. R. Burr Litchfield, *The King's Body: Sacred Rituals of Power in Medieval and Early Modern Europe*, University Park, PA.

Bevan, E. R. (1902), *The House of Seleucus*, 2 vols, London.

Bhandare, S. (2007), 'Not just a Pretty Face: Interpretations of Alexander's Numismatic Imagery in the Hellenic East', in H. Prabha Ray and D. T. Potts (eds), *Memory as History: The Legacy of Alexander in Asia*, New Delhi, 208–56.

Bichler, R. (1983), *'Hellenismus': Geschichte und Problematik eines Epochenbegriffs*, Darmstadt.

Bickermann, E. (1932), 'Bellum Antiochicum', *Hermes* 67, 47–76.

Bilde, P. et al. (1996), 'Introduction', in P. Bilde et al. (eds), *Aspects of Hellenistic Kingship*, Aarhus, 9–14.

Billows, R. A. (1989), 'Anatolian Dynasts: The Case of the Macedonian Eupolemos in Karia', *ClAnt* 8, 173–206.

Billows, R. A. (1990), *Antigonos the One-Eyed and the Creation of the Hellenistic State*, Berkeley.

Billows, R. A. (1995), *Kings and Colonists: Aspects of Macedonian Imperialism*, Leiden.

Bing, P. (2009), *The Scroll and the Marble: Studies in Reading and Reception in Hellenistic Poetry*, Ann Arbor.

Bland, R. (2012), 'From Gordian III to the Gallic Empire (AD 238–274)', in W. E. Metcalf (ed.), *The Oxford Handbook of Greek and Roman Coinage*, Oxford, 514–37.

Bloch, M. (1987), 'The ritual of the royal bath in Madagascar: the dissolution of death, birth and fertility in authority', in D. Cannadine and S. Price (eds), *Rituals of Royalty: Power and Ceremonial in Traditional Societies*, Cambridge, 271–97.

Boeke, H. (2007), *The Value of Victory in Pindar's Odes: Gnomai, Cosmology and the Role of the Poet*, Leiden.

Boehm, R. (2021), *City and Empire in the Age of the Successors: Urbanization and Social Response in the Making of the Hellenistic Kingdoms*, Berkeley.

Bohm, C. (1989), *Imitatio Alexandri im Hellenismus: Untersuchungen zum politischen Nachwirken Alexanders des Grossen in hoch- und späthellenistischen Monarchien*, Munich.

Boffo, L. (2001), 'Lo statuto di terre, insediamenti e persone nell'Anatolia ellenistica: Documenti recenti e problemi antichi', *Dike* 4, 233–55.

Boiy, T. (2000), 'Dating Methods during the Early Hellenistic Period', *JCS* 52, 115–21.

Boiy, T. (2004), *Late Achaemenid and Hellenistic Babylon*, Leuven.

Boiy, T. (2007), *Between High and Low: A Chronology of the Early Hellenistic Period*, Frankfurt am Main.

Boiy, T. (2011), 'The Reigns of the Seleucid Kings According to the Babylon King List', *JNES* 70, 1–12.

Borza, E. N. (1990), *In the Shadow of Olympus: The Emergence of Macedon*, Princeton.

Bosworth, A. B. (1980), *A Historical Commentary on Arrian's History of Alexander*, vol. 1: *Commentary on Books I–III*, Oxford.
Bosworth, A. B. (1988), *Conquest and Empire: The Reign of Alexander the Great*, Cambridge.
Bosworth, A. B. (1993), 'Perdiccas and the Kings', *CQ* n.s. 43, 420–7.
Bosworth, A. B. (1996), *Alexander and the East: The Tragedy of Triumph*, Oxford.
Bosworth, A. B. (1999), 'Augustus, the *Res Gestae* and Hellenistic Theories of Apotheosis', *JRS* 89, 1–18.
Bosworth, A. B. (2002), *The Legacy of Alexander: Politics, Warfare, and Propaganda under the Successors*, Oxford.
Bosworth, A. B. (2009), 'Johann Gustav Droysen, Alexander the Great and the Creation of the Hellenistic Age', in P. Wheatley and R. Hannah (eds), *Alexander & His Successors: Essays from the Antipodes*, Claremont, CA, 1–27.
Bottéro, J. (1992), *Mesopotamia: Writing, Reasoning, and the Gods*, Chicago.
Bourdieu, P. (1986), 'The Forms of Capital', in J. G. Richardson (ed.), *Handbook of Theory and Research for the Sociology of Education*, New York, 241–58.
Braund, D. (1997), 'Plutarch's *Pyrrhus* and Euripides' *Phoenician Women*: Biography and Tragedy on Pleonectic Parenting', *Histos* 1, 113–27.
Breitenberger, B. (2007), *Aphrodite and Eros: The Development of Erotic Mythology in Early Greek Poetry and Cult*, London.
Briant, P. (1973), *Antigone le Borgne: Les débuts de sa carrière et les problèmes de l'assemblée Macédonienne*, Paris.
Briant, P. (1979), 'Des Achéménides aux rois hellénistiques: continuités et ruptures', *ASNSP*, 1375–414.
Briant, P. (1988), 'Ethno-classe dominante et populations soumises dans l'empire achéménide: Le cas de l'Égypte', in A. Kuhrt and H. Sancisi-Weerdenburg (eds), *Achaemenid History*, III: *Method and Theory*, Leiden, 137–73.
Briant, P. (1990), 'The Seleucid Kingdom, the Achaemenid Empire and the History of the Near East in the First Millennium BC', in P. Bilde et al. (eds), *Religion and Religious Practice in the Seleucid Kingdom*, Aarhus, 40–65.
Briant, P. (1991), 'Chasses royales macédoniennes et chasses royales perses: Le thème de la chasse au lion sur la chasse de Vergina', *DHA* 17, 211–55.
Briant, P. (1994), 'Source gréco-hellénistiques, institutions perses et institutions macédoniennes: Continuités, changements et bricolages', in H. Sancisi-Weerdenburg, A. Kuhrt and M. Cool Root (eds), *Achaemenid History VIII: Continuity and Change*, Leiden, 283–310.
Briant, P. (2002), trans. P. T. Daniels, *From Cyrus to Alexander: A History of the Persian Empire*, Winona Lake, IN.
Bringmann, K. (2000), *Geben und Nehmen: Monarchische Wohltätigkeit und Selbstdarstellung im Zeitalter des Hellenismus*, Berlin.
Brosius, M. (2021), 'Achaimenid women', in E. D. Carney and S. Müller (eds), *The Routledge Companion to Women and Monarchy in the Ancient Mediterranean World*, London, 149–60.

Brown Ferrario, S. (2014), *Historical Agency and the Great Man in Classical Greece*, Cambridge.

Brügger, C. (2018), *Homer's Iliad: The Basel Commentary: Book XVI*, Berlin.

Buraselis, K. (2005), 'Kronprinzentum und Realpolitik: Bemerkungen zur Thronanwartschaft, Mitregentschaft und Thronfolge unter den ersten vier Ptolemäern', in V. Alonso Tronsoco (ed.), *ΔΙΑΔΟΧΟΣ ΤΗΣ ΒΑΣΙΛΕΙΑΣ: La figura del sucesor en la realeza helenística*, Madrid, 92–101.

Burckhardt, J. (1996), trans. S. Stern, ed. O. Murray, *The Greeks and Greek Civilization*, New York.

Burkert, W. (1979), *Structure and History in Greek Mythology and Ritual*, Berkeley.

Burstein, S. M. (2009), 'Alexander's Organization of Egypt: A Note on the Career of Cleomenes of Naucratis', in T. Howe and J. Reames (eds), *Macedonian Legacies: Studies in Ancient Macedonian History and Culture in Honor of Eugene N. Borza*, Claremont, CA, 10744.

Calder, W. M. (1981), 'Diadem and barrel-vault: a note', *AJA* 85, 334–5.

Calder, W. M. (1983), '"Golden Diadems" Again', *AJA* 87, 102–3.

de Callataÿ, F. (2012), 'Royal Hellenistic Coinages: From Alexander to Mithridates', in W. E. Metcalf (ed.), *The Oxford Handbook of Greek and Roman Coinage*, Oxford, 175–90.

de Callataÿ, F. and Kan, R. (2009), 'A New Silver Denomination of Lysimachus: a unique hermidrachm (from Mytilene?) with Athena Parthenos on the reverse', in S. Drougou et al. (eds), *ΚΕΡΜΑΤΑ ΦΙΛΙΑΣ: Τιμητικός Τόμος για τον Ιωάννη Τουρατσόγλου, Τόμος Α – Νομισματική – Σφραγιστική*, Athens, 109–15.

Callen King, K. (1991), *Achilles: Paradigms of the War Hero from Homer to the Middle Ages*, Berkeley.

Cameron, A. (1987), 'The construction of court ritual: The Byzantine *Book of Ceremonies*', in D. Cannadine and S. Price (eds), *Rituals of Royalty: Power and Ceremonial in Traditional Societies*, Cambridge, 106–36.

Cameron, Al. (1995), *Callimachus and His Critics*, Princeton.

Canepa, M. P. (2009), *The Two Eyes of the Earth: Art and Ritual of Kingship between Rome and Sasanian Iran*, Berkeley.

Canepa, M. (2010), 'Achaemenid and Seleucid Royal Funerary Practices and Middle Iranian Kingship', in H. Börm and J. Wiesehöfer (eds), *Commutatio et contentio: Studies in the Late Roman, Sasanian, and Early Islamic Near East, In Memory of Zeev Rubin*, Düsseldorf, 1–22.

Canepa, M. (2015), 'Dynastic Sanctuaries and the Transformation of Iranian Kingship between Alexander and Islam', in S. Babaie and T. Grigor (eds), *Persian Kingship and Architecture: Strategies of Power in Iran from the Achaemenids to the Pahlavis*, London, 65–118.

Cannadine, D. (1983), 'The Context, Performance and Meaning of Ritual: The British Monarchy and the "Invention of Tradition", *c.* 1820–1977', in E. Hobsbawm and T. Ranger (eds), *The Invention of Tradition*, Cambridge, 101–64.

Cannadine, D. (1987), 'Introduction: divine rites of kings', in D. Cannadine and S. Price (eds), *Rituals of Royalty: Power and Ceremonial in Traditional Societies*, Cambridge, 1–19.

Cannadine, D. and Price, S., eds (1987), *Rituals of Royalty: Power and Ceremonial in Traditional Societies*, Cambridge.

Capdetrey, L. (2007), *Le pouvoir séleucide: Territoire, administration, finances d'un royaume hellénistique (312–129 avant J.-C.)*, Rennes.

Capponi, L. (2021), *Cleopatra*, Bari.

Carlier, P. (1984), *La royauté en Grèce avant Alexandre*, Strasbourg.

Carlier, P. (2000), 'Homeric and Macedonian Kingship', in R. Brock and S. Hodkinson (eds), *Alternatives to Athens: Varieties of Political Organization and Community in Ancient Greece*, Oxford, 259–68.

Carney, E. (2000), *Women and Monarchy in Macedonia*, Norman, OK.

Carney, E. (2006), *Olympias: Mother of Alexander the Great*, London.

Carney, E. (2010), 'Putting women in their place: Women in public under Philip II and Alexander III and the last Argeads', in E. Carney and D. Ogden (eds), *Philip II and Alexander the Great: Father and Son, Lives and Afterlives*, Oxford, 43–54.

Carney, E. (2015), *King and Court in Ancient Macedonia: Rivalry, Treason and Conspiracy*, Swansea.

Cartledge, P. (1997), 'Introduction', in P. Cartledge, P. Garnsey and E. S. Gruen (eds), *Hellenistic Constructs: Essays in Culture, History, and Historiography*, Berkeley, 1–19.

Cartledge, P. (1998), 'The Machismo of the Athenian Empire – Or the Reign of the Phaulus?', in L. Foxhall and J. Salmon (eds), *When Men Were Men: Masculinity, Power and Identity in Classical Antiquity*, London, 54–67.

Chamoux, F. (2002), trans. M. Roussel, *Hellenistic Civilization*, Oxford.

Chaniotis, A. (1997), 'Theatricality beyond the Theater: Staging Public Life in the Hellenistic World', in B. le Guen (ed.), *De la scène aux gradins: Théâtre et representations dramatiques après Alexandre le Grand dans les cités hellénistiques*, Toulouse, 219–59.

Chaniotis, A. (2004), 'Justifying Territorial Claims in Classical and Hellenistic Greece: the beginnings of international law', in E. Harris and L. Rubenstein (eds), *The Law and the Courts in Ancient Greece*, London, 185–213.

Chaniotis, A. (2005a), *War in the Hellenistic World: A Social and Cultural History*, Oxford.

Chaniotis, A. (2005b), 'Victory's Verdict: The Violent Occupation of Territory in Hellenistic Interstate Relations', in J.-M. Bertrand (ed.), *La violence dans les mondes grec et romain*, Paris, 455–64.

Chapinal-Heras, D. (2021), *Experiencing Dodona: The Development of the Epirote Sanctuary from Archaic to Hellenistic Times*, Berlin.

Christesen, P. and Murray, S. C. (2010), 'Macedonian Religion', in J. Roisman and I. Worthington (eds), *A Companion to Ancient Macedonia*, Oxford, 428–45.

Christian, T. (2015), *Gebildete Steine: Zur Rezeption literarischer Techniken in den Versinschriften seit dem Hellenismus*, Göttingen.
Chrubasik, B. (2016), *Kings and Usurpers in the Seleukid Empire: The Men who Would be King*, Oxford.
Clarysse, W. (1991), 'Ptolemaeïsch Egypte: Een maatschappij met twee gezichten', *Handelingen van de Koninklijke Zuidnederlandse Maatschappij voor Taal- en Letterkunde en Geschiedenis* 45, 21–38.
Cohen, A. (1995), 'Alexander and Achilles – Macedonians and "Mycenaeans"', in J. B. Carter and S. P. Morris (eds), *The Ages of Homer: A Tribute to Emily Townsend Vermeule*, Austin, 483–506.
Cohen, A. (2010), *Art in the Era of Alexander the Great: Paradigms of Manhood and their Cultural Traditions*, Cambridge.
Collins, N. L. (1997), 'The Various Fathers of Ptolemy I', *Mnemosyne* 4th ser. 50, 436–76.
Collins, A. W. (2001), 'The Office of Chiliarch under Alexander and the Successors', *Phoenix* 55, 259–83.
Collins, A. W. (2012), 'The Royal Costume and Insignia of Alexander the Great', *AJPh* 133, 371–402.
Cornell, T. J. (2002), 'On War and Games in the Ancient World', in T. J. Cornell and T. B. Allen (eds), *War and Games*, 37–57, Woodbridge.
Courtieu, G. (2004), 'La visite d'Alexandre le Grand à Ilion / Troie', *Gaia* 8, 123–58.
Cummins, M. F. (2009), 'The Praise of Victorious Brothers in Pindar's Nemean Six and on the Monument of Daochus at Delphi', *CQ* n.s. 59, 317–34.
Currie, B. (2005), *Pindar and the Cult of Heroes*, Oxford.
Dahmen, K. (2007), *The Legend of Alexander the Great on Greek and Roman Coins*, London.
Dahmen, K. (2012), 'Alexander und das Diadem: Die archäologische und numismatische Perspektive', in A. Lichtenberger et al. (eds), *Das Diadem der Hellenistischen Herrscher: Übernahme, Transformation oder Neuschöpfung eines Herrschaftszeichens?*, Bonn, 281–92.
D'Agostini, M. (2018), 'Asia Minor and the many shades of civil war: Observations on Achaios the Younger and his claim to the kingdom of Anatolia', in K. Erickson (ed.), *The Seleukid Empire, 281-222 BC: War Within the Family*, Swansea, 59–82.
Dakaris, S. I. (1971), *Archaeological Guide to Dodona*, Ioannina.
Davies, J. K. (1984), 'Cultural, Social and Economic Features of the Hellenistic World', in F. W. Walbank et al. (eds), *The Cambridge Ancient History, 2nd edn, vol. VII, part I: The Hellenistic World*, Cambridge, 257–320.
Davies, J. L. (2002), 'The interpenetration of Hellenistic sovereignties', in D. Ogden (ed.), *The Hellenistic World: New Perspectives*, Swansea, 1–22.
Day, J. W. (2010), *Archaic Greek Epigram and Dedication: Representation and Reperformance*, Cambridge.
Deacy, S. (2008), *Athena*, London.
Dean, L. H. S. (2019), 'Introduction', in E. Woodacre et al. (eds), *The Routledge History of Monarchy*, London, 183–95.

Degen, J. (2019), 'Alexander III., Dareios I. und das speererworbene Land (Diod. 17, 17, 2)', *Journal of Ancient Near Eastern History* 6, 53–95.

De Lacy, P. (1952), 'Biography and tragedy in Plutarch', *AJPh* 73, 159–71.

De Lisle, C. (2021), *Agathokles of Syracuse: Sicilian Tyrant and Hellenistic King*, Oxford.

Demandt, A. (1996), 'Hellenismus – die modern Zeit des Altertums?', in B. Funcke (ed.), *Hellenismus*, Tübingen, 17–27.

Dieterle, M. (2007), *Dodona: Religionsgeschichtliche und historische Untersuchungen zur Entstehung und Entwicklung des Zeus-Heiligtums*, Hildesheim.

Djurslev, C. T. (2021), 'Four Beasts and a Baby: The "baleful birth" omen of Alexander's death in its Hellenistic context', *Mnemosyne* 74, 29–55.

Drews, R. (1983), *Basileus: The Evidence for Kingship in Geometric Greece*, New Haven.

Droysen, J. G. (1952), *Geschichte des Hellenismus*, vols 1–2, Basel.

Duff, T. (2004), 'Plato, tragedy, the ideal reader and Plutarch's *Demetrios and Antony*', *Hermes* 132, 271–91.

Dunn, C. and Wheatley, P. (2012), 'Craterus and the Dedication Date of the Delphi Lion Monument', *AHB* 26, 39–48.

Duplouy, A. (2006), *Le Prestige des Élites: Recherches sur les modes de reconnaissance sociale en Grèce entre les Xe et Ve siècles avant J.-C.*, Paris.

Dusinberre, E. R. (2013), *Empire, Authority, and Autonomy in Achaemenid Anatolia*, Cambridge.

Dyson, M. and Lee, K. H. (2000), 'Talthybius in Euripides' *Troades*', *GRBS* 41, 141–73.

Eckhardt, B. (2016a), 'The Seleucid Administration of Judea, the High Priesthood and the Rise of the Hasmoneans', *Journal of Ancient History* 4, 57–87.

Eckhardt, B. (2016b), 'The Hasmoneans and their Rivals in Seleucid and Post-Seleucid Judea', *Journal for the Study of Judaism* 47, 55–70.

Eckstein, A. M. (2006), *Mediterranean Anarchy, Interstate War, and the Rise of Rome*, Berkeley.

Eckstein, A. M. (2008), *Rome Enters the Greek East: From Anarchy to Hierarchy in the Hellenistic Mediterranean, 230–170 BC*, London.

Eckstein, A. M. (2009), 'Hellenistic Monarchy in Theory and Practice', in R. K. Balot (ed.), *A Companion to Greek and Roman Political Thought*, Oxford, 247–65.

Edwards, M. W. (1991), *The Iliad: A Commentary, Volume V: Books 17–20*, Cambridge.

Elliott, C. D. (2008), 'Purple Pasts: Color Codification in the Ancient World', *Law & Social Inquiry* 33, 173–94.

Elias, N. (1983), trans. E. Jephcott, *The Court Society*, New York.

Ellis, W. M. (1994), *Ptolemy of Egypt*, London.

Elsner, J. (1998), *Imperial Rome and Christian Triumph*, Oxford.

Emerson, R. M. (1983), 'Charismatic Kingship: A Study of State-Formation and Authority in Baltistan', *Politics & Society* 12, 413–44.

Emmons, B. (1954), 'Overstruck Coinage of Ptolemy I', *ANSMN* 6, 69–84.

Erciyas, D. B. (2005), *Wealth, Aristocracy and Royal Propaganda under the Hellenistic Kingdom of the Mithradatids*, Leiden.

Erickson, K. (2013), 'Seleucus I, Zeus and Alexander', in L. Mitchell and C. Melville (eds), *Every Inch a King: Comparative Studies on Kings and Kingship in the Ancient and Medieval Worlds*, Leiden, 109–28.
Erickson, K. (2019), *The Early Seleukids, Their Gods and Their Coins*, London.
Errington, R. M. (1970), 'From Babylon to Triparadeisus: 323–320 B.C.', *JHS* 90, 49–58.
Errington, R. M. (1983), 'The Historiographical Origins of Macedonian "Staatsrecht"', *Ancient Macedonia* 3, Thessalonica, 89–101.
Erskine, A. (2001), *Troy Between Greece and Rome: Local Tradition and Imperial Power*, Oxford.
Erskine, A. (2002a), 'Life After Death: Alexandria and the Body of Alexander', *G&R* 2nd ser. 49, 163–79.
Erskine, A. (2002b), 'O brother, where art thou? Tales of kinship and diplomacy', in D. Ogden (ed.), *The Hellenistic World: New Perspectives*, Swansea, 97–115.
Eyal, R. (2013), *The Hasmoneans: Ideology, Archaeology, Identity*, Göttingen.
Fantuzzi, M. and Hunter, R. (2004), *Tradition and Innovation in Hellenistic Poetry*, Cambridge.
Fearn, D. (2013), '*Kleos* versus Stone: Lyric Poetry and Contexts for Memorialization', in P. Liddel and P. Low (eds), *Inscriptions and Their Uses in Greek and Latin Literature*, Oxford, 231–53.
Felton, D. (2017), 'Thigh wounds in Homer and Vergil: Cultural reality and literary metaphor', in A. Park (ed.), *Resemblance and Reality in Greek Thought*, London, 239–58.
Fischer-Bovet, C. (2014), *Army and Society in Ptolemaic Egypt*, Cambridge.
Fischer-Bovet, C. (2015), 'Social unrest and ethnic coexistence in Ptolemaic Egypt and the Seleucid empire', *Past and Present* 229, 3–45.
Fischer-Bovet, C. and von Reden, S., eds (2021), *Comparing the Ptolemaic and Seleucid Empires: Integration, communication, and resistance*, Cambridge.
Fitzgerald, W. (1987), *Agonistic Poetry: The Pindaric Mode in Pindar, Horace, Hölderlin, and the English Ode*, Berkeley.
Fleischer, R. (1996), 'Hellenistic Royal Iconography on Coins', in P. Bilde et al. (eds), *Aspects of Hellenistic Kingship*, Aarhus, 28–40.
Flower, M. A. (2000), 'Alexander the Great and Pan Hellenism', in A. B. Bosworth and E. J. Baynham (eds), *Alexander the Great in Fact and Fiction*, Oxford, 96–135.
Flower, M. A. (2009), *The Seer in Ancient Greece*, Berkeley.
Foraboschi, D. (2000), 'The Hellenistic Economy: Indirect Intervention by the state', in E. Lo Cascio and D. Rathbone (eds), *Production and Public Powers in Classical Antiquity*, Cambridge, 37–43.
Fowler, D. (2000), *Roman Constructions: Readings in Postmodern Latin*, Oxford.
Fowler, R. and Hekster, O. (2005), 'Imagining Kings: From Persia to Rome', in R. Fowler and O. Hekster (eds), *Imaginary Kings: Royal Images in the Ancient Near East, Greece and Rome*, Munich, 9–38.

Franke, P. R. (1952-3), 'Geschichte, Politik und Münzprägung im frühen Makedonien', *JNG* 3-4, 99-111.

Franke, P. R. (1956), 'Literaturüberblicke der griechischen Numismatik Makedonien', *JNG* 7, 105-12.

Franko, M. (2003), 'Majestic Drag: Monarchical Performativity and the King's Body Theatrical', *The Drama Review* 47, 71-87.

Fraser, P. M. (1996), *The Cities of Alexander the Great*, Oxford.

Fredricksmeyer, E. A. (1981), 'Again the So-Called Tomb of Philip II', *AJA* 85, 330-4.

Fredricksmeyer, E. A. (1983), 'Once More the Diadem and Barrel-Vault at Vergina', *AJA* 87, 99-102.

Fredricksmeyer, E. A. (1986), 'Alexander the Great and the Macedonian Kausia', *TAPA* 116, 215-27.

Fredricksmeyer, E. A. (1991), 'Alexander, Zeus Ammon, and the conquest of Asia', *TAPA* 121, 199-214.

Fredricksmeyer, E. A. (1997), 'The Origins of Alexander's Royal Insignia', *TAPA* 127, 97-109.

Fredricksmeyer, E. A. (2000), 'Alexander the Great and the kingdom of Asia', in A. B. Bosworth and E. J. Baynham (eds), *Alexander the Great in Fact and Fiction*, Oxford, 136-66.

Friedrich, W.-H. (2003), *Wounding and Death in the Iliad: Homeric Techniques of Description*, London.

Fuchs, B. (2001), *Mimesis and Empire: The New World, Islam, and European Identities*, Cambridge.

Futo Kennedy, R. (2006), 'Justice, Geography and Empire in Aeschylus' Eumenides', *ClAnt* 25, 35-72.

Gabbert, J. J. (1997), *Antigonus II Gonatas: A Political Biography*, London.

Geertz, C. (1973), *The Interpretation of Cultures: Selected Essays*, New York.

Geertz, C. (1980), *Negara: The Theatre State in Nineteenth Century Bali*, Princeton.

Gehrke, H.-J. (1982), 'Der siegreiche König: Uberlegungen zur hellenistischen monarchie', *AKG* 64, 247-77. (Translated and updated edn: Gehrke, H.-J. (2013), 'The Victorious King: Reflections on the Hellenistic Monarchy', in N. Luraghi (ed.), *The Splendors and Miseries of Ruling Along: Encounters with Monarchy from Archaic Greece to the Hellenistic Mediterranean*, Stuttgart, 73-98.)

Gehrke, H.-J. (2007), 'Der Hellenismus als Kulturepoche', in G. Weber (ed.), *Kulturgeschichte des Hellenismus: Von Alexander dem Großen bis Kleopatra*, Stuttgart, 355-79.

Gerth, H. H. and Mills, C. W., eds (2009), *From Max Weber: Essays in Sociology*, London.

Glück, J. J. (1964), 'Reviling and monomachy as battle-preludes in ancient warfare', *Acta Classica* 7, 25-31.

Goldhill, S. (1991), *The Poet's Voice: Essays on Poetics and Greek Literature*, Cambridge.

Goukowsky, R. (1978-81), *Essai sur les origines du mythe d'Alexandre*, 2 vols, Nancy.

Graeber, D. (2017), 'Notes on the politics of divine kingship: Or, elements for an archaeology of sovereignty', in D. Graeber and M. Sahlins, *On Kings*, Chicago, 377–464.
Graeber, D. and Sahlins, M. (2017), 'Introduction', in D. Graeber and M. Sahlins, *On Kings*, Chicago, 1–22.
Grainger, J. D. (1990), *Seleukos Nikator: Constructing a Hellenistic Kingdom*, London.
Grainger, J. D. (2007), *Alexander the Great Failure: The Collapse of the Macedonian Empire*, London.
Grainger, J. D. (2002), *The Roman War of Antiochos the Great*, Leiden.
Granier, P. (1931), *Die makedonische Heeresversammlung*, Munich.
Green, P. (1978), 'Caesar and Alexander: aemulatio, imitatio, comparatio', *AJAH* 3, 1–26.
Green, P. (1989), 'After Alexander: Some Historiographical Approaches to the Hellenistic Age', in P. Green (ed.), *Classical Bearings: Interpreting Ancient History and Culture*, Berkeley, 165–92.
Green, P. (1990), *Alexander to Actium: The Historical Evolution of the Hellenistic Age*, Berkeley.
Green, P. (2007), *Alexander the Great and the Hellenistic Age*, London.
Greenwalt, W. S. (1993), 'The Iconographical Significance of Amyntas III's Mounted Hunter Stater', *Ancient Macedonia* 5, Thessalonica, 509–19.
Grimm, G. (1978), 'Die Vergöttlichung Alexanders des Grossen in Ägypten und ihrer Bedeutung für den Ptolemäischen Königskult', in H. Mähler and V. M. Strocka (eds), *Das Ptolemäische Ägypten: Akten des Internationalen Symposiums*, Berlin, Mainz, 103–9.
Gruen, E. S. (1984), *The Hellenistic World and the Coming of Rome*, Volume 1, Berkeley.
Gruen, E. S. (1985), 'The Coronation of the Diadochoi', in J. Eadie and J. Ober (eds), *The Craft of the Ancient Historian: Essays in Honor of Chester G. Starr*, Lanham, MD, 253–71.
Gruen, E. S. (1993), 'Introduction', in A. W. Bulloch et al. (eds), *Images and Ideologies: Self-Definition in the Hellenistic World*, Berkeley, 3–6.
Gruen, E. S. (1996), 'Hellenistic Kingship: Puzzles, Problems, and Possibilities', in P. Bilde et al. (eds), *Aspects of Hellenistic Kingship*, Aarhus, 116–25.
Guthke, K. S. (1992), *Last Words: Variations on a Theme in Cultural History*, Princeton.
Gutzwiller, K. (2014), 'Poetic Meaning, Place, and Dialect in the Epigrams of Meleager', in R. Hunter, A. Rengakos and E. Sistakou (eds), *Hellenistic Studies at a Crossroads Exploring Texts, Contexts and Metatexts*, Berlin, 75–96.
Hadley, R. A. (1974), 'Royal Propaganda of Seleucus I and Lysimachus', *JHS* 94, 50–65.
Hall, E. (1993), 'Asia Unmanned: Images of Victory in Classical Athens', in J. Rich and G. Shipley (eds), *War and Society in the Greek World*, London, 108–33.
Hall, J. A. (2012), 'Imperial universalism – further thoughts', in P. F. Bang and D. Kolodziejczyk (eds), *Universal Empire: A Comparative Approach to Imperial Culture and Representation in Eurasian History*, Cambridge, 304–9.
Hall, J. M. (1997), *Ethnic Identity in Greek Antiquity*, Cambridge.

Hammond, N. G. L. (1986), 'The Kingdom of Asia and the Persian Throne', *Antichthon* 20, 73–85.
Hammond, N. G. L. (1988), 'The King and the Land in the Macedonian Kingdom', *CQ* n.s. 38, 382–91.
Hammond, N. G. L. (1989), *The Macedonian State: The Origins, Institutions and History*, Oxford.
Hammond, N. G. L. (1991), 'The Royal Tombs at Vergina: Evolution and Identities', *ABSA* 86, 69–82.
Hammond, N. G. L. (1993), 'The Macedonian Imprint on the Hellenistic World', in P. Green (ed.), *Hellenistic History and Culture*, Berkeley, 12–37.
Hammond, N. G. L. (2000), 'The Continuity of Macedonian Institutions and the Macedonian Kingdoms of the Hellenistic Era', *Historia* 49, 141–60.
Hammond, N. G. L., Griffith, G. T. and Walbank, F. W. (1972–89), *A History of Macedonia*, 3 vols, Oxford.
Hardie, P. R. (1985), 'Imago Mundi: Cosmological and Ideological Aspects of the Shield of Achilles', *JHS* 105, 11–31.
Harrell, S. E. (2002), 'King or Private Citizen: Fifth-Century Sicilian Tyrants at Olympia and Delphi', *Mnemosyne* 4th ser. 55, 439–64.
Hatzopoulos, M. B. (1996), *Macedonian Institutions under the Kings: A Historical and Epigraphic Study*, 2 vols, Athens.
Hauben, H. and Meeus, A. (2014), 'Introduction: New Perspectives on the Age of the Successors', in H. Hauben and A. Meeus (eds), *The Age of the Successors and the Creation of the Hellenistic Kingdoms (323–276 B.C.)*, Leuven, 1–6.
Hazzard, R. A. (1995), *Ptolemaic Coins: An Introduction for Collectors*, Toronto.
Heckel, W. (1980), '*IG* II2 561 and the Status of Alexander IV', *ZPE* 40, 249–50.
Heckel, W. (1982), 'The Early Career of Lysimachos', *Klio* 64, 373–81.
Heckel, W. (1992), *The Marshals of Alexander the Great*, London.
Heckel, W. (2006), *Who's Who in the Age of Alexander the Great: Prosopography of Alexander's Empire*, Oxford.
Heckel, W. (2020), *In the Path of Conquest: Resistance to Alexander the Great*, Oxford.
Hekster, O. (2015), *Emperors and Ancestors: Roman Rulers and the Constraints of Tradition*, Oxford.
Hoffmann, O. (1906), *Die Makedonen: Ihre Sprache und ihr Volkstum*, Göttingen.
Hölbl, G. (2001), *A History of the Ptolemaic Empire*, London.
Holt, F. L. (2003), *Alexander the Great and the Mystery of the Elephant Medallions*, Berkeley.
Holt, F. L. (2016), *The Treasures of Alexander the Great: How One Man's Wealth Shaped the World*, Oxford.
Holton, J. R. (2014), 'Demetrios Poliorketes, Son of Poseidon and Aphrodite: Cosmic and memorial significance in the Athenian ithyphallic hymn', *Mnemosyne* 67, 370–90.
Holton, J. R. (2018a), 'The Reception of Alexander in the Ptolemaic Dynasty', in K. R. Moore (ed.), *Brill's Companion to the Reception of Alexander the Great*, Leiden, 96–118.

Holton, J. R. (2018b), 'The Ideology of Seleukid Joint Kingship: the Case of Seleukos, Son of Antiochos I', in K. Erickson (ed.), *The Seleukid Empire, 281–222 BC: War Within the Family*, Swansea, 101–28.

Hölscher, T. (1973), *Griechische Historienbilder*, Würzburg.

Hölscher, T. (2003), 'Images of War in Greece and Rome: Between Military Practice, Public Memory, and Cultural Symbolism', *JRS* 93, 1–17.

Hornblower, J. (1981), *Hieronymus of Cardia*, Oxford.

Hornblower, S. (1996), *A Commentary on Thucydides: Volume II: Books IV–V.24*, Oxford.

Houghton, A. and Lorber, C. (2002), *Seleucid Coins: A Comprehensive Catalogue: Part I, Seleucus through Antiochus III*, 2 vols, New York.

Howe, T. (2009), 'Alexander in India: Ptolemy as Near Eastern Historiographer', in T. Howe and J. Reames (eds), *Macedonian Legacies: Studies in Ancient Macedonian History and Culture in Honor of Eugene N. Borza*, Claremont, CA, 215–33.

Hunter, R. (2003), *Theocritus: Encomium of Ptolemy Philadelphus*, Berkeley.

Hunter, R. (2005), 'Speaking in Glossai: Dialect Choice and Cultural Politics in Hellenistic Poetry', in W. M. Bloomer (ed.), *The Contest of Language: Before and Beyond Nationalism*, Notre Dame, IN, 187–206.

Huttner, U. (1997), *Die politische Rolle der Heraklesgestalt im griechischen Herrschertum*, Stuttgart.

Instinsky, H. U. (1949), *Alexander am Hellespont*, Godesberg.

Janko, R. (1994), *The Iliad: A Commentary: Volume IV: Books 13–16*, Cambridge.

Joho, T. (2020), 'Burckhardt and Nietzsche on the *Agōn*: The dark luster of ancient Greece', in H. L. Reid et al. (eds), *Conflict and Competition: Agōn in Western Greece*, Sioux City, IA, 267–88.

Kahn, C. H. (1979), *The Art and Thought of Heraclitus: An edition of the fragments with translation and commentary*, Cambridge.

Kantorowicz, E. (1957), *The King's Two Bodies: A Study in Mediaeval Political Theology*, Princeton.

Kastan, D. S. (1986), 'Proud Majesty Made a Subject: Shakespeare and the Spectacle of Rule', *Shakespeare Quarterly* 37, 459–75.

Kholod, M. M. (2018), 'The Macedonian Expeditionary Corps in Asia Minor (336–335 BC)', *Klio* 100, 406–46.

Kingsley, B. M. (1984), 'The Kausia Diadematophoros', *AJA* 88, 66–8.

Kinns, P. (1983), 'The Amphictyonic coinage reconsidered', *NC* 143, 1–22.

Klooster, J. (2011), *Poetry as Window and Mirror: Positioning the Poet in Hellenistic Poetry*, Leiden.

Koenen, L. (1993), 'The Ptolemaic King as Religious Figure', in A. W. Bulloch et al. (eds), *Images and Ideologies: Self-Definition in the Hellenistic World*, Berkeley, 25–115.

Köhler, J. (1996), *Pompai: Untersuchungen zur hellenistischen Festkultur*, Frankfurt am Main.

Konstan, D. (2006), *The Emotions of the Ancient Greeks: Studies in Aristotle and Classical Literature*, Toronto.

Kosmin, P. (2014a), *The Land of the Elephant Kings: Space, Territory, and Ideology in the Seleucid Empire*, Cambridge, MA.

Kosmin, P. (2014b), 'Seeing Double in Seleucid Babylonia: Rereading the Borsippa Cylinder of Antiochus I', in A. Moreno and R. Thomas (eds), *Patterns of the Past: Epitēdeumata in the Greek Tradition*, Oxford, 173–98.

Kosmin, P. (2018), *Time and Its Adversaries in the Seleucid Empire*, Cambridge, MA.

Kraft, J. C., Kayan, I. and Erol, O. (1980), 'Geomorphic Reconstructions in the Environs of Ancient Troy', *Science* n.s. 209, 776–82.

Krentz, P. (2002), 'Fighting by the Rules: The Invention of the Hoplite Agōn', *Hesperia* 71, 23–39.

Kroll, J. (2007), 'The Emergence of Ruler Portraiture on Early Hellenistic Coins', in P. Schultz and R. von den Hoff (eds), *Early Hellenistic Portraiture: Image, Style, Context*, Cambridge, 113–22.

Kropp, A. J. M. (2013), *Images and Monuments of Near Eastern Dynasts, 100 BC–AD 100*, Oxford.

Kuhrt, A. (1987), 'Usurpation, conquest, and ceremonial: From Babylon to Persia', in D. Cannadine and S. Price (eds), *Rituals of Royalty: Power and Ceremonial in Traditional Societies*, Cambridge, 20–55.

Kurke, L. (1991), *The Traffic in Praise: Pindar and the Poetics of Social Economy*, Ithaca, NY.

Kuschel, B. (1961), 'Die neuen Münzbilder des Ptolemaios Soter', *JNG* 11, 9–18.

Kyriakou, P. (1995), *The Hapax Legomena in Apollonius Rhodius' Argonautica*, Stuttgart.

Kuttner, A. (1999), 'Hellenistic Images of Spectacle, from Alexander to Augustus', *Studies in the History of Art* 56, 96–123.

Kyle, D. J. (2015), *Sport and Spectacle in the Ancient World*, 2nd edn., Oxford.

Landucci Gattinoni, F. (1992), *Lisimaco di Tracia*, Milan.

Landucci Gattinoni, F. (2003a), *L'arte del potere: Vita e opere di Cassandro di Macedonia*, Stuttgart.

Landucci Gattinoni, F. (2003b), 'Tra monarchia nazionale e monarchia militare: il caso della Macedonia', *CSA* 1, 199–224.

Lane Fox, R. (1996), 'Text and Image: Alexander the Great, Coins and Elephants', *BICS* 41, 87–108.

Lane Fox, R. (2007), 'Alexander the Great: "Last of the Achaemenids"?', in C. Tuplin (ed.), *Persian Responses: Political and Cultural Interaction with(in) the Achaemenid Empire*, Swansea, 267–311.

Lane Fox, R. (2011), 'The First Hellenistic Man', in A. Erskine and L. Llewellyn-Jones (eds), *Creating a Hellenistic World*, Swansea, 1–30.

Lattey, C. (1917), 'The Diadochi and the Rise of King-Worship', *EHR* 32, 321–34.

Le Bohec-Bouhet, S. (2005), 'L'hériter du diadème chez les Antigonides', in V. Alonso Tronsoco (ed.), *ΔΙΑΔΟΧΟΣ ΤΗΣ ΒΑΣΙΛΕΙΑΣ: La figura del sucesor en la realeza helenística*, Madrid, 57–70.

Lehmann, P. W. (1980), 'The So-Called Tomb of Philip II: A Different Interpretation', *AJA* 84, 527–31.

Lehmann, G. A. (1988), 'Das neue Kölner Historiker-Fragment (*P. Köln* Nr. 247) und die *chronike suntaxis* des Zenon von Rhodos (*FGrHist*. 523)', *ZPE* 72, 1–17.

Lehmann, G. A. (2015), *Alexander der Große und die „Freiheit der Hellenen": Studien zu der antiken historiographischen Überlieferung und den Inschriften der Alexander-Ära*, Berlin.

Lehmann, S. (2012), 'Sieger-Binden im agonistischen und monarchischen Kontext', in A. Lichtenberger et al. (eds), *Das Diadem der Hellenistischen Herrscher: Übernahme, Transformation oder Neuschöpfung eines Herrschaftszeichens?*, Bonn, 181–208.

Leon, D. (2021), *Arrian the Historian: Writing the Greek Past in the Roman Empire*, Austin.

Le Rider, G. (2007), *Alexander the Great: Coinage, Finances, and Policy*, Philadelphia.

Le Rider, G. and de Callataÿ, F. (2006), *Les Séleucides et les Ptolémées: L'héritage monétaire et financier d'Alexandre le Grand*, Brussels.

Lévêque, P. (1957), *Pyrrhos*, Paris.

Lewis, N. (1986), *Greeks in Ptolemaic Egypt*, Oxford.

Lianou, M. (2010), 'The role of the Argeadai in the legitimation of the Ptolemaic dynasty: Rhetoric and practice', in E. Carney and D. Ogden (eds), *Philip II and Alexander the Great: Father and Son, Lives and Afterlives*, Oxford, 123–34.

Lichtenberger, A. (2012), 'Gibt es eine vorhellenistische makedonische Tradition für das Diadem?', in A. Lichtenberger et al. (eds), *Das Diadem der Hellenistischen Herrscher: Übernahme, Transformation oder Neuschöpfung eines Herrschaftszeichens?*, Bonn, 281–92.

Liotsakis, V. (2019), *Alexander the Great in Arrian's Anabasis: A Literary Portrait*, Berlin.

Llewellyn-Jones, L. (2017), 'Reviewing space, context and meaning: The Eurymedon vase again', in D. Rodriguez Perez (ed.), *Greek Art in Context: Archaeological and Art Historical Perspectives*, London, 97–115.

Lloyd, G. E. R. (1989), *The Revolutions of Wisdom: Studies in the Claims and Practice of Ancient Greek Science*, Berkeley.

Lloyd, A. B. (2011), 'From Satrapy to Hellenistic Kingdom: The Case of Egypt', in A. Erskine and L. Llewellyn-Jones (eds), *Creating a Hellenistic World*, Swansea, 83–106.

Lorber, C. C. (2005), 'A Revised Chronology for the Coinage of Ptolemy I', *NC* 165, 45–64.

Lorber, C. C. (2011), 'Theos Aigiochos: The Aegis in Ptolemaic Portraits of the Divine King', in P. Iossif, A. Chankowski and C. C. Lorber (eds), *More than Men, Less than Gods: Studies in Royal Cult and Imperial Worship*, Leuven, 293–356.

Lorber, C. C. (2012), 'The Coinage of the Ptolemies', in W. E. Metcalf (ed.), *The Oxford Handbook of Greek and Roman Coinage*, Oxford, 211–34.

Lund, H. S. (1992), *Lysimachus: A Study in Early Hellenistic Kingship*, London.
Lungstrum, J. and Sauer, E. (1997), 'Creative Agonistics: An Introduction', in
   J. Lungstrum and E. Sauer (eds), *Agonistics: Arenas of Creative Contest*, New York, 1–32.
Ma, J. (1999), *Antiochos III and the Cities of Western Asia Minor*, Oxford.
Ma, J. (2003), 'Kings', in A. Erskine (ed.), *A Companion to the Hellenistic World*, Oxford, 177–95.
Ma, J. (2008), 'Paradigms and Paradoxes in the Hellenistic World', in B. Virgilio (ed.), *Studi Ellenistici* 20, 371–86.
Ma, J. (2013), 'Hellenistic Empires', in P. F. Bang and W. Scheidel (eds), *The Oxford Handbook of the State in the Ancient Near East and Mediterranean*, Oxford, 324–52.
Mackie, C. J. (1999), 'Scamander and the Rivers of Hades in Homer', *AJPh* 120, 485–501.
Mamroth, A. (1949–52), 'Die Tetradrachmen Königs Philippos II von Makedonien', *Berliner Numismatische Zeitschrift* 1, 13–16.
Mann, C. (2013), 'The Victorious Tyrant: Hieron of Syracuse in the Epinicia of Pindar and Bacchylides', in N. Luraghi (ed.), *The Splendors and Miseries of Ruling Alone: Encounters with Monarchy from Archaic Greece to the Hellenistic Mediterranean*, Stuttgart, 25–48.
Manni, E. (1951), *Demetrio Poliorcete*, Rome.
Manning, J. G. (2003), *Land and Power in Ptolemaic Egypt: The Structure of Land Tenure, 332–30 BCE*, Cambridge.
Manning, J. G. (2010), *The Last Pharaohs: Egypt under the Ptolemies, 305–30 BC*, Princeton.
Marini, N. (2007), *Demetrio, Lo Stile*, Rome.
Markle, M. M., III (1976), 'Support of Athenian Intellectuals for Philip: A Study of Isocrates' *Philippus* and Speusippus' *Letter to Philip*', *JHS* 96, 80–99.
Marks, J. (2010), 'Context as Hypertext: Divine Rescue Schemes in the *Iliad*', in F. Montanari and A. Rengakos (eds), *Trends in Classics* 2, 300–22.
Masséglia, J. (2015), *Body Language in Hellenistic Art and Society*, Oxford.
Martin, K. (2012), 'Der König als heros? Das Diadem und die Binden von (Gründer-)heroen', in A. Lichtenberger et al. (eds), *Das Diadem der Hellenistischen Herrscher: Übernahme, Transformation oder Neuschöpfung eines Herrschaftszeichens?*, Bonn, 249–78.
Martin, L. H. (2000), 'Kingship and the Consolidation of Religio-Political Power during the Hellenistic Period', *Religio: Revue pro religionistiku* 8, 151–60.
McCauley, B. (1998), 'The Transfer of Hippodameia's Bones: A Historical Context', *CJ* 93, 225–39.
McKechnie, P. (2009), 'Omens of the death of Alexander the Great', in P. Wheatley and R. Hannah (eds), *Alexander & His Successors: Essays from the Antipodes*, Claremont, CA, 206–26.
Meadows, A. (2012), 'Deditio in Fidem: The Ptolemaic Conquest of Asia Minor', in C. Smith and L. M. Yarrow (eds), *Imperialism, Cultural Politics, & Polybius*, Oxford, 113–33.

Meadows, A. (2014), 'The Spread of Coins in the Hellenistic World', in P. Bernholz and R. Vaubel (eds), *Explaining Monetary and Financial Innovation: A Historical Analysis*, Berlin/New York, 169–95.
Meeus, A. (2008), 'The Power Struggle of the Diadochoi in Babylon, 323 BC', *AncSoc* 38, 39–82.
Meeus, A. (2009a), 'Kleopatra and the Diadochoi', in P. Van Nuffelen (ed.), *Faces of Hellenism: Studies in the History of the Ancient Mediterranean (4th Century BC–6th Century AD)*, Leuven, 63–92.
Meeus, A. (2009b), 'Some institutional problems concerning the succession to Alexander the Great: *Prostasia* and *chiliarchy*', *Historia* 58, 287–310.
Meeus, A. (2009c), 'Alexander's image in the age of the Successors', in W. Heckel and L. A. Tritle (eds), *Alexander the Great: A New History*, Oxford, 235–50.
Meeus, A. (2012), 'Diodorus and the Chronology of the Third Diadoch War', *Phoenix* 66, 74–96.
Meeus, A. (2013), 'Confusing aim and result? Hindsight and the disintegration of Alexander's empire', in A. Powell (ed.), *Hindsight in Greek and Roman History*, Swansea, 113–48.
Meeus, A. (2014), 'The territorial ambitions of Ptolemy I', in H. Hauben and A. Meeus (eds), *The Age of the Successors and the Creation of the Hellenistic Kingdoms (323–276 BC)*, Leuven, 263–306.
Mehl, A. (1980/1), 'Doriktetos Chora: Kritische Bemerkungen zum "Speererwerb" in Politik und Völkerrecht der hellenistischen Epoche', *AncSoc* 11/12, 173–212.
Mehl, A. (1986), *Seleukos Nikator und sein Reich*, Leuven.
Meyer, D. (2005), *Inszeniertes Lesevergnügen: Das inschriftliche Epigramm und seine Rezeption bei Kallimachos*, Stuttgart.
Meyers, E. M. and Chancey, M. A. (2012), *Alexander to Constantine: Archaeology in the Land of the Bible, Volume III*, New Haven.
Mikalson, J. D. (1998), *Religion in Hellenistic Athens*, Berkeley.
Mileta, C. (2002), 'The King and His Land: Some Remarks on the Royal Area (basilike chora) of Hellenistic Asia Minor', in D. Ogden (ed.), *The Hellenistic World: New Perspectives*, Swansea, 157–75.
Mileta, C. (2012), 'Ein Agon um Macht und Ehre. Beobachtungen zu den agonalen Aspekten der Königserhebungen im ›Jahr der Könige‹', in A. Lichtenberger et al. (eds), *Das Diadem der Hellenistischen Herrscher: Übernahme, Transformation oder Neuschöpfung eines Herrschaftszeichens?*, Bonn, 315–34.
Millar, F. (1992), *The Emperor in the Roman World*, 2nd edn, Ithaca, NY.
Millar, F. (1993), *The Roman Near East, 31 BC–AD 337*, Cambridge, MA.
Mitchell, L. (2013), *The Heroic Rulers of Archaic and Classical Greece*, London.
Mitchell, L. and Melville, C. (2013), '"Every Inch a King": Kings and Kingship in the Ancient and Medieval Worlds', in L. Mitchell and C. Melville (eds), *Every Inch a King: Comparative Studies on Kings and Kingship in the Ancient and Medieval Worlds*, Leiden, 1–21.

Momigliano, A. D. (1975), *Alien Wisdom: The Limits of Hellenization*, Cambridge.
Momigliano, A. D. (1994), 'J. G. Droysen between Greeks and Jews', in G. W. Bowersock and T. J. Cornell (eds), *A. D. Momigliano: Studies on Modern Scholarship*, Berkeley, 147–61.
Moore, K. R., ed. (2018), *Brill's Companion to the Reception of Alexander the Great*, Leiden.
Morgan, K. (2015), *Pindar and the Construction of Syracusan Monarchy in the Fifth Century BC*, Oxford.
Mørkholm, O. (1991), *Early Hellenistic Coinage: From the Accession of Alexander to the Peace of Apamea (336–188 BC)*, Cambridge.
Mossman, J. M. (1988), 'Tragedy and Epic in Plutarch's *Alexander*', *JHS* 108, 83–93.
Mossman, J. M. (1992), 'Plutarch, Pyrrhus, and Alexander', in P. Stadter (ed.), *Plutarch and the Historical Tradition*, London, 90–108.
Moyer, I. S. (2011a), *Egypt and the Limits of Hellenism*, Cambridge.
Moyer, I. S. (2011b), 'Court, Chora, and Culture in Late Ptolemaic Egypt', *AJPh* 132, 15–44.
Mullen, J. S. (2018), 'Beyond Persianization: The Adoption of Near Eastern Traditions by Alexander the Great', in K. R. Moore (ed.), *Brill's Companion to the Reception of Alexander the Great*, Leiden, 233–53.
Müller, O. (1973), *Antigonos Monophthalmos und 'Das Jahr der Könige': Untersuchungen zur Begründung der hellenistischen Monarchien 306–4 v. Chr.*, Saarbrücken.
Murray, O. (2006), 'Burckhardt and the Archaic Age', in L. Burkchardt and H.-J. Gehrke (eds), *Jacob Burckhardt und die Griechen*, Basel, 247–61.
Murray, W. (2012), *The Age of Titans: The Rise and Fall of the Great Hellenistic Navies*, Oxford.
Musgrave, J. H. et al. (1984), 'The Skull from Tomb II at Vergina: King Philip II of Macedon', *JHS* 104, 60–78.
Nagle, D. B. (1996), 'The Cultural Context of Alexander's Speech at Opis', *TAPA* 126, 151–72.
Nagy, G. (1974), *Comparative Studies in Greek and Indic Meter*, Cambridge, MA.
Naiden, F. S. (2019), *Soldier, Priest, and God: A Life of Alexander the Great*, Oxford.
Nawotka, K. (2003), 'Freedom of the Greek cities in Asia Minor in the age of Alexander the Great', *Klio* 85, 15–41.
Newell, E. T. (1927), *The Coinages of Demetrius Poliorcetes*, London.
North, J. (2008), 'Caesar at the Lupercalia', *JRS* 98, 144–60.
Oakley, F. (2006), *Kingship: The Politics of Enchantment*, London.
Oakley, S. P. (1985), 'Single combat in the Roman Republic', *CQ* n.s. 35, 392–410.
Ober, J. (2008), *Democracy and Knowledge: Innovation and Learning in Classical Athens*, Princeton.
Ober, J. (2015), *The Rise and Fall of Classical Greece*, Princeton.
Ogden, D. (1997), *The Crooked Kings of Ancient Greece*, London.
Ogden, D. (1999), *Polygamy, Prostitutes and Death: The Hellenistic Dynasties*, Swansea.

Ogden, D. (2002), 'From Chaos to Cleopatra', in D. Ogden (ed.), *The Hellenistic World: New Perspectives*, Swansea, ix–xxv.
Ogden, D. (2011), *Alexander the Great: Myth, Genesis and Sexuality*, Exeter.
Ogden, D. (2015), 'Alexander, Agathos Daimon, and Ptolemy: The Alexandrian Foundation Myth in Dialogue', in N. Mac Sweeney (ed.), *Foundation Myths in Ancient Societies: Dialogues and Discourses*, Philadelphia, 129–50.
Ogden, D. (2017), *The Legend of Seleucus: Kingship, Narrative and Mythmaking in the Ancient World,* Cambridge.
O'Neil, J. (2000), 'The Creation of New Dynasties after the Death of Alexander the Great', *Prudentia* 32, 118–37.
O'Sullivan, L. (2020), 'Reinventing *Proskynesis*: Callisthenes and the Peripatetic School', *Historia* 69, 260–82.
Palagia, O. (1986), 'Imitation of Herakles in Ruler Portraiture: A Survey, from Alexander to Maximinus Daza', *Boreas* 9, 137–51.
Palagia, O. (2000), 'Hephaestion's Pyre and the Royal Hunt of Alexander', in A. B. Bosworth and E. J. Baynham (eds), *Alexander the Great in Fact and Fiction*, Oxford, 167–206.
Palagia, O. (2014), 'The frescoes from the Villa of P. Fannius Synistor in Boscoreale as reflections of Macedonian funerary paintings of the early Hellenistic period', in H. Hauben and A. Meeus (eds), *The Age of the Successors and the Creation of the Hellenistic Kingdoms (323–276 BC)*, Leuven, 207–31.
Palagia, O. (2018), 'The Reception of Alexander in Hellenistic Art', in K. R. Moore (ed.), *Brill's Companion to the Reception of Alexander the Great*, Leiden, 140–61.
Parker, B. J. (2011), 'The construction and performance of kingship in the Neo-Assyrian empire', *Journal of Anthropological Research* 67, 357–86.
Parker, R. (2011), *On Greek Religion*, Ithaca, NY.
Paschidis, P. (2013), '*Agora* XVI 107 and the royal title of Demetrius Poliorcetes', in V. Alonso Troncoso and E. M. Anson (eds), *After Alexander: The Time of the Diadochi (323–281 BC)*, Oxford, 121–41.
Paspalas, S. A. (2000), 'The Taurophonos Leon and Craterus' monument at Delphi', in G. R. Tsetskhladze, A. J. N. W. Prag and A. M. Snodgrass (eds), *Periplous: Papers on Classical Art and Archaeology presented to Sir John Boardman*, London, 211–19.
Paspalas, S. A. (2005), 'Philip Arrhidaios at Court – An Ill-Advised Persianism? Macedonian Royal Display in the Wake of Alexander', *Klio* 87, 72–101.
Patterson, L. E. (2010), *Kinship Myth in Ancient Greece*, Austin.
Peek, W. (1961), 'Zur Löwenjagd des Krateros', *Philologus* 105, 297–8.
Perdrizet, P. (1897), '*Venatio Alexandri*', *JHS* 19, 273–9.
Peremans, W. (1987), 'Les Lagides, les élites indigènes et la monarchie bicéphale', in E. Lévy (ed.), *Le système palatial en Orient, en Grèce et à Rome*, Leiden, 327–43.
Pfeiffer, S. (2008), *Herrscher- und Dynastiekulte im Ptolemäerreich: Systematik und Einordnung der Kultformen*, Munich.
Pollitt, J. J. (1986), *Art in the Hellenistic Age*, Cambridge.

Pötscher, W. (1966), 'Zeus Naios und Dione in Dodona', *Mnemosyne* 4th ser. 19, 113–47.
Potolsky, M. (2006), *Mimesis*, London.
Prag, J. R. W. and Quinn, J. C. (2013), 'Introduction', in J. R. W. Prag and J. C. Quinn (eds), *The Hellenistic West: Rethinking the Ancient Mediterranean*, Cambridge, 1–13.
Préaux, C. (1939), *L'Économie royale des Lagides*, Brussels.
Préaux, C. (1965), 'Réflexions sur l'entité héllenistique' *Chronique d'Egypte* 40, 129–39.
Préaux, C. (1989), *Le monde héllenistique, vol. 1*, 3rd edn, Paris.
Price, M. J. (1991), *Coinage in the Name of Alexander the Great and Philip Arrhidaeus*, 2 vols, London.
Pritchett, W. K. (1985), *The Greek State at War, part IV*, Berkeley.
Quigley, D. (2004), 'Introduction: The character of kingship', in D. Quigley (ed.), *The Character of Kingship*, Oxford, 1–23.
Rapin, C. (2017), 'Alexandre le Grand en Asie Centrale: Géographie et Stratégie de la Conquête des Portes Caspiennes à l'Inde', in C. Antonetti and P. Biagi (eds), *With Alexander in India & Central Asia: Moving East & Back to West*, Oxford, 37–121.
Ready, J. L. (2007), 'Toil and trouble: The acquisition of spoils in the *Iliad*', *TAPA* 137, 3–43.
Regev, E. (2011), 'Royal Ideology in the Hasmonaean Palaces in Jericho', *Bulletin of the American Schools of Oriental Research* 363, 45–72.
Ristvet, L. (2015), *Ritual, Performance, and Politics in the Ancient Near East*, Cambridge.
Ritter, H.-W. (1965), *Diadem und Königsherrschaft: Untersuchungen zu Zeremonien und Rechtsgrundlagen des Herrschaftsantritts bei den Persern, bei Alexander dem Großen und im Hellenismus*, Munich.
Ritter, H.-W. (1984), 'Zum sogennanten Diadem des Philippsgrabes', *AA* (1984), 105–11.
Ritter, H.-W. (1987), 'Die Bedeutung des Diadems', *Historia* 36, 290–301.
Rodríguez Pérez, D. (2011), 'Contextualizing Symbols: "The Eagle and the Snake" in the Ancient Greek World', *Boreas* 33, 1–18.
Roisman, J. (2008), 'Greek Perspectives on the Justness and Merits of the Trojan War', *College Literature* 35, 97–109.
Roisman, J. (2012), *Alexander's Veterans and the Early Wars of the Successors*, Austin.
Rosen, K. (1979), 'Politische Ziele in der frühen hellenistischen Geschichtschreibung', *Hermes* 107, 460–77.
Roskam, G. (2009), *Plutarch's Maxime cum principibus philosopho esse disserendum: An interpretation with commentary*, Leuven.
Rostovtzeff, M. (1941), *The Social and Economic History of the Hellenistic World*, 3 vols, Oxford.
Roy, J. (1998), 'The Masculinity of the Hellenistic King', in L. Foxhall and J. Salmon (eds), *When Men were Men: Masculinity, Power and Identity in Classical Antiquity*, London, 111–35.
Rutherford, R. B. (2019), *Homer: Iliad book XVIII*, Cambridge.
Rutter, N. K. (1997), *The Greek Coinages of Southern Italy and Sicily*, London.

Ruzicka, S. (2012), *Trouble in the West: Egypt and the Persian Empire, 525-332 BCE*, Oxford.
Sahlins, M. (2011), 'Twin-born with Greatness: The Dual Kingship of Sparta', *HAU: Journal of Ethnographic Theory* 1, 63-101.
Sammons, B. (2017), *Device and Composition in the Greek Epic Cycle*, Oxford.
Samuel, A. E. (1983), *From Athens to Alexandria: Hellenism and Social Goals in Ptolemaic Egypt*, Leuven.
Samuel, A. E. (1989), *The Shifting Sands of History: Interpretations of Ptolemaic Egypt*, Lanham, MD.
Sanders, E. (2014), *Envy and Jealousy in Classical Athens: A Socio-Psychological Approach*, Oxford.
Schäfer, C. (2002), *Eumenes von Kardia und der Kampf um die Macht im Alexanderreich*, Frankfurt am Main.
Scodel, R. (2008), *Epic Facework: Self-presentation and social interaction in Homer*, Swansea.
Scott, M. (2010), *Delphi and Olympia: The Spatial Politics of Panhellenism in the Archaic and Classical Periods*, Cambridge.
Schmitthenner, W. (1968), 'Über Eine Formveränderung der Monarchie Seit Alexander d. Gr.', *Saeculum* 19, 31-46.
Scholz-Cionca, S. (2017), 'The Dancing Despot: Toyotomi Hideyoshi and the Performative Symbolism of Power', in Z. Ben-Dor Benite et al. (eds), *The Scaffolding of Sovereignty: Global and Aesthetic Perspectives on the History of a Concept*, New York, 186-207.
Selden, D. (1998), 'Alibis', *ClAnt* 17, 289-412.
Sens, A. (2004), 'Doricisms in the New and Old Posidippus', in B. Acosta-Hughes et al. (eds), *Labored in Papyrus Leaves: Perspectives on an Epigram Collection Attributed to Posidippus (P.Mil.Vogl. VIII 309)*, Cambridge, MA, 65-83.
Seyer, M. (2006), 'The Royal Hunt – The Symbolic Meaning of an Ancient Topos', in A. Prinz (ed.), *Hunting Food – Drinking Wine*, Vienna, 171-98.
Sharpe, K. (2006), 'Sacralization and Demystification: The Publicization of Monarchy in Early Modern England', in J. Deploige and G. Deneckere (eds), *Mystifying the Monarch: Studies on Discourse, Power, and History*, Amsterdam, 99-116.
Sherwin-White, S. and Kuhrt, A. (1993), *From Samarkhand to Sardis: A New Approach to the Seleucid Empire*, London.
Shipley, G. (1993), 'Distance, Development, Decline? World-Systems Analysis and the "Hellenistic" World', in P. Bilde et al. (eds), *Centre and Periphery in the Hellenistic World*, Aarhus, 271-84.
Shipley, G. (2000), *The Greek World after Alexander, 323-30 BC*, London.
Shipley, G. (2018), *The Early Hellenistic Peloponnese: Politics, Economies, and Networks 338-197 BC*, Cambridge.
Skeat, T. C. (1969), *The Reigns of the Ptolemies*, Munich.
Smith, R. R. R. (1988), *Hellenistic Royal Portraits*, Oxford.

Smith, R. R. R. (1994), 'Spear-won land at Boscoreale: on the royal paintings of a Roman villa', *JRA* 7, 100–28.

Sommerstein, A. H., ed. (1989), *Aeschylus: Eumenides*, Cambridge.

Spawforth, (2007), 'The Court of Alexander the Great between Europe and Asia', in A. J. S. Spawforth, (ed.), *The Court and Court Society in Ancient Monarchies*, Cambridge, 82–120.

Squillace, G. (2018), 'Alexander after Alexander: Macedonian Propaganda and Historical Memory in Ptolemy and Aristobulus' Writings', in K. R. Moore (ed.), *Brill's Companion to the Reception of Alexander the Great*, Leiden, 119–39.

Stanwick, P. E. (2003), *Portraits of the Ptolemies: Greek Kings as Egyptian Pharaohs*, Austin.

Stephens, S. A. (2003), *Seeing Double: Intercultural Poetics in Ptolemaic Alexandria*, Berkeley.

Stephens, S. A. (2005), 'Battle of the Books', in K. Gutzwiller (ed.), *The New Posidippus: A Hellenistic Poetry Book*, Oxford, 229–48.

Stewart, A. S. (1993), *Faces of Power: Alexander's Image and Hellenistic Politics*, Berkeley.

Strauss Clay, J. (1983), *The Wrath of Athena: Gods and Men in the Odyssey*, London.

Strootman, R. (2010), 'Queen of Kings: Kleopatra VII and the Donations of Alexandria', in M. Facella and T. Kaizer (eds), *Kingdoms and Principalities in the Roman Near East*, Stuttgart, 139–57.

Strootman, R. (2011), 'Kings and Cities in the Hellenistic Age', in O. M. van Nijf and R. Alston (eds), *Political Culture in the Greek City after the Classical Age*, Leuven, 141–54.

Strootman, R. (2014a), *Courts and Elites in the Hellenistic Empires: The Near East after the Achaemenids, c. 330 to 30 BCE*, Edinburgh.

Strootman, R. (2014b), '"Men to whose rapacity neither sea nor mountain sets a limit": The aims of the diadochs', in H. Hauben and A. Meeus (eds), *The Age of the Successors and the Creation of the Hellenistic Kingdoms (323–276 BC)*, Leuven, 307–22.

Strootman, R. (2020), '"To be magnanimous and grateful": The Entanglement of Cities and Empires in the Hellenistic Aegean', in M. D. Gygax and A. Zuiderhoek (eds), *Benefactors and the Polis: The Public Gift in the Greek Cities from the Homeric World to Late Antiquity*, Cambridge, 137–78.

Svenbro, J. (1993), trans. J. Lloyd, *Phrasikleia: An Anthropology of Reading in Ancient Greece*, Ithaca, NY.

Taeger, F. (1957), *Charisma: Studien zur Geschichte des antiken Herrscherkultes, Band I: Hellas*, Stuttgart.

Tarn, W. W. (1913), *Antigonus Gonatas*, Oxford.

Tarn, W. W. (1921), 'Heracles Son of Barsine', *JHS* 41, 18–28.

Tarn, W. W. (1933), 'Alexander the Great and the Unity of Mankind', *PBA* 19, 123–66.

Tatum, W. J. (1996), 'The Regal Image in Plutarch's Lives', *JHS* 116, 135–51.

Tejada, J. V. (2004), 'Warfare, History and Literature in the Archaic and Classical Periods: The Development of Greek Military Treatises', *Historia* 53, 129–46.

Thomas, R. (1995), 'The Place of the Poet in Archaic Society', in A. Powell (ed.), *The Greek World*, London, 104–29.

Thomas, R. (2007), 'Fame, Memorial, and Choral Poetry: The Origins of Epinikian Poetry – an Historical Study', in S. Hornblower and C. Morgan (eds), *Pindar's Poetry, Patrons, and Festivals: From Archaic Greece to the Roman Empire*, Oxford, 141–66.

Thompson, M. (1968), 'The Mints of Lysimachus', in C. M. Kraay and G. K. Jenkins (eds), *Essays in Greek Coinage Presented to Stanley Robinson*, Oxford, 163–82.

Thonemann, P. (2012), 'Alexander, Priene, and Naulochon', in P. Martzavou and N. Papazarkadas (eds), *Epigraphical Approaches to the Post-Classical Polis*, Oxford, 23–36.

Thonemann, P. (2015), *The Hellenistic World: Using Coins as Sources*, Cambridge.

Thornton, T. C. G. (1963), 'Charismatic kingship in Israel and Judah', *Journal of Theological Studies* 14, 1–11.

Trampedach, K. (2013), 'Between Hellenistic Monarchy and Jewish Theocracy: The Contested Legitimacy of Hasmonean Rule', in N. Luraghi (ed.), *The Splendors and Miseries of Ruling Alone: Encounters with Monarchy from Archaic Greece to the Hellenistic Mediterranean*, Stuttgart, 231–59.

Trofimova, A. (2012), *Imitatio Alexandri in the Hellenistic Art: Portraits of Alexander the Great and Mythological Images*, Rome.

Troxell, H. A. (1997), *Studies in the Macedonian Coinage of Alexander the Great*, New York.

Turner, E. (1984), 'Ptolemaic Egypt', in F. W. Walbank et al. (eds), *The Cambridge Ancient History, 2nd edn, vol. VII, part I: The Hellenistic World*, Cambridge, 118–74.

Tuplin, C. (2014), 'The military dimension of Hellenistic kingship: an Achaemenid heritage?', in F. Hoffmann and K. S. Schmidt (eds), *Orient und Okzident in hellenistischer Zeit*, Munich, 245–76.

Ulf, C. (2011), 'Ancient Greek competition – a modern construct?', in N. Fisher and H. van Wees (eds), *Competition in the Ancient World*, Swansea, 85–111.

Valeri, V. (1985), *Kingship and Sacrifice: Ritual and Society in Ancient Hawaii*, Chicago.

Van der Spek, R. (2014), 'Seleukos, Self-Appointed General (Strategos) of Asia (311–305 B.C.), and the Satrapy of Babylonia', in H. Hauben and A. Meeus (eds), *The Age of the Successors and the Creation of the Hellenistic Kingdoms (323–276 BC)*, Leuven, 323–44.

Van Nijf, O. (2001), 'Local heroes: athletics, festivals and elite self-fashioning in the Roman east', in S. Goldhill (ed.), *Being Greek under Rome: Cultural Identity, the Second Sophistic and the Development of Empire*, Cambridge, 306–34.

Van Wees, H. (1988), 'Kings in Combat: Battle and Heroes in the Iliad', *CQ* n.s. 38, 1–24.

Van Wees, H. (2011), 'Rivalry in history: an introduction', in N. Fisher and H. van Wees (eds), *Competition in the Ancient World*, Swansea, 1–36.

Versluys, M. J. (2017), *Visual Style and Constructing Identity in the Hellenistic World: Nemrud Dag and Commagene under Antiochus I*, Cambridge.
Virgilio, B. (2003), *Lancia, diadema e porpora: Il re e la regalità ellenistica*, 2nd edn, Pisa.
Vlassopoulos, K. (2013), *Greeks and Barbarians*, Cambridge.
von Graeve, V. (1970), *Der Alexandersarkophag und seine Werkstatt*, Berlin.
von Hesberg, H. (1999), 'The King on Stage', *Studies in the History of Art* 56, 64–75.
von Reden, S. (2007), *Money in Ptolemaic Egypt: From the Macedonian Conquest to the End of the Third Century BC*, Cambridge.
Voutiras, E. (1984), 'Zur historischen Bedeutung des Krateros-Weihgeschenkes in Delphi', *WJA* 10, 57–62.
Walbank, F. W. (1950), Review of Instinsky (1949), *JHS* 70, 79–81.
Walbank, F. W. (1957–79), *A Historical Commentary on Polybius*, 3 vols, Oxford.
Walbank, F. W. (1984), 'Monarchies and Monarchic Ideas', in F. W. Walbank et al. (eds), *The Cambridge Ancient History*, 2nd edn, vol. VII, part I: *The Hellenistic World*, Cambridge, 62–100.
Walbank, F. W. (1996), 'Two Hellenistic Processions: A Matter of Self-Definition', *Scripta Classica Israelica* 15, 119–30.
Wallace, S. (2018a), '*Metalexandron*: Receptions of Alexander in the Hellenistic and Roman Worlds', in K. R. Moore (ed.), *Brill's Companion to the Reception of Alexander the Great*, Leiden, 162–96.
Wallace, S. (2018b), 'Alexander the Great and Democracy in the Hellenistic World', in M. Canevaro and B. Gray (eds), *The Hellenistic Reception of Classical Athenian Democracy and Political Thought*, Oxford, 45–72.
Walzer, M. (1967), 'On the role of symbolism in political thought', *Political Science Quarterly* 82, 191–204.
Weiler, B. (2010), 'Crown-Giving and King-Making in the West ca. 1000–ca. 1250', *Viator* 41, 57–88.
Wheatley, P. V. (1998), 'The Date of Polyperchon's Invasion of Macedonia and Murder of Heracles', *Antichthon* 32, 12–23.
Wheatley, P. V. (2002), 'Antigonus Monophthalmus in Babylonia, 310–308 BC', *JNES* 61, 39–47.
Wheatley, P. V. (2009), 'The Diadochi, or Successors to Alexander', in W. Heckel and L. A. Tritle (eds), *Alexander the Great: A New History*, Oxford, 53–68.
Wheatley, P. V. (2014), 'Seleukos and Chandragupta in Justin XV 4', in H. Hauben and A. Meeus (eds), *The Age of the Successors and the Creation of the Hellenistic Kingdoms (323–276 BC)*, Leuven, 501–15.
Wheatley, P. V. and Dunn, C. (2020), *Demetrius the Besieger*, Oxford.
Whitmarsh, T. (2002), 'Alexander's Hellenism and Plutarch's Textualism', *CQ* n.s. 52, 174–92.
Wiemer, H.-U. (2007), 'Alexander – die letzte Achaimenide? Eroberungspolitik, locale Eliten und altorientalische Traditionen im Jahr 323', *Historische Zeitschrift* 284, 283–309.

Will, E. (1979), 'Le monde hellénistique et nous', *Ancient Society* 10, 79–95.

Will, E. (1985), 'Pour une "anthropologie coloniale" du monde hellénistique', in J. W. Eadie and J. Ober (eds), *The Craft of the Ancient Historian: Essays in Honor of Chester G. Starr*, Lanham, MD, 273–301.

Willers, D. (1979), 'Zwei Löwenjagdgruppen des vierten Jahrhunderts v. Chr.', *HASB* 5, 21–6.

Willrich, H. (1899), 'Krateros und der Grabherr des Alexandersarkophages von Sidon', *Hermes* 34, 231–50.

Winter, J. (2010), 'Sites of memory', in S. Radstone and B. Schwarz (eds), *Memory: History, Theories, Debates*, New York, 312–24.

Woodacre, E. (2019), 'Understanding the mechanisms of monarchy', in E. Woodacre et al. (eds), *The Routledge History of Monarchy*, London, 1–19.

Woodacre, E. et al., eds (2019), *The Routledge History of Monarchy*, London.

Worthington, I. (2016), *Ptolemy I: King and Pharaoh of Egypt*, Oxford.

Yardley, J. C. and Atkinson, J. E. (2009), *Curtius Rufus: Histories of Alexander the Great, Book 10*, Oxford.

Yardley, J. C. and Heckel, W. (1997), *Justin: Epitome of the Philippic History of Pompeius Trogus: Books 11–12: Alexander the Great*, Oxford.

Yardley, J. C., Wheatley, P. V. and Heckel, W. (2011), *Justin: Epitome of the Philippic History of Pompeius Trogus, Volume II: Books 13–15: The Successors to Alexander the Great*, Oxford.

Zahrnt, M. (1996), 'Alexanders Übergang über den Hellespont', *Chiron* 26, 129–47.

Zanker, G. (2004), *Modes of Viewing in Hellenistic Poetry and Art*, Madison.

Zanker, P. (1988), trans. A. Shapiro, *The Power of Images in the Age of Augustus*, Ann Arbor.

Zervos, O. H. (1967), 'The Early Tetradrachms of Ptolemy I', *ANSMN* 13, 1–16.

Index

Achilles
  Alexander's ancestor 25
  Athena 80–1
  Briseis 130
  comparison with Alexander 72, 74–5, 149, 163 n.29, 168 n.12
  Homeric shield 44, 94–5
  kleos ('fame') 51
  Patroclus 72, 75
  Pyrrhus of Epirus 92–6
  Scamander 131
Achaemenid Persian empire
  acculturation policies 19–20, 26
  customs and traditions 37–8, 100–1, 130
  as Hellenistic genealogy 19–23, 148, 154 n.34, 157 n.106
  imperial kingship model 113
  lion-symbolism 90
  ruling elite class 20, 154
  satrapal coinage 60–1
  Trojan metonymy 52, 55, 59–60, 132
Adea-Eurydice 24
aegis (garment)
  Achilles 80–1, 149
  Alexander 78, 80–4, 120, 149
  Apollo 170 n.49
  Athena 80, 170 n.50
  Ptolemy 83–4, 149
  Zeus 170 n.49–50
Agathocles (Syracusan king) 95–6, 120
agonism (*see* competition)
Alexander I 56–7
Alexander (III) the Great (*see also* imitation)
  Achilles 25, 74, 80–1, 91
  blended royal model 19
  body 67, 79, 81, 83, 88
  bronze coinage 60, 63
  city-foundations 22
  court 26, 37, 66–7
  and Craterus 37–40, 43–5, 52–5, 66–8
  death 1–2, 4, 22, 23, 27–9, 36–8
  death-omens 118–19
  diadem 115–25, 149
  diadochan coinage 78, 119–25
  education 24
  Egypt 21
  gold coinage 25, 61–2, 81, 92
  government 22
  Heracles 60–3, 74, 90, 92–3
  Homer and the Trojan War 25, 43, 51–2, 64, 74
  India 71, 75
  international image 25
  last words 27–8, 147, 159 n.158
  Lysimachus 85–6, 90–1, 118–19, 121, 149
  monetization 15–16, 23, 60
  'Persianization' 20, 26, 37
  'Porus medallions' 78
  portraits 92, 133–4
  Ptolemy 71–2, 74–5, 78, 120, 124, 136, 149
  Pyrrhus of Epirus 91–4
  Seleucus 118–20, 122
  silver coinage 16, 60–1, 63, 78, 92, 96
  spear-won land 127–30, 132–4, 139, 142, 144, 149
  temple patronage 92
Alexander IV
  death 85–6, 103–4, 137–8, 171 n.73, 175 n.30
  joint king 1, 2, 5, 36–7, 138
  regnal years 2, 153 n.6, 177 n.63
Alexinus of Elis 70
Antigonus (I) Monophthalmus ('One-Eyed') 25, 139
  accession 1–3, 35, 103–11, 124–5, 149, 175–6 n.41, 176 n.44–8
  Athens 104
  Babylonia 104, 153 n.6
  coinage 119

defeat at Ipsus (301 BC) 85, 119, 121, 140–2
flight from Perdiccas (321/20 BC) 38
invasion of Egypt (306 BC) 138–9, 153 n.2, 184 n.76
marriage to Cleopatra (attempted) 86, 161 n.5
paeans 70
peace of 311 BC 85
self-coronation 107, 111–13, 149
succession-planning 107–8, 113–15
war with Eumenes 38, 68–9, 136–7, 141
war with Seleucus 104
Antigonus (II) Gonatas 8, 92, 114
Antiochus I
   coinage 122–4
   joint king 115, 179 n.101
   sale of Pitane 143
Antiochus III 127–9, 142–4, 150
Antiochus IV 142
Antipater
   death 85
   epimeleia (regency) 85, 135, 136
   Lamian War 38, 65
   marriage alliances 38, 85
   physical stature 65–6, 167 n.25
   regency in Europe 36–8, 51
   reputation 69
   war against Perdiccas 38, 40, 68, 85, 136, 162 n.19
Antipater (I), son of Cassander 96–7, 173 n.127
Apis bull 21
Apollonius Rhodius 75, 183 n.34
Archelaus I 57–8
Archon 50–1, 161 n.5
aretē ('excellence') 24, 73–4, 77, 81, 169 n.18
Argead dynasty 2
   dissolution 29, 35–7, 103, 136
   Greek identity 56–7
   as Hellenistic genealogy 21–6, 31, 63–4, 100–1, 148–9, 174 n.9
   Heraclid ancestry and connection 56–64, 78, 84, 93
   and Lysimachus 84, 87, 89
   marriage links 23–4, 159 n.35, 171 n.74
   numismatic traditions 57–62, 93, 97
Aristodemus of Miletus 105–7, 176 n.44

Arrhidaeus (Macedonian satrap) 36, 78–9, 161 n.5
Asander 36, 161 n.5
Athena
   Alexander's coinage 25, 61–2, 81, 92, 119, 132
   Athenian ideology 131
   Hellespont altar 127
   heroic protector 80–1, 170 n.46, 170 n.50
   Lysimachus' coinage 121
Athens
   claims in Asia Minor 131
   Antigonus and Demetrius 103–4
   Lamian War 38
   memorial ideology 164 n.65
   monuments at Delphi 42
   Philip II 59
   Salamis victory (480 BC) 61, 132

Babylonia
   Alexander's death-omens 117–9
   Antigonus' takeover (316/15 BC) 136–7, 140
   dating systems 109, 153 n.6, 177 n.63
   mint and coinage 119
   Macedonian satrapal rule 50, 158 n.125
   'seeing double' 8, 155 n.41
   Seleucid rule 21, 50, 104, 124, 136, 140
Babylon Settlement (323 BC) 26
   Craterus' absence 38
   satrapal division 22, 78, 85, 86
Balacrus 38
bricolage 25–7

Callimachus 75
Cassander 4, 25, 136, 138, 184 n.72
   accession 2, 3, 103, 108–9, 177 n.58
   battle of Ipsus (301 BC) 140
   coinage 97, 119
   conflict with Polyperchon 69, 85
   control of Greece 103–4
   death 96
   marriage to Cleopatra (attempted) 86, 161 n.5
   murder of Alexander IV 85–6, 137, 175 n.39
   peace of 311 BC 85, 184 n.72
   settlement after Ipsus 121, 140–1

Chandragupta 104
Cleitus 36, 161 n.5
Cleopatra (Alexander's sister) 23–4, 86, 161 n.5
Cleopatra VII 4, 102
coinage (*see also names of individual rulers*)
   functions 59
   Greek traditions 119–20
   international circulation 23, 25
   mediatization 15–16
   production 156 n.83
   trust 61
   value as evidence 18, 157 n.95
   weight standards 23
competition
   athletic contests 48, 56–7
   as historiographical term 27–8, 110–11, 160 n.160
   Hellenistic political system 11, 21, 54, 72, 113, 136, 148
   imitatio Alexandri 93–4
   as interpretative model 6, 9, 10, 27–33, 104, 109–10, 149–50, 160 n.159–77
   Rome 110–11, 160 n.169
coronation
   as ritual act 10–11, 111–15
   self-coronation 2, 11, 107, 111–15
Corupedium, battle of (281 BC) 128, 142–3
Craterus 148–9, 162 n.13
   Argead tradition 63–64
   Babylon Settlement (323 BC) 38
   career 37–9
   death 38–9, 68–9
   Delphic monument 37–55, 63, 65, 69, 84, 89–90, 162–3 n.22–4
   marriage to Phila 38
   paeans 69–70
   royal style and behaviour 64–8
   traditionalism 37, 67–8, 161 n.9
Craterus II (son of Craterus) 38, 40–1, 69, 162–3 n.24

Delphi 37–55, 63, 65, 70, 84, 89, 90, 148
Demeter 173 n.113
Demetrius of Phalerum 104
Demetrius Poliorcetes ('Besieger of Cities') 4, 25
   accession 1–3, 35, 103–11, 124–5, 149, 175–6 n.41, 176 n.44–8
   Athens 103–4
   coinage 92, 119, 121–2, 150
   defeat at Gaza (312 BC) 140
   defeat at Ipsus (301 BC) 85, 119, 121, 140–2
   invasion of Egypt (306 BC) 138–9, 153 n.2, 184 n.76
   ithyphallic hymn 166 n.109
   Lamia 88
   Lysimachus 88–9
   Macedonian takeover (296/95 BC) 97
   marriage to Phila 38–9, 69
   paeans 70
   Plutarch 17, 35
   succession to Antigonus 107–8, 113–15
   thalassocracy 140
diadem
   Alexander the Great 115–25
   cultural origins 100–1
   etymology and definition 100
   Hasmonean 99–100
   Hellenistic royal accession 103–15
   Hellenistic royal succession 113–15
   Julius Caesar 101–3
   post-Hellenistic 151
Diodorus Siculus
   on Alexander's death 27
   on Alexander at the Hellespont 127, 130
   on Alexander's lineage 81
   on Alexander's throne 116–18
   on coinage 59
   on Heracles-cult 97
   on leadership qualities 67
   on monomachy 73
   on Ptolemy 77–8, 135–40, 142, 169 n.35
   on 'spear-won land' 127, 130, 135–42
   on rivalry and competition 2–3, 110–11
   on the 'Year of the Kings' (306–4 BC) 1–3, 104–9, 112, 114, 115, 153 n.3
Diodotus (II) Tryphon 114
Dione 91–2
Dodona 91–2, 95
doriktētos chōra (*see* spear-won land)
Dromichaetes 115
Droysen, Johann Gustav (1808–84) 6–7

Eryx (Sicily) 96
Eumenes of Cardia 36, 161 n.5
   Craterus 38, 67–9, 161 n.9
   defeat and death 38, 136–7, 141
   empty throne stratagem 103, 117
   monomachy with Neoptolemus
      168 n.16

fetial priests 130
Flamininus, T. Quinctius 128

Gaza, battle of (312 BC) 140

Heracles 80, 149
   Alexander 60–3, 74, 90, 92–3
   Alexander's coinage 16, 60–1, 63, 78,
      92, 96, 119
   Argead importance 56–63, 78, 84, 89,
      97
   cult in central Greece 97
   Hellespont altar 127
   Pyrrhus of Epirus 95–7
   Sicily 96
   Trojan War 59–60
Hermippus of Cyzicus 70
Hesiod 55, 75
Homeric poetry 80, 164 n.65, 130,
      165 n.70, 182–3 n.31
   agonism 160 n.162, 160 n.176
   anax ('chief') and rulers 24, 52, 90,
      133
   fame 48–9, 51
   influence on Arrian 71–2, 168 n.8
   as literary model 43–5, 47, 51–5, 71–2,
      75
   society in 24, 44–5, 51, 73, 160 n.162,
      164 n.46
honour 28, 41, 43–6, 50–1, 64, 73–4,
      160 n.162, 164 n.46–8, 177–8 n.72

imitation 31–3, 109, 111, 121, 150,
      163 n.24, 169 n.28
   heroic 71–8, 82–3, 149
   imitatio Alexandri 25–7, 40, 74–5, 88,
      90–1, 93–4, 135, 159 n.149, 163 n.29
   numismatic 120–1

kleos ('fame') 43, 48–51, 55, 69, 164 n.62–5,
      165 n.70–1

Lanassa (wife of Agathocles and Pyrrhus)
   95–6
Leonnatus 36, 66, 161 n.5
Lycophron 183 n.34
Lysimachus 4, 25, 96–7, 128, 136, 137, 138
   accession 2, 3, 103, 108–9
   Babylon Settlement (323 BC) 85
   battle of Ipsus (301 BC) 121, 140–1,
      184 n.72
   Belevi tomb 87–8, 89
   coinage 86–7, 119, 121–2
   defeat and death 128, 142–3
   diadem-omen 118–19, 120, 178 n.79
   Dromichaetes 115
   Leontophoros ('lion-carrier' ship) 88
   lion-symbolism 86–91, 149
   marriage to Cleopatra (attempted) 86,
      161 n.5
   marriage to Nicaea 85
   peace of 311 BC 85, 184 n.72
   sōmatophylax (royal bodyguard) 85
   Thrace 85, 90

Menoitius 97
multipolarity 4–5, 10

Nike 25, 61, 119–21, 132

Octavian 150
Odysseus 43, 45, 54, 80, 163 n.42–4
Olympias 24
Ophellas 36

Patroclus 71–2, 74–5, 81, 97, 168 n.9,
      168 n.12
Perdiccas (regent) 36, 38, 85, 136–7,
      162 n.13
   war with Ptolemy 66–7, 77–81, 120,
      135–6, 138–9, 144, 153 n.2
   empty throne stratagem 103, 117
Perdiccas III 59
performance, performativity
   poetic 45–7, 59, 164 n.65, 167 n.129
   royal 3, 5–6, 9, 10–19, 21, 25, 29–30,
      32–3, 37, 40, 43–4, 45, 47, 56–8,
      62–3, 65–8, 84, 100, 107–11, 113,
      115, 132, 139, 147–9, 158 n.115,
      164 n.46
Peucestas 36, 161 n.5